RATIONALITY, HUMILITY, AND SPIRITUALITY IN CHRISTIAN LIFE

RATIONALITY, HUMILITY, AND SPIRITUALITY IN CHRISTIAN LIFE

Dennis Hiebert

CASCADE *Books* • Eugene, Oregon

RATIONALITY, HUMILITY, AND SPIRITUALITY IN CHRISTIAN LIFE

Copyright © 2020 Dennis Hiebert. All rights reserved. Except for brief quotations in critical publications or reviews, no part of this book may be reproduced in any manner without prior written permission from the publisher. Write: Permissions, Wipf and Stock Publishers, 199 W. 8th Ave., Suite 3, Eugene, OR 97401.

Cascade Books
An Imprint of Wipf and Stock Publishers
199 W. 8th Ave., Suite 3
Eugene, OR 97401

www.wipfandstock.com

PAPERBACK ISBN: 978-1-5326-5687-3
HARDCOVER ISBN: 978-1-5326-5688-0
EBOOK ISBN: 978-1-5326-5689-7

Cataloguing-in-Publication data:

Names: Hiebert, Dennis.

Title: Rationality, humility, and spirituality in christian life. / Dennis Hiebert.

Description: Eugene, OR: Cascade Books, 2020. | Includes bibliographical references and index.

Identifiers: ISBN 978-1-5326-5687-3 (paperback) | ISBN 978-1-5326-5688-0 (hardcover) | ISBN 978-1-5326-5689-7 (ebook)

Subjects: LCSH: Faith and reason—Christianity | Rationalism | Humility—Religious aspects | Spirituality—Christianity | Christian life | Critical realism.

Classification: BV4501.2 H54 2020 (paperback) | BV4501.2 (ebook)

Manufactured in the U.S.A.   03/13/20

To my friend Jake Friesen,
whose noble spirit death could not defeat.

"Going home without my sorrow
Going home sometime tomorrow
Going home to where it's better than before"
Leonard Cohen, "Going Home"

By asking me to be his private spiritual conversation
partner throughout his final weeks,
Jake led me to believe I might have something to say.

"My soul waits in silence for God alone."

PSALM 62:1

About the Cover

We live side by side inside what we learn, inside a particular and peculiar time and place, inside a socially constructed and constraining community and culture. We enter and exit our (dis)similar, (ir)religious abodes through doors framed differently, yet functioning similarly. We peer out and ponder the wider, worrisome world from windows adorned with meticulously managed life and beauty. However colorful and serviceable they may be, to inhabit only cramped, constricting quarters is to forego vast, open spaces shrouded in a mysterious "cloud of unknowing."

CONTENTS

Tables | ix
Acknowledgments | xi
Introduction | xv

1 ESSAY ONE: RATIONALITY | 1
2 ESSAY TWO: HUMILITY | 53
3 ESSAY THREE: SPIRITUALITY | 100
   EPILOGUE | 161

Bibliography | 167
Index | 189

TABLES

Religious and/or Spiritual Self-Identification | 113
Words Associated with Spirituality and Religion | 117

ACKNOWLEDGMENTS

A TREATISE CAN COME together in any number of odd ways, and this one had its own unique formulation. I did not initially set out to write what you have in your hands, at least not in the coherent three-part configuration you have before you. When I submitted a manuscript on intellectual humility to *Christian Scholar's Review*, the editors suggested the topic was too large for a journal article, and should be expanded into a monograph. They even recommended that I submit a proposal to Wipf and Stock Publishers, not knowing that I had already published with Cascade Books of Wipf and Stock previously. One year earlier I had also published a separate journal article exploring the problems of rationality in Christian life, and as I pondered the possibilities of another book, those problems presented themselves to me as grounds for Christian intellectual humility. Attempting to discern the consequences of that pairing for Christian life then led naturally enough to questions about spirituality, a resurgent topic in recent decades which had already fascinated me for a while. Thus the three primary components of this work fell into ordered place. And hence my first appreciation goes to the editors of *Christian Scholar's Review* for their simple suggestion that became this reality.

The expansion from article to book, certainly not unique in academia, continued. Earlier, condensed iterations of each of the three essays comprising this volume have been published as research articles in academic journals as follows:

"'Come Healing of the Reason:' Problematic Practices of Rationality in Christian Faith." *Didaskalia* 26 (2016) 49–84.

"Clothing Christian Convictions in Intellectual Humility." *Cultural Encounters: A Journal for the Theology of Culture* 15 (2019) 39–59.

"'The Massive Subjective Turn:' Sociological Perspectives of Spirituality." *Journal of Sociology and Christianity* 8 (2018) 55–75.

My gratitude therefore also goes out to the editors of these respective journals and their anonymous reviewers who provided much helpful feedback that refined my analyses, especially in areas of scholarship in which my knowledge is even more limited.

As a professor of sociology, my workplace has also obviously facilitated this endeavor. I have taught at Providence University College for several decades, and in addition to encouraging and enabling research and writing as all universities do, it has aided this project in one particularly notable way. Being positioned in a small, Canadian, Christian liberal arts university has saved me from being buried in a large department of a single academic discipline, where all members think and speak the same academic language. It has also molded me into more of a generalist who knows a little about a lot, rather than a specialist who knows a lot about a little. I have benefitted enormously from almost all my faculty colleagues being scholars in multiple other academic disciplines. My normal, daily, professional interaction constantly engages scholarship in fields other than my own, which no doubt has contributed to the interdisciplinary character of this work—I have long recognized that I am not so much an original thinker as a synthesizer of the thoughts of others. While birthed in the sociology of religion, this work has been nurtured by the various other scholarly perspectives my everyday colleagues have brought to it, for which I am also most thankful.

Other colleagues, forums, and conferences, such as the Christian Sociological Association, have heard earlier, partial renditions of these ideas, and also provided useful feedback. However, the most informative and formative feedback came from a benevolent and faithful cadre of readers who critiqued drafts of these essays as I completed them. Chris Summerville, Mike Powell, Zach Reimer, David Wiebe, Kurt Armstrong, Patrick Franklin, Randy Holm, Mel Letkeman, Heather Macumber, Glen Klassen, Paul Chamberlain, Marie Raynard, Laura Vander Velden, Ryan Turnbull, Hilary DeRoo, Ben Schatzlein, Brianne Collins, Morgan Mulenga, and Jeff Wheeldon all read parts or all of my drafts and offered valuable comments and suggestions, each from their own unique perspective and expertise. More than one astutely detected an autobiographical undertone throughout. All have enhanced what in its limitations remains mine.

Two others deserve extra special mention and thanks. I met Mike Powell less than a year ago, and somehow our first conversation turned toward this project. Providentially, he then soon became its copy editor, and his rigorous attention to detail has significantly enhanced its readability. Meanwhile, Val Hiebert (no relation), my closest colleague and friend the past twenty years, graciously endured my comparatively petty fretting about this project while grieving the death of her husband, to whom this book is dedicated. One cannot complete a project such as this without both exceptional technical and exceptional personal support.

Finally, more than any other person, Judy has again been as faithfully supportive of this project as any marital partner could be, generously providing time, space, and domestic enablements as needed. Nevertheless, preferring to experience the finished product as other readers will, she chose not to read any of it during the long labor of love leading to its publication. So I can only eagerly anticipate how she will resonate with it, confident that our mutual spiritual sojourn all these years, though not always perfectly in step, has taken us both far from where we began, together.

PERMISSIONS

Come Healing
Words and Music by Leonard Cohen and Patrick Leonard
Copyright © 2012 Old Ideas LLC and No Tomato Music
All Rights on behalf of Old Ideas LLC Administered by Sony/ATV Music Publishing LLC, 424 Church Street, Suite 1200, Nashville, TN 37219
All Rights for No Tomato Music Administered Worldwide by Kobalt Songs Music Publishing
International Copyright Secured All Rights Reserved
Reprinted by Permission of Hal Leonard LLC

"Forty Years in the Wilderness," Written by Bruce Cockburn, © 2016 Holy Drone Corp.

Going Home
Words and Music by Leonard Cohen and Patrick Leonard
Copyright © 2012 Old Ideas and No Tomato Music
All Rights on behalf of Old Ideas Administered by Sony/ATV Music Publishing LLC, 424 Church Street, Suite 1200, Nashville, TN 37219
All Rights on behalf of No Tomato Music Administered Worldwide by Kobalt Songs Music Publishing
International Copyright Secured All Rights Reserved
Reprinted by Permission of Hal Leonard LLC

POEMS by C.S. Lewis copyright © C.S. Lewis Pte. Ltd. 1964. Reprinted by permission.

Marlene's Designer Portraits

INTRODUCTION

For much of the twentieth century, most social scientists considered secularization to be an irresistible force. The inevitability of increasing faithlessness became an article of faith, as scholars assumed that modernization would lead inexorably to near total secularity. Religion would be reduced to what the classical sociologist Emile Durkheim termed the "cult of the individual."[1] However, by the dawn of the twenty-first century, many social scientists had rejected the secularization thesis,[2] observing in its place extensive cultural processes of religious stabilization, revitalization, polarization, and even sacralization.[3] They acknowledged that, while religion in the global North continued to wane, the global South remained "as furiously religious as it ever was."[4] They also differentiated between secularization at the macro-societal level, the meso-organizational level, and the micro-individual level of human life.[5] Doing so revealed that, while secularization is by many measures plainly evident at the macro and meso levels, it is not as operative at the micro level. Religious institutions, language, and symbols may no longer dominate society and culture, and religious organizations may be shrinking as church attendance declines and churches close at unprecedented rates, but private belief in the reality of a supernatural divine and individual spiritual longing for connection with the transcendent persist, and are in many ways resurgent. Clearly, long-term cultural trends in

---

1. Marske, "Durkheim's 'Cult of the Individual.'"
2. For example, see Stark, "Secularization, R.I.P."
3. In *The Market as God*, Harvey Cox employs the concept of sacralization to characterize the current regard for and function of capitalism. Robert Nelson does the same in *The New Holy Wars: Economic Religion vs. Environmental Religion in Contemporary America*, explicating two new forms of religion based on what each has sacralized, ironically both derived from the historic religion of Christianity.
4. Berger, *Desecularization of the World*, 2.
5. Dobbelaere, *Secularization*.

religion are at the very least more complex than simple, uniform, linear, religious decline.

Nevertheless, Western Euro-American culture is by now unquestionably and thoroughly post-Christendom. The geopolitical state of Christendom forged in the fourth century under the Roman Emperor Constantine began to crumble and disintegrate eras later when confronted by the Enlightenment in the eighteenth century, the rise of the nation-state in the nineteenth century, and the turn to consumerism of the broadest, even non-material sense in the twentieth century.[6] Christendom gradually lost its religious monopoly to religious pluralism, and lost its political authority to political secularism. Now in post-Christendom, Christian ideals and values no longer overtly ground public thought and action, Christian ethics no longer overtly guide social institutions, and the Bible no longer overtly governs morality with any collective authority.[7] Though post-Christendom is often conflated with post-Christian, the latter is best understood as something else, that is, as a society in which there is no longer a significant percentage of Christians, much less a significant Christian presence. A post-Christian culture denotes that most collective expressions of and personal commitments to Christianity have been abandoned, and that Christianity has therefore become essentially absent. In this sense, it is entirely possible for a society to be post-Christendom without yet being post-Christian, which in fact best describes current Western Euro-American culture.

To be post-Christian at the micro-individual level is comparatively straightforward. A post-Christian is any individual who no longer identifies, affiliates, practices, or believes as a Christian after having done so earlier in his or her life. If she or he has not converted to an alternative religious identity, affiliation, practice, and belief, she or he has nonetheless de-converted, disengaged, secularized, and become an ex-Christian.[8] The Barna Group has constructed "Post-Christian Metrics" comprised of fifteen factors that serve as criteria for whether an individual qualifies as post-Christian.[9] They have also documented a "sharp rise" in the number of post-Christian Americans from 37 percent in 2013 to 44 percent in 2015.

6. Hall, *End of Christendom*.

7. Nevertheless, Christianity's deeply formative influence on Western cultural values remains everywhere evident. In effect, as Charles Taylor argued in "A Catholic Modernity?" secular modernity is at heart a championing of Christian social ethics in secular terms. For example, the most compelling justification for human rights is the Christian understanding that all humans are equally in the image of God. See Witte and Alexander, *Christianity and Human Rights*.

8. One of their leading websites is https://www.ex-christian.net/.

9. https://www.barna.com/research/2015-sees-sharp-rise-in-post-christian-population/.

INTRODUCTION

Christianity has faced multiple, relatively unique challenges in every time and place, in every era and culture, in every chapter and circumstance of its long and winding history. The causal variables of those challenges have been myriad, and in the historical moment, have often seemed overwhelming. Today's challenges of secularization, post-Christendom, and post-Christianity are in that sense not unique, but in that they threaten the very existence of Christianity, their magnitude cannot be overstated. Nor can any single analysis of these current challenges pretend to be complete, just as no simple solutions can guarantee a positive way forward. But cumulative analysis from various scholarly perspectives is crucial, and every caring and critical voice joins the chorus of others seeking to understand the factors, both internal and external, that contribute to the ethos of Christian life.

The following interdisciplinary analysis of contemporary Christian life is drawn primarily from the academic discipline of sociology, but secondarily also from psychology, philosophy, history, culture studies, religious studies, and biblical studies. It seeks to identify and elucidate certain selected aspects of contemporary Christian life that are problematic, and therefore constitute some of the challenges confronting it. The first aspect is the extreme and at times excessive rationality built into the cognitive and organizational structure of contemporary Christianity. The second is the need for Christians to embody an authentic attitude of humility, and in particular the intellectual humility that overbearing rationality makes less likely. The third is how Christians actually experience and live their faith, as more of an externally determined and regulated religiosity, or an internally differentiated and open spirituality. In light of the critique of rationality in Christian life, and the call for intellectual humility in Christians, what might vibrant Christian spirituality be and do at this point in history? Ultimately, the following analysis is a call to Christians to think critically about the structure, attitude, and experience of their personal and collective faith in connected and coherent ways that they may not have previously. Each of the structure of rationality, the attitude of humility, and the experience of spirituality will be elucidated in separate essays as follows.

ESSAY ONE: RATIONALITY

The autonomous rationality of modernity has infected Christianity in ways that have profoundly shaped its current character and health. Interdisciplinary analysis reveals the shifting location and function of rationality in Christian faith, and explicates two social practices of rationality that, in their extreme, prove problematic. Both the practice of rationalization as illuminated by sociology as well as the practice of rationalism as illuminated by philosophy are shown to reduce Christian faith by diminishing and even denying its non-rational elements. It will be argued that just as Christianity is metaphysical and God is supernatural, so too Christian faith is meta-rational or super-rational. In matters of Christian faith, rationality makes a good servant but a bad master. Therefore a way must be made for more affective, narrative, and incarnational forms of Christian faith that is not anti-rational, but anti-rational*ist*.

ESSAY TWO: HUMILITY

Along with the polarization of public life in Western societies, recent work in ethics and epistemology as well as the rise of positive psychology have brought attention to issues of intellectual humility, a virtue most challenged and tested by religious convictions. Philosophical perspectives give rigorous definition to humility in general and intellectual humility in particular, as well as the opposing vice of intellectual arrogance. Social scientific perspectives reveal how intellectual humility correlates with other personal virtues, how it intersects with concepts of the self and identity, and how it functions in both micro relational dynamics and macro cultural dynamics. Religious studies explores the effects of intellectual humility at the intrapersonal, interpersonal, and cultural levels of religion. In response, the biblical call to humility will be reviewed, and the grounds for Christian intellectual humility considered. Christian practice of intellectual humility has been mixed, but is best evidenced by faith as open-minded trust rather than as correct belief.

ESSAY THREE: SPIRITUALITY

The rapid rise in the number of persons who identify as religious "nones," "somes," "dones," or simply "spiritual but not religious" is one manifestation of "the massive subjective turn of modern culture."[10] However, due to the elusive character of spirituality, the social sciences have struggled to define it as it is claimed and practiced both inside and outside religious traditions. Empirical research nevertheless shows a pronounced turn away from religiosity toward spirituality. Social scientific theories of cultural change provided by religious outsiders help explain that turn at the macro level, while contrasting Christian evaluations provided by religious insiders offer

---

10. Taylor, *Ethics of Authenticity*, 26.

perspectives of what it signifies about Christian faith. The history of Christian spirituality can be traced through the texts, practices, and lifestyles promoted by the branches of Christianity, and the various views of spirituality within them. Though Christian spirituality is typically at its core a "personal relationship with God," what that means remains uneven and open, especially in Christian mysticism.

THEORETICAL PERSPECTIVE: CRITICAL REALISM

Throughout the analysis that follows, the working assumptions will be those of critical realism as pioneered by Roy Bhaskar, Margaret Archer, and others in the 1970s and 1980s, and now increasingly prominent in philosophy and sociology.[11] "Critical realism is not an empirical program; it is not a methodology; it is not even truly a theory, because it explains nothing. It is, rather, a meta-theoretical position" committed to "ontological realism, epistemic relativism, judgmental rationality, and a cautious ethical naturalism."[12] Above all, it is committed to post-positivism, which rejects the position that only scientifically or logically verifiable assertions are justifiable. Many have characterized critical realism as the attempt to steer a third, middle way between the Scylla of modern naïve realism on one side, and the Charybdis of postmodern anti-realism on the other. As such, it adheres to neither the extremes of positivism nor relativism, empiricism nor interpretivism, essentialism nor constructivism. Understanding reality to be stratified and emergent in multiple dimensions, critical realism is also firmly anti-reductionistic, and in significant ways, both post-disciplinary and post-postmodern. Fact is deemed to be ultimately inseparable from value. Reality is deemed to be open, not closed.

The basic thesis and defining feature of critical realism is that much of reality exists independently from human awareness of it.[13] Indeed, one of its seminal distinctions is between the real, the actual, and the empirical.[14] Pictured as three concentric circles, the real is the largest, outer, all-inclusive circle, comprised of all the material, non-material, and social "mechanisms" that exist, whether humans are aware of them or not, each with their own structures and causal capacities. The actual is the middle circle, comprised of all the mechanisms that have been activated, producing events in time

11. See Gorski, "What is Critical Realism?" Leading Christian proponents include Bernard Lonergan, Michael Polanyi, Alister McGrath, and Christian Smith.
12. Archer, "What is Critical Realism?" para. 2 and 3.
13. Sayer, *Realism and Social Science*.
14. Bhaskar, *Possibility of Naturalism*.

and space, whether observed by humans or not. The empirical is the smallest, inner circle, comprised of all the mechanisms that have been both activated and observed, the domain of our direct or indirect experience of the real or actual. Therefore, "what we observe (the empirical) is not identical to all that happens (the actual), and neither is identical to that which is (the real). The three must not be conflated."[15]

The compatibility of the critical realist perspective with the project at hand is readily apparent. Indeed, the fit is so perfect that, were it not for its origins and growing acceptance in secular philosophy and social science, critical realism would appear made for contemporary Christian scholarship. So if it is true that much of reality exists independently from human awareness of it, then space has already been opened and a call already sent for a critique of rationality that exposes its limitations, for an intellectual humility that is the only honest way of inhabiting that space, and for an openness to spirituality that holds potential for the fullest human being. New Testament scholar N. T. Wright is representative of relevant Christian scholarship when he writes, "I propose a form of *critical realism*. This is a way of describing the process of 'knowing' that acknowledges the *reality of the thing known, as something other than the knower* (hence 'realism'), while fully acknowledging that the only access we have to this reality lies along the spiraling path of *appropriate dialogue or conversation between the knower and the thing known* (hence 'critical')."[16]

PERSPECTIVAL APPROACH: EMIC AND ETIC

I write as both a Christian and a sociologist, someone who practices both personal Christian faith and professional social scientific scholarship. I have been a Jesus-follower all my life, but only came to formal, academic sociology in mid-life, recognizing then to my surprise, as many sociologists do, that I had always thought sociologically. I had dabbled in academic theological formation earlier, but I am not a professional theologian nor a biblical scholar. Like many others in their own unique configuration, I am both a person of Christian faith and an observer of Christian faith.

Therefore I bring to the analysis that follows what anthropology first termed, and what social scientists more broadly now differentiate, as both emic and etic approaches to my subject matter.[17] An emic approach is that of the "subjective," local, religious insider; whereas an etic approach

---

15. Smith, *What is a Person?*, 93.
16. Wright, *New Testament*, 35.
17. Harris, "History and Significance."

is that of the "objective," universal, social scientific outsider. An emic approach depicts how reality is viewed and explained by "natives" within the social group being studied; whereas an etic approach depicts how outside observers define, categorize, understand, and explain the same group using different, scholarly, "non-native" terminology and explanations. An emic approach is first order; whereas an etic approach is second order. They may disagree occasionally about "what is really going on" in Christian life, but both accounts must be taken seriously, as awkward and even uncomfortable as that may be for some. And they will inevitably overlap and perhaps blur at times in the following pages, but I am convinced that both are necessary to understand and practice Christian life better. So, to echo Bruce Cockburn, after well beyond forty years in the wilderness, I've got to take up my load and cover some ground before everything comes undone.

> Forty years in the wilderness getting to know the beasts
> Projected and reflected on the greatest and the least
> Forty years of days and nights—angels hovering near
> Kept me moving forward though the way was far from clear
> And they said
>
> Take up your load
> Run south to the road
> Turn to the setting sun
> Sun going down
> Got to cover some ground
> Before everything comes undone[18]

---

18. Cockburn, "Forty Years in the Wilderness."

1

ESSAY ONE: RATIONALITY

A. INTRODUCTION TO RATIONALITY

Story

LIFE OF PI is a multiple award-winning novel by Yann Martel published in 2001.[1] The 2012 film adaptation directed by Ang Lee also won multiple Golden Globe and Academy Awards, including Best Picture. It tells the tale of an Indian boy, Piscine "Pi" Patel, who is raised Hindu, but at age 14 is introduced to Christianity, and then at 15 to Islam. He decides to follow all three religions because he "just wants to love God." He is told by his father and the mentors of the three religions that doing so is irrational and therefore impossible. He must choose one. At age 16, Pi and his family together with their zoo animals embark for Canada, but are shipwrecked on a Japanese freighter. Pi's family is lost, but he survives, stranded on a lifeboat in the Pacific Ocean with a Bengal tiger as well as three other animals who are soon devoured by each other, and the last by the tiger. While adrift at sea with the tiger, Pi experiences various fantastic events. After 227 days, the lifeboat washes onto a beach in Mexico and the tiger disappears into the nearby jungle. While Pi is recovering in the hospital, he tells his story to two investigators from the Japanese Ministry of Transport. The officials reject it as unbelievable. So Pi tells them an alternate story, replacing the animals with the ship's cook, a sailor, his mother, and himself. Pointing out

---

1. Martel, *Life of Pi*.

that neither story can be proven, and that neither explains the cause of the shipwreck, he asks the officials which story they prefer. They then choose the more astounding story with the animals. Pi thanks them and adds, "So it goes with God."

According to Martel, his novel contains three themes: "Life is a story . . . You can choose your story . . . A story with God is the better story."[2] That life is a story is hardly debatable. A human life is undeniably a chain of events that happen to a central human being in the company of others, beginning some place and ending in another. But that is merely neutral narrative. When structure and meaning are built into an otherwise random and confusing flow of events, it becomes something more significant. It becomes a story, an interpretation of beginnings, happenings, and endings, and an attempt to make sense and gain understanding.[3] Humans can not only choose their actions, within limits, but they can create their own meanings and interpretations of those actions, or adopt meanings given to them. Either way, lived meaning remains a choice. And a story with God in it draws meaning and interpretation from a grander, cosmic, master narrative, a metanarrative that provides meaning not only for all life, human or non-human, but for all that exists. Christianity is frequently described as a metanarrative comprised of four acts—creation, fall, redemption, and restoration—and as the one "story that interprets all other stories."[4] Hence Pi's naïve desire to be Christian as well as Muslim and Hindu is reckoned to be irrational and impossible.

Yet, according to postmodernism, the very notion of metanarratives is merely a characteristic of a modernist worldview, that intellectual framework within which one explains the meaning of life. The essence of the postmodern critique of modernity is the latter's love for all-encompassing truths and ideologies, and its concomitant detestation for the "other" and diversity.[5] Jean-François Lyotard famously defined postmodernism as "incredulity toward metanarratives"[6] such as modern science, that is, as "mistrust or skepticism about the totalizing stories of modernism and their grounds for universal legitimacy."[7] Philosopher Abigail Doukhan delineated three structures of all metanarratives, expressly including the Christian metanarrative,[8]

2. Renton, "Yann Martel Interview."
3. Martin, *Write Your Best Story*.
4. Horton, *Christian Faith*, 17.
5. Lyotard, *Postmodern Explained*.
6. Lyotard, *Postmodern Condition*, 14.
7. Taylor, "Christian Narrative," para. 1.
8. There is an ongoing debate whether Christianity should be understood as a

as being willfully universal, essentially coercive, and necessarily simplistic.[9] Nevertheless, the main problem with metanarratives is their "allergy to otherness" which Lyotard suggested leads ultimately to the gas chambers of Auschwitz. Pi clearly failed to embody that particular modernist allergy.

What then should be done with the central Christian claim of Jesus as the way, the truth, and the life?[10] Lyotard himself acknowledged alternative modes of discourse capable of conveying truth content. In fact he disavowed "that there are no longer any credible narratives at all. By metanarratives or grand narratives I mean precisely narrations with a legitimating function. Their decline does not stop countless other stories (minor or not so minor) from continuing to weave the fabric of everyday life."[11] He termed this non-legitimizing alternative discourse "storytelling."

Strikingly, Doukhan maintained that the biblical narrative is itself structured as storytelling in a mode which "both escapes the pitfalls of [modern] metanarrativistic discourse and the relativistic/subjectivist trap of postmodern story telling."[12] Contrary to metanarratives, "biblical stories are not universal, but rather, profoundly particular,"[13] depicting the raw humanity and uniqueness of each person's approach to God. By being simply *told*, they are also deeply non-coercive.

> While the modernist approach to the truth content of an ideology necessitates an effort of 'legitimization,' that is to say, of foundation, or appeal to reason, the biblical approach consists in merely retelling the stories. The biblical narrative thus does not *argue* its position in a way that would appeal to human

---

metanarrative. While many understand it as such, James K. A. Smith, for one, has maintained for years that such a conception is simply a myth spread in evangelical circles. Christians "should find in Lyotard not an enemy but an ally; orthodox Christian faith actually requires that we, too, stop believing in metanarratives" (*Who's Afraid of Postmodernism?*, 64). Yet, along with providing more nuanced distinctions Lyotard made between petite and grand narratives, and the grand narratives of antiquity compared to the grand narratives of modernity, Ron Kubsch provides evidence that Lyotard did indeed designate Christianity as a grand emancipation narrative and treated it as one ("Why Christianity").

9. Doukhan, "Christianity for Postmoderns."

10. "Jesus said to him, 'I am the way, and the truth, and the life. No one comes to the Father except through me'" (John 14:6 NRSV). The word "only" does not appear in the first sentence, though it is often inferred from the second.

11. Lyotard, *Postmodern Explained*, 19.

12. Doukhan, "Christianity for Postmoderns," 48–49.

13. Doukhan, "Christianity for Postmoderns," 49.

> reason or cognition as would a metanarrative, but rather simply *testifies* to an event that took place at a given time in history.[14]

Furthermore, the biblical stories avoid the typical over-simplification that "points to a single and simple goal, one that can be easily followed by all, thereby allowing for no nuances or critiques."[15]

> Rather than opting for a one size fits all paradigm of truth, thereby occulting the diversity and pluralism of walks with God in the Bible, why not opt for a storytelling approach whereby the full richness and plenitude of the biblical truth is shared? ... Rather than opting for a coercive approach to the truth, intent on argumentation and justification of the foundations of one's faith, why not opt for the simple witness of the event of salvation as narrated in the biblical stories, in both New and Old Testament, leaving it to the Spirit to convict of the truth content of those stories? ... Rather than opting for a simplistic narrative of the Christian faith, why not recover its mystery as a truth both above and beyond the limitations of human reason, thereby not excluding doubt, questions, and interrogations on the part of the believer?[16]

Rather than telling Pi his desire to love God by following all three religions is irrational, why not let truth prevail as it is worked out in his life?

Rationality

As a boy, Piscine chose the nickname "Pi" to pay tribute to the irrational number which is the ratio of the circumference of a circle to its diameter. An irrational number is any real number that cannot be expressed as a ratio of two integers, and cannot be represented as a terminating or recurring decimal. That Pi should want to identify with the irrational is not exceptionally radical, given that concepts and entities defined as irrational are actually far more common than usually assumed, even in mathematics and sciences. In mathematics, that seemingly most rational academic discipline in which "$2 + 2 = 4$,"[17] most real numbers are irrational, as mathematics defines irrational. Over in physics, that seemingly most empirical hard science which

---

14. Doukhan, "Christianity for Postmoderns," 50.
15. Doukhan, "Christianity for Postmoderns," 46.
16. Doukhan, "Christianity for Postmoderns," 51.
17. Though it could equal other numbers when using something other than a base ten numeral system.

examines physical matter, sub-fields such as classical mechanics, quantum mechanics, and relativity theory are rife with contradictions, paradoxes, or mysteries that rationality has not been able to unravel.[18] And in religion, that seemingly most formative, personal, and collective life force, knowledge has traditionally not been built on the rational and the empirical. In postmodern parlance, a religion, like a culture or a science, is a grand story or metanarrative replete with its own language or set of symbols straining toward some usually supernatural referent of truth and/or love, according to its own epistemology or method of knowing. Across world religions historically, rational logic, mathematical probabilities, and empirical evidence have not been central to the faith and conviction of most individual religious adherents. As Old Testament scholar Antony Campbell opined, "There is a wonderful absurdity to Christian faith, weighed against the even greater absurdity of anything less."[19]

Yet at the macro cultural level, rationality has always from earliest times been at work in the history of religion, first reducing the bewildering array of gods in religion down to a clear and coherent set, and then down to one, before rendering the remaining god superfluous. Sociologist Robert Bellah's influential account of religious evolution identifies five historical stages, with transition from each stage to the next being a function of rationality.[20] In Primitive religion, spirits were deemed no greater than humans, and humans identified with them through ritual. In Archaic religion, spirits were deemed supernaturally powerful, and humans communicated with them through prayer and sacrifice, even while reality remained monistic. In Historic (Abrahamic) religion, the spiritual became transcendent, monotheistic, and entirely differentiated from the secular, indeed in tension with the secular. In Early Modern religion marked by the Protestant Reformation, the negative view of the world was modified, as salvation was worked out in this world through faithfulness in personal relationship with God. Finally, in Modern religion, the dualistic view of reality broke down as the supernatural collapsed into the natural, and religion became mostly ethical life in this world, privatized and autonomous from organizational control.[21] In Max Weber's words, "Reason favored the primacy of universal gods, and every consistent crystallization of a pantheon followed systematic rational

18. Yanofsky, *Outer Limits of Reason*.
19. Campbell, *Whisper of Spirit*, i.
20. Bellah, "Religious Evolution."
21. Luckmann, *Invisible Religion*.

principles."²² Reason eventually dispensed with the gods altogether, leaving us with godless, functional religion, or what some might term spirituality.

With the rise of modernity and the historically unprecedented autonomy of rationality in the Enlightenment, Western Christian religion in particular has been subject to growing pressure to become ever more rationalistic in different and expanded ways. To the extent that Christianity has succumbed to that pressure, however unevenly in different times, places, and contexts, rationality has deeply shaped the current character of Christianity, profoundly altering its pre-modern, early church character.²³

The following analysis first overviews the character of rationality, along with its shifting location and function in Christian faith, before identifying two social practices of rationality, both stemming from the Enlightenment, that, in the extreme, prove problematic. The first, as described by sociology, is the practice of rationalization, which is the imperative to decipher and practice the most efficient means to every end. The second, as described by philosophy, is the practice of rationalism, which is the imperative to employ reason as the ultimate arbiter of all truth. Both of these social practices will be shown to reduce Christian faith by diminishing and even denying its non-rational elements and ways of being and knowing.

Therefore, it will be argued that, in matters of Christian faith, rationality makes "a good servant but a bad master."²⁴ In other words, when rationality is used by Christians for delimited purposes, it can be a helpful tool. But when rationality rules Christianity as its *de facto* lord, mostly trouble ensues. To be wholly Christian then, is to be anti-rational*ist* without being anti-rational, which is to value and practice rationality without being ruled by it or limited to it. Both the Christian means-end rationality of rationalization and the Christian cognitive fundamentalism of rationalism can, must, and are making way for more narrative, affective, and incarnational forms of Christian faith. To be Christian is not only or even necessarily an outgrowth of rational action or thought, but to live the Christian story, to feel Christ-like passions, and to enact Christ-like behavior. Or in the words of the prophet, "to do justice, and to love kindness, and to walk humbly with your God" (Mic 6:8).

---

22. Weber, *Economy and Society*, 417.
23. Byrne, *Religion and the Enlightenment*.
24. Livingstone, "Farewell to Arms," 253.

B. THE CHARACTER OF RATIONALITY

Definitions

It is simplistic to speak of rationality in the singular, because rationalities may be those "of modern academic philosophy, [or] those provided by more or less organized communities of shared belief."[25] Hence, what is rational in the classroom is not necessarily what is rational in the village. As such, Enlightenment rationality, for example, is itself a historical, partisan subculture, just as the rationality of a pre-historic tribe was. But in its simplest, generic form, rationality is the state of being reasonable, of weighing and evaluating reasons to believe or act according to one's overarching view of the world. To reason is to make sense of things consciously and critically for the purpose of establishing what are then held to be facts, and thereby justifying subsequent beliefs or acts. For example, understandings of the origin of the world can be thoroughly rational, and justify subsequent beliefs about the world and actions toward it. Conversely, non-rationality is belief or action not weighed or evaluated by critical reason, but driven primarily by tradition, custom, norms, consensus, habit, values, ideals, meaning-making, emotions, intuition, or even the unconscious. In all these ways, understandings of the origin of the world can also be completely non-rational, yet likewise justify subsequent beliefs and actions.

Both rationality and non-rationality are internally coherent to their practitioners, but rationality employs a critical cognitive process that non-rationality does not.[26] The narrower confines of logical rationality—also known as critical thinking when less formal—differentiates between deductive and inductive reasoning. In deductive or top-down reasoning, a conclusion is judged to be valid when it follows logically from sound premises. When the premises are true and the reasoning is valid, then necessarily the conclusion is true. The classic form of deductive reasoning is the syllogism, a deductive argument containing two premises and a conclusion. For example, if all humans are mortal, and Jane is human, then Jane is surely mortal. In contrast, inductive or bottom-up reasoning infers a conclusion on the basis of observable evidence; the soundness or justification of the conclusion is judged according to its ability to account for the evidence and explain anomalies. Therefore, if Joe has arrived on time for the last thousand days, he will probably arrive on time today. Because the premises of deductive arguments are intended to provide conclusive support for their conclusions,

---

25. MacIntyre, *Whose Justice? Which Rationality?*, 3.

26. The concepts of rationality and non-rationality employed here are drawn primarily from Max Weber's *Economy and Society*.

deductive reasoning professes to reach conclusions that are certainly true. However, because the premises of inductive arguments are intended to provide anywhere from relatively weak to strong, but not conclusive, support for their conclusions, inductive reasoning professes only to reach conclusions that are probably true.[27] Joe will probably arrive on time today, but today might be the exception.

A further, rougher distinction can be made between theoretical reason as a cognitive function of belief in contrast to practical rationality as an optimizing strategy for action, a difference that will be elaborated in later sections of this analysis. But both theoretical reason and practical rationality are always grounded in the background assumptions and conditions of one model of truth or another, rendering the conclusions of rationality to be dependent upon one's conception of truth. For example, if the belief of a particular formulation of truth is that benefitting oneself is the foremost value, then rationality will lead to action that is self-interested even to the point of what some would deem selfishness. Conversely, if the belief of a model is that benefitting the group is the foremost value, then purely selfish behavior will be deemed irrational. Similarly, it is rational for a woman living in a post-industrial, technologically advanced, postmodern welfare state to bear few children, because she is not dependent on them for her personal, long-term well-being and security. Yet it is equally rational for a woman living in an agricultural, technologically less developed, pre-modern minimalist state to bear many children, because in those circumstances, she is dependent on them for her personal, long-term well-being and security.

Truth

Even the truth that rationality seeks is not singular or universal, as it can take several alternate forms depending on several contextual variables or theoretical perspectives.[28] Four leading forms of truth are pertinent here. Originating with Plato and Aristotle, the most common model or conception of truth is *correspondence theory*, which holds as true beliefs that conform to reality external to the self, or statements that accurately describe the actual state of the real world. As such, this form of truth is most useful for empirical questions about the natural world.[29] Second, *coherence theory*

---

27. Moore and Parker, *Critical Thinking*.
28. Blackburn and Simmons, *Truth*.
29. The conception of "the empirical" employed here is the same as that of the meta-theoretical position of critical realism, but the conceptions of "the actual" and "the real" are not.

requires a proper fit of elements within a whole system of thought or action, and holds as true beliefs that lend mutual inferential support to each other within that system. This becomes problematic for the complexities of psychological and sociological aspects of human life, because of their frequent disjunctions. Third, *pragmatic theory* holds as true beliefs that are verified by their usefulness when put into practice. As William James put it, "the 'true' is only the expedient in our way of thinking, just as the 'right' is only the expedient in our way of behaving."[30] Fourth, *constructivist theory* holds as true beliefs that are constructed by social processes which are historically and culturally specific, and shaped by the power struggles within a specific community of discourse. This theory is more useful for questions about culture than about nature, such as questions about gender, because cultures are constructed in ways that nature is not. What all theories of truth have in common is that weighing and evaluating reasons to believe or act is employed to pursue truth. Each theory is a way of making sense of things consciously and critically for the purpose of establishing truth.

All religious truth in general, and Christian truth in particular, utilizes a combination of these theories of truth. Moreover, all these theories, except for the latter, are commonly and readily granted credibility and embraced by people of Christian faith themselves. The relocations of the Hebrew people, the life of Jesus, and the activities of Paul are accepted as historical facts that correspond to actual people in time and place. The various texts and themes of the Bible and the cumulative traditions of the church are fit together into a coherent theological system. Positive personal experience and community dynamics are taken as evidence that Christianity "works" for good when put into practice. Nevertheless, while almost all Christians accept the narrative of creation, fall, redemption, and restoration, rational arguments about the theological details have divided Christianity into hundreds, likely thousands of branches and denominations, depending on how they are defined.[31]

---

30. James, *Pragmatism*, 98.

31. The most commonly cited number of denominations, 33,000, is from the *World Christian Encyclopedia*, 2001. "World Christianity consists of 6 major ecclesiastico-cultural blocs, divided into 300 major ecclesiastical traditions, composed [sic] of over 33,000 distinct denominations in 238 countries: Independents—22,000 denominations; Protestants—9000 denominations; Marginals—1600 denominations; Orthodox—781 denominations; Catholics—242 denominations; Anglicans—168 denominations" (1:16). The Center for Global Christianity at Gordon-Conwell Theological Seminary, a primary source for the Pew Research Center, estimates there are currently 47,000 denominations. Add to this house churches, emergent churches, and non-denominational churches, which the Association of Religion Data Archives numbers at 35,496, and the plurality is astounding.

As acceptable to Christians as correspondence, coherence, and pragmatic theories of truth are, resistance typically emerges and stiffens at the suggestion that Christian truth is a social construction. The "social construction of reality" thesis seems to unnerve many Christians, as if it implies that their truth is not independently, objectively true. Yet science is also a social construction, and few suggest that it is therefore nothing but a grand false illusion. The social construction of reality thesis posits that society is creatively invented and actively produced by human beings, not something given to humans. It describes "the process whereby people continuously create, through their actions and interactions, a shared reality that is experienced as objectively factual and subjectively meaningful."[32]

Notably, in their landmark, definitive work entitled *The Social Construction of Reality: A Treatise in the Sociology of Knowledge*,[33] Peter Berger and Thomas Luckmann made it very clear from the outset that they were not interested in philosophical arguments about ontology (What is real?) or epistemology (How do we know?). They had more pragmatic and empirical interests—how do we live? They were only concerned with "whatever passes for 'knowledge' in a society, regardless of the ultimate validity or invalidity (by whatever criteria) of such 'knowledge,'" and were focused on "the processes by which any body of knowledge comes to be socially accepted as reality."[34] Similar to critical realism, the meta-theory or philosophy of reality and human knowledge described and adopted in the introduction to this book, Berger and Luckmann never conflate human knowledge about reality with reality itself. The constructivist theory of truth is therefore more about how truth is apprehended than about what it is. In this sense, Christian beliefs about God are clearly historical social constructions, even while Christian faith that is fully self-aware rests in the full true reality of God that presumably lies beyond those constructions.[35]

Social Practices

Rationality is therefore not just the individual's contextualized use of reason to establish and justify belief and action. In whatever form, rationality becomes a social practice embedded in the social structure of a collectivity.[36]

32. Wallace and Wolf, *Contemporary Sociological Theory*, 277.
33. Berger and Luckmann, *Social Construction*.
34. Berger and Luckmann, *Social Construction*, 3.
35. For a Christian critique of the social construction of reality, see Clark and Gaede, "Knowing Together."
36. Leading theorists who have elaborated the concept of social practices include

In the ongoing sociological debate about the primary efficacy of individual actors versus social conditions, individual agency versus social structure, the micro versus the macro, social practice theory focuses on the pre-theoretical assumptions of belief and action. Social practices are the taken-for-granted beliefs and routinized actions which simultaneously and dialectically create both the consciousness of actors and the structural conditions that make those practices possible.[37]

For example, a friendship between two individuals takes for granted certain beliefs about friendship and routinized actions within friendship. These beliefs and actions simultaneously and dialectically create both the consciousness of the two friends as friends and the structural conditions of friendship that make their interactions possible. The two individuals initially create the friendship, and each time they interact they subsequently re-create it. Their friendship becomes an objective reality not only to the friends themselves, but to all others who observe it as well, with all understanding the meaning of the relationship as such. As a reality external even to the two individuals involved, friendship then acts back on both individuals, obligating them to do what friends do in terms of sharing time, energy, resources, and so on.

Social practices pertain to the whole range of how we manage our bodies, handle objects, treat subjects, describe things, and understand the world. They shape thought, knowledge, desire, and the discourse that is both the genesis and product of practice. Seen in this light, both the individual agent and the social structure in which the individual believes and acts are products of the routines that lie at the heart of social practices. And rationality, or its absence, or opposite, is often therefore not just an individual belief or action, but a social practice.

So too is religion. Earlier in his career, Christian Smith conceptualized religion as a moral order of belief.[38] However, in his later book entitled *Religion: What It Is, How It Works, and Why It Matters*, Smith represents many scholars who have come to understand religion primarily as socially prescribed practices. Religion is "a complex of culturally prescribed practices, based on premises about the existence and nature of superhuman powers, whether personal or impersonal, which seek to help practitioners gain access to and communicate or align themselves with these powers, in hopes of realizing human goods and avoiding things bad."[39] Contrary to

Pierre Bourdieu, Anthony Giddens, and Alasdair MacIntyre.
37. Ritzer and Stepnisky, *Sociological Theory*.
38. Smith, *Moral, Believing Animals*.
39. Smith, *Religion*, 22.

Weber's conceptualization, "religion is not most fundamentally a cognitive or existential meaning system. Rather it is essentially a set of practices . . . 'making meaning' is not the heart of religion."[40] Smith goes on to differentiate interventionist, behavior-regulating, and discursive types of religious practices, and to describe the mutual influence of practices and premises. The point for our interests here is that rationality and religion are overlapping social practices.

Isms

The hundreds of "isms" identifiable in public life[41] constitute an entire subcategory of competing social practices. The Greek suffix *ismos* means the action of engaging in something, such as terrorism or patriotism, but as the suffix is employed in English, an ism can also mean a state of being, such as barbarism or alcoholism, or a movement in the arts, such as impressionism or realism.[42] Yet the majority of isms are philosophical or religious belief systems that have become politicized and ideological. Hence fascism, humanism, or Christianism[43] are sets of conscious and unconscious ideas about what is real, and ideals about what ought to be made real, that function as comprehensive normative visions, or systems of meaning applied to public matters.

When rationality is practiced as Enlightenment rationalism, unaided reason is regarded as the sovereign method of knowing, imbued with the power to grasp indubitable truths about the world.[44] Mind is given authority over the senses, the *a priori* over the *a posteriori*. Deductive reasoning from foundational or first principles is held up as the solely sufficient means to truth and the ultimate test of truth, and therefore independent from and superior to the observation of science, the revelation of religion, the authority of tradition, or the subjectivity of personal insight or collective common sense. Ironically, such rationalism has functioned both negatively to deny

---

40. Smith, *Religion*, 41.

41. *The Phrontistery* lists 234 philosophical isms. http://phrontistery.info/isms.html#top.

42. Saint-Andre, *Ism Book*.

43. Christianism and Christianist are terms used to describe conservative Christians who pursue political power for the purpose of implementing their positions as public policy. *The Merriam-Webster Dictionary* chose Christianism as the World of the Year in 2015. See Sullivan, "My Problem with Christianism."

44. Early proponents included René Descartes, Baruch Spinoza, and Gottfried Wilhelm Leibniz.

the supernatural, as in secular humanism, and affirmatively to aid the understanding of revealed truth, as in many forms of modern theology.

Enlightenment rationalism is most conventionally contrasted with a second Enlightenment ism, empiricism, which is the belief and practice of regarding sense evidence to be the beginning and end of knowledge.[45] Empiricism is a different type of foundationalism, built not upon *a priori* assumptions and reason, but upon the "self-evident" truths of observation and experience. A contemporary example of an extreme form of empiricism is scientism, which is frequently critiqued as a form of reductionism by critical realists. Empiricism denies the reality of metaphysical and theological truth, or even the utility of conceptual reflection alone. So Emile Durkheim, for example, maintained that "religion can affirm nothing that science denies, and deny nothing that science affirms."[46]

Nevertheless, rationality and science are far from antithetical, because science is itself a particular kind of rationality, by virtue of its use of both the reasoning of logic plus the experience of the senses in the instrumental reasoning known as the scientific method. Francis Bacon construed rationalists as spiders spinning their webs out of themselves, and empiricists as ants collecting materials to make some sense and use of them. Empiricism has led in turn to the more radical stance of positivism in the nineteenth century,[47] the belief that knowledge is reliable only if it is immediately observable and scientifically testable. Empiricism then led further to logical positivism in the twentieth century,[48] the belief that only carefully constructed logical propositions about strictly limited factual domains could be true or false. Today in the twenty-first century, critical realism is "wary of simple correspondence concepts of truth" in both rationalism and empiricism.[49]

Rather than empiricism, the truer opposite of Enlightenment rationalism is a constellation of social practices that have in common varying degrees of non-rationality. Crucially, this non-rationality must not be mistaken for either irrationality or anti-rationality. Irrationality violates rationality, whereas anti-rationality opposes rationality. But in the language of logic and deductive reasoning, the complement "not-*a*," which in this case is non-rationality, is not necessarily the denial, rejection, or refutation of "*a*," which here is rationality. "Not-*a*" is simply everything other than

45. Early proponents included Thomas Hobbes, John Locke, and David Hume.

46. Durkheim, *Elementary Forms*, 433.

47. Positivism is most associated with the early-nineteenth-century founder of sociology, Auguste Comte.

48. Logical positivism is most associated with the Vienna Circle of the early twentieth century.

49. Sayer, *Realism and Social Science*, 2.

"*a*." Non-rationality is simply everything other than rationality. "Not-*a*" is simply contrary to "*a*," without necessarily contradicting "*a*." The non-rationality of aesthetics, for example, simply has nothing to do with the critical cognitive process of rationality, just like the non-logical is not necessarily illogical or anti-logical, but simply has nothing to do with the logical. Belief in either theism or atheism, the case in point here, is non-rational to the extent that they are both inferences about the world that are not subject to the verification or falsification that would put them in the category of either the entirely rational or irrational.

The Romantic era that peaked in the first half of the nineteenth century was a reaction to Enlightenment rationality.[50] Romanticism, the social practice that legitimates emotion, imagination, and intuition as authentic and authoritative sources of knowledge, was built on the non-rational. So too was transcendentalism,[51] the social practice that presupposed an ideal reality higher than the physical world of human perception and experience, and sought to transcend both rationalism and empiricism. Other putatively non-rational epistemologies include emotionalism, intuitionism, mysticism, nativism, perspectivism, relativism, sensationalism, solipsism, subjectivism, syncretism, and so on. To be sure, a great deal of human belief and action occurs in the realm of the non-rational. But in modernity, Enlightenment conceptions of rationality have been the primary cultural imperative and social practice, as most other isms have been defined in terms of their kind and degree of departure from it.

C. THE SHIFTING LOCATION OF RATIONALITY IN RELIGION

Definitions

To observe that modernity has made rationality more central to religion is not yet to identify exactly where rationality is located or where it is more prominent within the expansive realm of religion. Doing so requires first differentiating between religion, spirituality, and faith.

Whether religion is understood as culturally prescribed practices or as an external, collective moral order,[52] it is undeniably a collective phenomenon, external to or beyond the individual. In Durkheim's classic functional definition of religion—religion defined by what it does rather than

---

50. Leading proponents included Giambattista Vico and Samuel Taylor Coleridge.
51. Leading proponents included Ralph Waldo Emerson and Henry David Thoreau.
52. Smith, *Moral, Believing Animals*.

defined substantively by what it is—"religion is a unified system of beliefs and practices relative to sacred things, that is to say, things set apart and forbidden—beliefs and practices which unite into one single moral community called a Church all those who adhere to them."[53] Ronald Johnstone's contemporary definition of religion draws on Berger's frequently referenced metaphor of religion as a sacred canopy.[54] "Religion is a set of beliefs and rituals by which a group of people seeks to understand, explain, and deal with a world of complexity, uncertainty, and mystery, by identifying a sacred canopy of explanation and reassurance under which to live."[55] Both definitions emphasize the collective: "unified system(s) . . . which unite into one single moral community . . . all those who adhere," and "a group of people . . . identify a sacred canopy . . . under which to live." Both definitions also emphasize the rational—"a unified system of beliefs," and "a set of beliefs . . . [that] seeks to understand, explain, and deal with a world of complexity, uncertainty, and mystery"—while notably omitting the spiritual.

Though the differences between religion and spirituality will be explored in more detail in Essay Three, as initial distinctions, spirituality is individual instead of collective, internal instead of external, and an experiential dynamic instead of a moral order. In Donald Swenson's succinct phrasing, religion is the sacred between or among, whereas spirituality is the sacred within.[56] As experience more than cognition, spirituality is something felt more than thought. Nor is spirituality merely the privatized, individualized religiosity wrought by modernity,[57] as portrayed in Smith's update of Berger's sacred canopy.

> In the modern world, religion does survive and can thrive, not in the form of 'sacred canopies,' but rather in the form of 'sacred umbrellas.' Canopies are expansive, immobile, and held up by props beyond the reach of those covered. Umbrellas, on the other hand, are small, handheld, and portable—like the faith-sustaining religious worlds that modern people construct for themselves. As the old, overarching sacred canopies split apart and their ripped pieces of fabric fell toward the ground, many innovative religious actors caught those falling pieces of cloth

---

53. Durkheim, *Elementary Forms*, 62.
54. Berger, *Sacred Canopy*.
55. Johnstone, *Religion in Society*, 97.
56. Swenson, *Society, Spirituality, and the Sacred*.
57. McGuire, *Religion*.

in the air and, with more than a little ingenuity, remanufactured them into umbrellas.[58]

In contradistinction to both religion and spirituality, faith is best understood as an individual existential commitment that is holistically cognitive, affective, volitional, and behavioral. Faith is an exercise of not just the mind, but the whole being, including the heart and will and body. Whether religious or not, the sum of faith retains a substantial proportion of non-rationality, despite frequent earnest attempts to make it as reasonable as possible. Even if the object of religious faith cannot be made deductively certain due to its supernatural qualities, it can at least be made inductively as probable as possible, so as to reduce the span of the inevitable "leap of faith"[59] that remains necessary after reason has had its say.

At the personal level, faith, according to James Fowler, is a human universal, in as much as all humans seek meaning of some kind.[60] In essence, faith is a relationship of trust and loyalty between the self and some other, in the context of what is deemed to be of ultimate value and power. Faith is also a specific structure of knowing, not a particular content of what is known, because faith can be placed in many different things—God, government, marriage, or science. As the character of the elder in George Bernard Shaw's play *Too True to be Good* lamented,

> The science I pinned my faith to is bankrupt: its tales were more foolish than all the miracles of the priests, its cruelties more horrible than all the atrocities of the Inquisition. . . . [I]ts counsels that were to have established the millennium have led straight to European suicide. . . . For its sake I helped to destroy the faith of millions of worshippers in the temples of a thousand creeds. And now look at me and behold the supreme tragedy of the atheist who has lost his faith—his faith in atheism, for which more martyrs have perished than for all the creeds put together.[61]

---

58. Smith, *American Evangelicalism*, 106.

59. The phrase is commonly attributed to Søren Kierkegaard, though he never used it directly. Nevertheless, he did write of many different leaps or breaks from reason and science related to Christian faith, and felt that a leap of faith was vital in accepting Christianity, due to the paradoxes that exist within it. See his *Philosophical Fragments* and *Concluding Unscientific Postscript*. "Like Dostoevsky, Kierkegaard, who plays an important role in the spiritual struggle for meaning on the part of the modern writer, casts off the bondage of logic and the tyranny of science." Glicksberg, *Literature and Religion*, 12.

60. Fowler, *Stages of Faith*.

61. Shaw, *Too True to be Good*, Act 3, 99.

Significantly, Fowler distinguishes between two kinds of knowing that occur in faith. The "logic of rational certainty" aspires to disinterested, objective truths that need to be impersonal, propositional, demonstrable, and replicable. The "logic of conviction," on the other hand, is imaginative, affective, ecstatic, unconsciously structuring, and ultimately self-constituting of the knower in relation to the known. As a non-rational method of knowing, the logic of conviction does not negate the logic of rational certainty, but by being more inclusive, it contextualizes, qualifies, and anchors rational certainty. Ultimately, faith is more action than belief, what Fowler terms "faithing." Faith is a verb, something we do, not a noun, or an object we possess. Faith is not sitting in the airport lounge merely professing belief that the pilot is competent, sober, and not on a suicide mission. Faith is putting self at stake by boarding the plane. Fowler's full, formal definition of faith is as follows:

> People's evolved and evolving ways of experiencing self, others and world (as they construct them), as related to and affected by the ultimate conditions of existence (as they construct them), and of shaping their lives' purposes and meanings, trusts and loyalties, in light of the character of being, value and power determining the ultimate conditions of existence (as grasped in their operative images—conscious and unconscious—of them).[62]

Peter Enns puts it in plainer language: "faith isn't something in your head (or heart)."[63] Faith in the New Testament was "not about the content of what to think" or feel.[64] While faith, like belief, includes content—the what—faith is more about trust—the who. Faith is the continual act of trusting, the practice of trusting.

Similarly, Brian McLaren differentiates between conceptual beliefs, which are expressed in propositions, such as "I believe *that* . . . ," and relational beliefs, which are expressed in relationships of trust and loyalty, such as "I believe *in* . . . "[65] As faithing, relational beliefs reveal more about the commitment of the subject of belief, that is, the believer, than about the object of belief. "The situation becomes more complex when an object of relational belief—like a religion or a church, for example—demands statements of conceptual belief as proof of loyalty or requirement for belonging. The situation is even more highly charged when an object of relational

---

62. Fowler, *Stages of Faith*, 92–93.
63. Enns, *Sin of Certainty*, 98.
64. Enns, *Sin of Certainty*, 98.
65. McLaren, *Great Spiritual Migration*, 233–34.

belief provides rewards and punishments based on conceptual beliefs,"[66] sanctions such as honor or shame, acceptance or rejection. In *The Predicament of Belief*,[67] Philip Clayton and Steven Knapp recommended a minimal conceptual belief *about* Jesus that shifts focus onto relational belief *in* Jesus, that is, faith in Jesus. Christians, they recognized, will believe at different descending levels of certainty, from universally compelling belief, to rationally defensible belief, to personalized belief, to vacillating belief, to wishful belief, to metaphorical belief.

Returning to the social practices of isms, fideism—literally faith-ism—is also antithetical to rationalism in a vein different from romanticism. Alvin Plantinga defined fideism as an "exclusive or basic reliance upon faith alone, accompanied by a consequent disparagement of reason and utilized especially in the pursuit of philosophical or religious truth."[68] Faith is seen as independent of Enlightenment rationality, frequently hostile to it, and often superior to it. As Tertullian famously put it, "What indeed has Athens to do with Jerusalem?"[69] And as Blaise Pascal famously put it later, "The heart has its reasons which reason knows not."[70] Ultimately forsaking reason, if not disparaging it, and relying on faith alone, what the fideist objects to is not so much reason *per se*, but the evidentialism that insists no belief should be held unless it is supported by Enlightenment-style evidence. William Clifford's declaration that "[i]t is wrong always, everywhere, and for every one, to believe anything upon insufficient evidence" is one example of such evidentialism.[71] Yet it is not as if the faith of the fideist has no basis or evidence. More often than not, their faith is based on non-rational experience rather than reason, in what has been termed experientialism.[72] Experience becomes the final court of appeal, as the self-attesting character of experience is used to verify the truthfulness of any claim, resonating with pragmatic theories of truth. However, mainstream theology of each of the Catholic, Orthodox, and Protestant branches of Christianity tends to reject experience alone as an adequate foundation of truth.

---

66. McLaren, *Great Spiritual Migration*, 234.
67. Clayton and Knapp, *Predicament of Belief*.
68. Plantinga, "Reason and Belief in God," 87.
69. See Tertullian, "On Prescription Against Heretics" and "On the Flesh of Christ," in Roberts and Donaldson, *Ante-Nicene Fathers*, 3:246.
70. Pascal, *Pensées*, 97. Other, more recent proponents include Søren Kierkegaard, William James, and Ludwig Wittgenstein.
71. "Ethics of Belief," in Clifford, *Lectures and Essays*, 346.
72. Leading proponents include Friedrich Schleiermacher, Rudolph Otto, and Martin Heidegger.

Elements of Religion

But non-rational experience is not easily excised from the definitional heart of religion.[73] Various social scientific models identify the most common elements of religion, and non-rational experience is most frequently located at the genesis or core of religion.[74] Three other characteristic elements of religion are also usually included in such models. First, *myths* are narratives that alone or in combination with other elements render a cosmology, a way of explaining the origin, history, and evolution of the universe. While many religious adherents take them literally, others understand them as truth-telling stories that are not necessarily historical accounts, because their empirical factuality cannot be determined, and is ultimately irrelevant. The narrative veracity of these explanatory verbalizations produces the intellectual framework of a worldview that often remains implicit and unconsciously taken for granted. Nevertheless, the structured set of beliefs derived from the myth establish that religion's orthodoxy. Second, religious *rituals* are repeated, consecrated (sacred) behaviors that symbolically express the moods and motivations of a belief system, and function to socialize, bond, remind, regulate, and empower its adherents. These actions establish that religion's orthopraxy. Third, religious *ethos* is a cluster of codes of behavior—values, norms, morality—that, instead of being a way of *viewing* life, constitutes a way of *doing* life. Instead of describing what is, the codes of behavior in a religious ethos describe what ought to be done. Religious ethos also establishes the underlying attitude toward the individual and the world, and prevents the profane from intruding upon the sacred.

Social scientific models of the arrangement of these elements of religion more often than not place the non-rational experience of spirituality, or the sacred within, at the center of religion for both the individual and the religion as a whole. Religious experience refers to all those ineffable yet noetic aspects that have an internal presence to the individual,[75] including feelings, perceptions, moods, attitudes, attributions, and the like. Myths then explain experience, rituals extend experience, ethos maintains experience, and religious organizations rise up to frame and house religious experience. Together, myth, ritual, ethos, and experience are more powerful than rational systems of belief because their images capture imagination, carry emotional power, and mobilize resources beyond what abstract propositions

---

73. Alston, *Perceiving God*.

74. Social scientists whose model of religion locates non-rational experience at the genesis or core of religion include Emile Durkheim, Clifford Geertz, Donald Swenson, Keith Roberts, and David Yamane.

75. James, *Varieties of Religious Experience*.

and rational systems can do. As Andrew Greeley put it, to understand religion, we need to focus on its poetry, not its prose, on its imaginative and narrative infrastructure, not on its cognitive superstructure.[76] "The origins and raw power of religion are at the imaginative (that is, experiential and narrative) level for both the individual and for the tradition."[77]

In a sense, non-rational experience is not only the center of religion, but also its root. Rationality is implicated in both the beginning and the end of religion chronologically, in the beginning by its absence, and in the end by its overwhelming presence. Swenson argues that all religions begin with the non-rational experience of what becomes a charismatic leader.[78] So Christianity, for example, begins when the disciples abandon their everyday lives in response to Jesus's invitation to "Follow me." Experience then produces myth, myth produces ritual, and ritual produces ethos. At the other end of a religion's timeline, Thomas O'Dea argues that secularization is due to the rationalization of thought in general, and to systematizing religious beliefs into logical rational terms in particular.[79] Matters that once were mysteries to be pondered become problems to be solved, as religion transforms "from *mythos* to *logos*," demythologizing the world, human culture, and even its very own sacred Scriptures. Like Berger and others, O'Dea points to rational, this-worldly Protestantism in particular as contributing much to the modern secularization process.

O'Dea's conception of religion is based on Rudolph Otto's *The Idea of the Holy*,[80] who in turn had based his conception of the holy, or *numinous* as he termed it, on Immanuel Kant's distinction between *phenomena*, the world of physical objects approached by science and defended by reason, and *noumena*, the world beyond empirical observation. Otto took the non-rational experience of the holy, the *"mysterium tremendum et fascinosum,"* to be the universal foundation of religion. Filled with awe and fear, and feeling overwhelmed by the absolute unapproachability of the holy, Wholly Other, like Moses before the burning bush, the individual senses their utter unworthiness and dependence, like the Hebrew prohibition against even voicing the name of Yahweh. At the same time, there is power, energy, urgency, vitality, passion, will, force, fascination, attraction, and ultimate goodness that commands an ethical imperative. Intellectualizing about the non-rational experience of the holy, in an attempt to "make sense" out of it or explain it,

---

76. Greeley, *Religion as Poetry*.
77. Greeley, *Catholic Imagination*, 4.
78. Swenson, *Society, Spirituality, and the Sacred*.
79. O'Dea, *Sociology of Religion*.
80. Otto, *Idea of the Holy*.

only came after the fact, with myth and ritual simply trying to recreate some semblance of that experience. And like those before and after him, Otto also lamented the tendency of modern Western culture to reduce the holy to rational concepts about God.

Cultural Shifts

The pre-modern Latin root of the English word "religion," *religio*, meant a living, personal, subjective experience, a "particular way of seeing and feeling the world,"[81] a matter of the heart. Nevertheless, in modern times, religion became more of an institutionalized system of beliefs, something whose propositions were either true or false, a matter of the mind. Today, the postmodern cultural shift away from religiosity toward spirituality, and the subsequent uncoupling of spirituality from religious institutions, has renewed the role of non-rationality in the practice of faith. Religion is now mostly experienced as "life-as," connoting life lived in conformity to "objective" roles, duties, and obligations. Spirituality, in contrast, is experienced as "subjective-life," connoting life lived in authentic connection with the inner depths and experiences of one's unique self-in-relation.[82] Whereas the religious source of significance is found in adhering to a transcendent tradition that bestows order and meaning from the outside, the spiritual source of significance is found in turning away from self-sacrificial deference to external authority toward being true to internalities. What Charles Taylor called "the massive subjective turn"[83] of contemporary Western culture is less a Great Turning than a Great Returning to an ancient understanding of Christian faith.[84]

Harvey Cox, for example, in a rather sweeping generalization that applies mostly to the global West/North, discerned three ages of Christian history similar to the pre-modern, modern, and postmodern divides, but with a middle age of earlier onset and thus longer duration than modernity.[85] During the Age of Faith (the first several centuries after Christ until Constantine), being Christian meant a communal living out of trust and loyalty to Jesus, following the work he had begun, and embracing his hope. During the Age of Belief (from Constantine until the twentieth century), being Christian meant accepting the creeds, catechisms, and dogma of the

81. Smith, *Meaning and End of Religion*, 21.
82. Heelas and Woodhead, *Spiritual Revolution*, 6.
83. Taylor, *Ethics of Authenticity*, 26.
84. Bass, *Christianity After Religion*.
85. Cox, *Future of Faith*.

institutionalized church. Now, during the Age of Spirit begun in the twentieth century, being Christian has come to mean connection to God through mystery, wonder, and awe, in decidedly non-dogmatic, non-institutional, and non-hierarchical ways. The Age of Faith was characterized by faith *in* God, the Age of Belief by belief *about* God, and the Age of Spirit by experience *of* God. Faith is now resurgent, even while dogma is dying. Like Fowler, for Cox too, faith is not mere belief. Faith is a deep-seated existential confidence *in* the divine, whereas belief is intellectual assent to tenets *about* the divine, though obviously religious faith must arise from some beliefs about the divine.

Diana Butler Bass took the shift away from religiosity toward spirituality, and from belief toward faith, a step further by unpacking the character and order of believing, behaving, and belonging.[86] She asserted that the modern assumption that belief is merely the intellectual content of faith, our rehearsal of ideas about God, is itself misguided. Replacing focus on faith *in* God with focus on tenets *about* God produced modern, fundamentalist, institutionalized, and therefore problematic religion. Preoccupation with the question "what do I believe" led inexorably to religious dogma. The more spiritual question "how do I believe" is equally important, pushing people into a deeper engagement with the world beyond dictated information *about* the divine, to personal experience *of* the divine. Even the question "whom do I believe" is more experiential, pushing the question of authority beyond mere expertise to issues of relationship and authenticity. Returning to belief as more experiential, and not merely intellectual assent, shifts the focus from the correctness of cognitive content back to the act of faith as a verb—practicing trust, loyalty, and love. To believe in God, Bass concluded, is not merely to weigh the rational or empirical evidence for the existence of God, but to trust and take refuge in the holy, Wholly Other.

Second, regarding behaving, Bass also noted that for its first few centuries, Christianity was understood primarily as spiritual practices that offered a meaningful way of life in the world, not a tight set of doctrines about the world and its creator-redeemer. This echoes and affirms Christian Smith's shift, reviewed earlier, from defining religion as a moral order of belief back to defining it primarily as a set of prescribed practices. Again, "religion is not most fundamentally a cognitive or existential meaning system. Rather it is essentially a set of practices."[87] It was possible in the early church, and still is today, to be a practicing Christian though not always a believing one. Contrary to the emphasis in John's Gospel and Paul's Letters,

86. Bass, *Christianity After Religion*.
87. Smith, *Religion*, 41.

according to the Synoptic Gospels, Jesus himself consistently answered the question "What must I do to be saved?" by requiring active obedience, not mere belief.[88]

Third, regarding belonging, Bass described the Christian self as constituted by relationship, not cognition. Contrary to René Descartes's sense of the self as a proposition—*cogito ergo sum*: "I think, therefore I am"—and consistent with George Herbert Mead's sense of self as socially emergent—individual selves are the products of social interaction and not the (logical or biological) preconditions of that interaction[89]—Christian spirituality proceeds from self as preposition. When Bass "confess[es] that I no longer hold propositional truths about Christianity; rather, I experience prepositional truths of being found *in* God *through* Christ *with* others *toward* the kingdom,"[90] she fails to see the propositional truth claims implicit in the objects of her prepositional phrases, but she succeeds in placing emphasis on the relational prepositions. Like the southern African concept of *Ubuntu*—"I am because we are"—this Christian concept of self and other opposes classic Western individualism.[91]

Her more compelling argument is what Bass termed the current Great Reversal. Protestants gradually shifted away from emphasizing spiritual practices toward emphasizing belief first, behavior second, and belonging as an ancillary eventuality. The intra-Christian contest of truth claims that ensued produced an intellectualized and impersonal religion that defined people by what propositions they believed. But according to Bass, Christian spirituality unfolds in the exact opposite order: belonging first, behaving second, and belief as an eventuality. This is the chronology of spirituality lived out by the children of Israel in the Old Testament. Marvin Wilson noted that "In Hebrew thought, the essence of true godliness is tied primarily to a relationship, not to a creed."[92] Likewise, Christianity did not begin with Peter's confession, but with the disciples having chosen earlier to follow Jesus, to join in and belong. Peter's confession of belief eventually grew out of the belonging of relationship. Christian faith did not begin by precisely refining ideas about God via seminal exercises in systematic theology. It was originally about how to act toward each other, what to do in this world. All Germanic languages other than English have in fact introduced a terminological distinction between truth as "fidelity" and truth

---

88. Neufeld, "Gospel in the Gospels."
89. Mead, *Mind, Self and Society*.
90. Bass, *Christianity After Religion*, 192.
91. Breems, "Relational Being as Icon."
92. Wilson, *Our Father Abraham*, 138.

as "factuality." Bass used contemporary Amish and African Christianity as examples of Christianity in its ancient and proper order, of spirituality and faith as experiential practice, unencumbered with complex creeds and confessions, a spirituality more of the heart and hands than the head.

The constant challenge of social history is to ascertain how ordinary people actually lived throughout successive eras, in contrast to how intellectual elites thought they ought to live. In this case, the challenge is to ascertain the social practice of Christian faith in contrast to the history of theology. What has been the truly operative faith of the Christian laity, who for much of Judeo-Christian history have been largely illiterate, compared to faith as ordered and ordained by Christian theologians, philosophers, and clerics? What has been the "lived religion" of Christians, the "actual experience of [Christian] persons," versus "the prescribed [Christian faith] of institutionally defined beliefs and practices?"[93] All of the above suggests that the role of Enlightenment rationality in Christian faith can easily be overdrawn, and when it is, prove to be problematic. Modern rationality, it has been said here, is having good reasons that justify the cognitive function of belief and the optimizing strategy for action. Overplaying modern rationality in belief leads to rationalism, while overplaying modern rationality in action leads to rationalization. From the perspective of critical realism, both rationalism and rationalization are structures and causal capacities (the real) that have been activated (the actual) and observed (the empirical). They are also emergent social practices not reducible to Enlightenment rationality alone. Therefore, these two problematic social practices, the first philosophical and the second sociological, warrant closer examination, best done in reverse order.

D. RATIONALIZATION OF ACTION

Definitions

In its psychological sense, rationalization means to attribute one's actions to rational and credible motives, or to attribute one's attitude to rational and credible realities, without acknowledging one's true motives or realities, much less recognizing one's subconscious motives or realities. Rationalization in this sense is the defense mechanism of creating an excuse or more attractive explanation for dubious actions or attitudes. For example, we can convince and deceive both the other and ourselves that our action really was "the most loving thing to do."

93. McGuire, *Lived Religion*, 12.

But in its sociological sense, rationalization means the gradual historic displacement of tradition, values, affect, intuition, and mystery by reason and rational calculation in all aspects of everyday life and in every social institution, including religion. Rationalization in this sense is the collective process of determining and selecting the most efficient means to an end. For example, capitalism now organizes commercial enterprises in ways that will maximize their financial profit, not in ways that "it's always been done."

More than any other founder of sociology, Max Weber delineated and explicated the rationalization of modern society. Indeed, though he was critical of Karl Marx's materialistic economic determinism for being a reductive, mono-causal view of history, Weber himself came close to an equivalent idealistic determinism in attributing to rationality the foremost formative role in the rise of modernity. "The fate of our times is characterized by rationalization and intellectualization and, above all, by the disenchantment of the world. Precisely the ultimate and most sublime values have retreated from public life either into the transcendental realm of mystic life or into the brotherliness of direct and personal human relations."[94]

Yet it is difficult to extract a clear definition of rationalization from Weber's work, just as he never overtly defined religion even as he studied it extensively.[95] Like religion, rationalization comes in so many different forms that a single definition may well be precluded. Thus the full range of the meaning of rationalization can only be distilled from a combination of Weber's many other concepts. His conceptions of action and authority, each with their own typologies, have become part of the vocabulary of sociology, and serve well to elucidate rationalization.[96]

First, action must be understood as more than behavior. Mere behavior is meaningless because it occurs without thought, whereas action is subjectively meaningful to the actor because it is the product of conscious processes. For example, there is a profound difference between a blink and a wink. A blink is a mindless physiological function of the body lubricating or protecting the eye, whereas a wink is loaded with multiple potential meanings that require mental processing, and are vulnerable to sometimes socially disastrous misinterpretation. A blink is a cognitively unmediated physical response to the stimulus of a dry or irritated eye. A wink is a physical, communicative encoding of a subtle and potentially enormously complicated message being sent. While the movement of the eyelid is identical

---

94. Weber, "Science as a Vocation."
95. Weber, *Sociology of Religion*.
96. Ritzer and Stepnisky, *Sociological Theory*.

in both cases, a blink is meaningless behavior, whereas a wink is meaningful action.

Psychological behaviorism that merely observes the relationships between stimulus and response is inadequate to grasp full human functioning, because it fails to identify all stimuli—eyelid movement caused by thought, not by dryness—and to take into account the interpretation of the stimulus that determines the response—what the observer of the eyelid movement took it to be or mean.[97] Though touching a hot stove produces mindless behavior, the vast majority of human responses are not behavioral reactions to a stimulus alone, but rather are actions determined by an interpretation of a stimulus. Therefore, just as understanding belief requires a shift in focus from the "what" of belief to the "why" of belief, so too does the understanding of action.

A full range of sources of action exist, from the non-rational to the rational. Weber's typology of action identified two sub-categories of non-rational action and another two sub-categories of rational action, though they usually occur in some combination.[98] First, non-rational action is *affectual* when it is the result of emotion, such as parents sacrificing for their children because they are emotionally invested in them. Second, non-rational action is *traditional* when it follows custom by habitually replicating the way things have been done in the past, such as children uncritically adopting gender roles that their parents have modelled for them. Third, and on the other hand, rational action is *value-rational* when it is chosen on the basis of the actor's belief in some larger set of values, such as parents disciplining their children according to their cultural ideals. Finally, rational action is *means-end rational* when it pursues most effectively and efficiently the ends that actors have chosen, shaped by their view of the people and objects in their environment, such as a family reconstructing its division of labor in order to optimize its functioning.

Other theorists have suggested that Weber's third type of action, value-rational action, is not purely rational, but only rational in the sense of adhering to some systematic value. Given that values themselves are not necessarily rational, such action is also not necessarily rational. Religious submission to some supposed higher power is a salient case in point. Thus it is argued that human action remains primarily non-rational when it is guided by emotions, traditions, ideals, morals, norms, habits, unconscious desires, and/or the quest for meaning—the first three of Weber's types of action. In contrast, truly rational action, the fourth type, is less encompassing,

---

97. Mead, *Mind, Self and Society*.
98. Weber, *Economy and Society*, 24–26.

and is motivated primarily by a strategic or calculated attempt to maximize rewards or benefits while minimizing costs, what Weber termed means-end rationality, and what others term instrumental rationality. In short, values motivate non-rational action, whereas interests motivate rational action.[99]

Rational Choice Theory

Self-interested means-end rationality has grown ever more dominant in contemporary society, to the point where theorizing all social relations is itself increasingly built on it. Rational choice theory, an outgrowth from economics, is one of the fastest growing perspectives of the last generation.[100] It understands all human action to be driven by individual self-interest seeking to profit from calculations of what the actor perceives to be costs and rewards in a world of scarcity. It goes on to explore how interaction between rationally motivated individuals can produce norms, networks, group solidarity, and the control of resources, as well as how these factors, once created, act back on and constrain the individual's decisions and behavior. For many theorists, rational choice theory has now become the new paradigm in the sociology of religion,[101] displacing the old, Weberian cultural paradigm.

This new paradigm explains religion as the desire for certain rewards that are actually not available in society, such as life after death. In the temporal absence of such rewards, humans seek compensators, which are beliefs, immediately unverifiable, that rewards for sacred beliefs and actions will be obtained in the distant future. So Pascal's wager, for example, is to bet one's life on the existence of God and live accordingly, because the maximal eternal rewards delivered for doing so, if true, far outweigh the minimal temporal costs if false. While this explains religious belief and action at the micro personal level, it also leads to the notion of religious economies at the macro collective level, replete with markets of current and potential customers, firms seeking to serve the market, and competing product lines, all of which thrive best without interference from the state. The old paradigm of religion which focused on the meaning it provided for life is said to be inadequate, especially in the religious free-market conditions of modern pluralism.[102] Yet this new paradigm is problematically one-dimensional in its focus on rationality, is clearly less applicable to Eastern religions not built

99. Appelrouth and Edles, *Classical and Contemporary Sociological Theory*.

100. Leading proponents include James Coleman, George Homans, and Peter Blau.

101. Leading proponents include Rodney Stark, Roger Finke, and Laurence Iannaccone.

102. Stark and Finke, *Acts of Faith*.

on rational ways of living as Christianity in the West is built, and is reductionist in its failure to take culture into account.[103]

Employing rational choice theory reveals that rationality in religion is therefore much more than reasons for individual belief, or even reasons for individual action, but extends to the organization of collective belief and action as well. Nevertheless, the rise of rational choice theory also reveals that rationality is increasingly asserting itself in the very social scientific explanation of religion itself. Despite its dark view of humans as cold-hearted, self-centered, profit-seeking calculators, rational choice theory makes sense and rings true to the contemporary Western mind. Hence, it turns out that rational choice theory is itself another cultural artifact, even while it denies the formative effects of culture on how people think. Contrary to the claims of rational choice theory, it would seem that rational choice theory is itself further evidence that humans are more accurately conceived as enculturated beings, or "moral, believing, narrating animals,"[104] not merely rationalistic calculators, unless their culture shapes them to be so. If and when their culture does shape them so, their belief in rationality will indeed narrate their lives. Hence, rational choice theory is a "historically situated moral project . . . [that] embodies and reinforces key elements of the secular Enlightenment story . . . [of] modern liberal democratic capitalism."[105] It is a case of the cultural becoming the scientific, which constitutes some evidence that culture is more formative than rationality.

Authority

Turning to Weber's concept of authority furthers his analysis of and argument for the rationalization of modern Western society.[106] To begin, authority must be differentiated from power. Unlike power, which is control seen by those subject to it as illegitimate because it is taken by coercion, authority is control seen by those subject to it as legitimate, and is therefore granted by consent. For example, someone can use an army tank to control vehicle traffic at an intersection of roads by threatening, or, if necessary, enacting destructive force on any vehicle that does not comply with their directives. That is power. Alternately, someone can control vehicle traffic by wearing a police officer's uniform, standing in the middle of the intersection, and waving their arms. That is authority. Society has legitimated the right of

---

103. Swenson, *Society, Spirituality, and the Sacred*; Smith, *Moral, Believing Animals*.
104. Smith, *Moral, Believing Animals*, 118.
105. Smith, *Moral, Believing Animals*, 59–60.
106. Weber, *Economy and Society*.

various officers of the law, by virtue not of their person but of the offices they hold, to make certain binding decisions on others. Thus the exercise of authority always reveals more about those subject to it than about whatever they deem authoritative. Authority, like beauty, is in the eye of the beholder.

Authority does not reside inherently in any person, organization, text, or tradition. For example, to say that any particular text is sacred and therefore authoritative is to say more about the one making the claim than about the text itself, because there are obviously those people for whom that text is not sacred, much less authoritative. They have not granted that text that status, and therefore that text does not have that function for them. Both the sacred and authority, like beauty, are in the eye of the beholder. Even in Christian theology, the authority of the biblical text is properly seen as a derivative rather than an inherent authority, as theologians such as Karl Barth and John Webster have argued. Unlike power, which is social control taken by force, authority is social control given by legitimacy.[107]

Weber's typology of authority identified three historic types based on different sources of legitimacy. First, traditional authority is legitimated by respect for long-established cultural patterns, and exemplified in the realm of religion by the Christian ecclesia, or "church tradition." Second, charismatic authority is legitimated by the perception of exceptional personal qualities in someone, and exemplified by the founders of many new religious movements, including Jesus. Charisma mobilizes people who perceive those singular qualities in that person to acts of great devotion and obedience, enabling charismatic authorities to initiate and activate a break with existing traditions. But both traditional and charismatic authority are non-rational. The third type, rational-legal authority, is legitimated by codified rules and regulations, and exemplified by church bureaucracies, the Roman Catholic Church being the largest and longest-standing bureaucracy in all of human history.

The most critical phase of any new religious movement is when the charismatic founder dies and charismatic authority is lost. If traditional or rational-legal authority structures are not quickly established, the movement will also die. When no longer able to sit at the feet of the guru, messiah, or sage, surviving adherents will organize their community, ritualize their worship, and rationalize their beliefs in a process known as the

---

107. Nevertheless, in Weberian conception, power is inherently neither nefarious nor corrupting, but rather the ethically neutral ability to exert one's will despite resistance, with equal potential to be used for good or evil. A parent can use their superior physical strength to snatch their toddler from the path of an oncoming vehicle, or to abuse their toddler. In *Playing God*, Andy Crouch argued journalistically that power is a God-sanctioned key to human flourishing.

"institutionalization of religion." But even if and when the movement is stabilized by traditional or rational-legal authority, it will, over time, likely be confronted occasionally by new charismatic authorities that challenge those forms of authority, the way the charismatic Protestant reformers challenged the Roman Catholic Church. But while charismatic authority is a powerful force able to overcome traditional or rational-legal authority structures, it is also temporary and unstable. Therefore any new or revolutionary religious movement can only be sustained beyond the life of its charismatic leader by, ironically, the routinization of charisma, that is, by transforming back into the very same traditional or rational-legal structure of authority that charisma supplanted.

Today, because modernity borne of Enlightenment has such a pervasive disrespect for the non-rationality of tradition, and such a persistent distrust of the volatility of charisma, only rational-legal authority is normally respected, trusted, and self-sustaining. Moderns have become imprisoned in what Weber famously termed the "iron cage" of rationalization, which not only locks people into a way of life, but is impervious to external assault.

Extremes of Rationalization

In his massive corpus, Weber examined the effects of rationalization on social structures such as the economy, the polity, law, the city, and even art forms, but more to our interests here, also on religion.[108] For example, rationalization is implicated in his articulation of the original sociological distinction between priests and prophets. Religious priests are specialists who speak *for* the religious establishment from within it on the basis of their status and prestige in its traditional or rational-legal authority structure. Conversely, religious prophets speak *to* the religious establishment from its margins with only whatever charisma they are attributed. According to Swenson, "the focus of the priest is to secure some permanency of the message of the prophet, to insure the economic existence of the enterprise, and to control the authority of the collective."[109] Priests are typically more rationalized than prophets, especially evident in the rise of a professionally trained priesthood that is larger and more literate, specialized, organized, and appreciated than the prophets who are all the opposite.

No one has advanced Weber's rationalization thesis further than George Ritzer with his equally influential McDonaldization thesis, perhaps

---

108. Weber, *Economy and Society*.
109. Swenson, *Society, Spirituality, and the Sacred*, 117.

the end-point of the rationalization process.[110] McDonaldization is the process by which the principles of the fast-food restaurant are coming to dominate more and more sectors of not only Western society, but in the push of cultural imperialism and globalization, are creating a homogenized McWorld at large.[111] The five basic dimensions that govern both employees and customers of McDonald's are a) efficiency, the effort to discover the best possible means to whatever end is desired, b) calculability, the emphasis on quantity of products and speed of service, often to the detriment of quality, c) predictability, the assurance that everything is much the same everywhere and every time, d) control, the physical and social technologies that determine what will happen, and e) the irrationality of rationality, the paradoxical reality that instrumental rationality becomes irrational when the ends sought are sabotaged by the means employed.

The last dimension, the irrationality of rationality exemplified by McDonald's, is evident on multiple fronts and depths in their restaurants world-wide, from the material particularity of the long lines that slow the process, to the excessively processed edibles themselves, to the non-material, ultimate dehumanization endemic to the whole process. Everyone involved becomes an appendage to the machine, and mere fragments of persons in their engagement. Worker activity is deskilled as much as possible, customers are fed prefabricated food and interactions at the service counter, and contact with other human beings is minimized. Communality dissolves into commonality.

At its darkest, "considered as a complex purposeful operation, the Holocaust may serve as a paradigm of modern bureaucratic rationality."[112] Applying the basic principles of industrialization in general, and the factory system in particular, the Nazis employed utmost rationality in their objective to destroy as many specific human beings as possible. As detailed by Zygmunt Bauman, far from being the result of irrationality, premodern barbarity, crazed lunatics, or a breakdown of modernity, the Holocaust was a product of modernity "in keeping with everything we know about our civilization, its guiding spirit, its priorities, its immanent vision of the world."[113] The efficiency of the gas chambers, the calculability of the death rate, the predictability of the trains delivering their cargo, and the physical and social technologies that controlled inmates and guards alike, were all products of modern rationality.

110. Ritzer, *McDonaldization of Society*.
111. Barber, *Jihad vs. McWorld*.
112. Bauman, *Modernity and the Holocaust*, 149.
113. Bauman, *Modernity and the Holocaust*, 8.

> Like everything else done in the modern—rational, planned, scientifically informed, expert, efficiently managed, co-ordinated—way, the Holocaust left behind and put to shame all its alleged pre-modern equivalents, exposing them as primitive, wasteful, and ineffective by comparison. Like everything else in our modern society, the Holocaust was an accomplishment in every respect superior.[114]

Of course, the characteristic of rationalization most evident in the Holocaust is the irrationality of rationality in not just dehumanizing but exterminating humans on a mass scale. But without modern rationalization, "the Holocaust would be unthinkable."[115]

Rationalization of Christianity

The question that must then be addressed is whether and to what extent rationalization has likewise infected modern Western Christianity, and if so, to what extent the particular aspects of McDonaldization have infected modern Western Christian organizations. Are Christian church and para-church organizations now prone to legitimating efficiency, calculability, predictability, and control as God's values and methods? Are non-rational values such as authentic community and openness to the Spirit now secondary and optional aspects of corporate ministry? Different Christian observers talk of McMinistry—gospel as therapy—and McMissions—"short-term tourists for Jesus."[116] John Drane, for one, dissected what he considered the now half-live corpse of the contemporary church in order to ascertain what had reduced it to irrelevant robotics. His findings were that the rationalized McChurch now delivers bite-sized, pre-packaged fast talk, where size and quantity are the measures that matter most, where the promise of no surprises quells the free wind of the Spirit, and where control substitutes for accountability.[117] What then comes as no surprise is that the effects of rationalization on the church and its individual adherents mirror the effects on society and its members.

Though both Weber and Ritzer see much good in rationalization, both also share equally grave concerns about how what appears as progress functions as regress. Weber despaired of the personal alienation wrought by bureaucracies, and the public disenchantment of the world wrought by

---

114. Bauman, *Modernity and the Holocaust*, 89.
115. Bauman, *Modernity and the Holocaust*, 13.
116. Hiebert, "McDonaldization."
117. Drane, *McDonaldization of the Church*.

rationalization which crushes the human spirit, rendering life more methodical and less meaningful. Ritzer lamented the feeble, never-ending, contemporary attempts to re-enchant the world through the "cathedrals of consumption" of popular culture.[118] There is little reason to believe that Christian cathedrals can avoid such effects while engaging in the same practices. Add to such effects that relying increasingly on human methods means relying less on the divine, and McDonaldization, like the rationalization that birthed it, becomes a powerful force of secularization as well, Christianity undermining itself by its social practices. Martin Heidegger argued that this instrumental rationality was the greatest danger facing modern humans.[119]

In a follow-up volume entitled *After McDonaldization* where he searched for remedies, Drane called for pragmatic Christian faith that prioritizes personal experience over reason as the primary way in which people's perspectives are shaped.[120] He argued that the notion that people live according to an explicit, coherent "worldview" needs to be replaced with the recognition that people's individual lifestyles and implicit, incoherent personal perspectives are what shape their sense of being, not some rational, overarching understanding of how the world is supposed to work.[121]

E. RATIONALISM IN BELIEF

Historical Developments

While action is predominantly the purview of sociology, belief is predominantly the purview of philosophy, the realm in which rationality is more conventionally understood to function. Inasmuch as Christian faith is an individual existential commitment, the rationalization of individual and collective action serves as the current social context in which the relative rationality of belief occurs. Both the rationalization and rationalism of Christian faith are more characteristic of religiosity than spirituality, and hence are currently being challenged by the cultural shift away from the former toward the latter, what Dietrich Bonhoeffer called "religionless Christianity."[122] Contrary to Smith's sociological argument that religion is essentially prescribed practices, Protestants in particular have tended to

---

118. Ritzer, *Enchanting a Disenchanted World*.
119. Heidegger, *Question Concerning Technology*.
120. Drane, *After McDonaldization*.
121. Meanwhile, there is talk in the blogsphere of the McDonaldization of Christian philosophy as well. See for example Bothwell, "McDonaldization."
122. Bonhoeffer, *Papers and Letters from Prison*.

view their faith as essentially prescribed premises, or beliefs. Their theology of salvation has been built primarily on belief as in John 3:16, not on action as in Matthew 25:31–46. And the social practice of rationalism in Christian belief has its own history that nonetheless runs parallel to the rationalization of Christian action, both arising as consequences of Enlightenment modernity.

In *Apostles of Reason: The Crisis of Authority in American Evangelicalism*, historian Molley Worthen chronicles how, minus the magisterial authority of the Roman Catholic Church, Protestants over time turned ever more to reason as the foremost means to truth.[123] Previously, until the canon of Scripture was closed in the fifth century, Christians believed and acted according to the authority of church tradition. Thereafter, the Roman Catholic dyad of tradition and Scripture prevailed until the Reformation, when reason was added to form the well-known Anglican triad of the sources and criteria of Christian faith. Subsequently, experience was added in the late eighteenth century, in what became known as the Wesleyan quadrilateral. The United Methodist Church, for example, asserts that Christian faith is revealed in Scripture, illumined by tradition, vivified in personal experience, and confirmed by reason.[124] But confronted by modernity, connected by the rise of literacy among the laity, compelled to show evidence that the Bible was true, and concerned to fathom what it actually might mean, twentieth-century American fundamentalism and then evangelicalism brought reason to faith in an unprecedented manner and to an unprecedented degree.

Of course, none of the four grounds of Christian faith are truly autonomous or self-sufficient. As Lesslie Newbigin put it, "reason does not operate except within a continuing social tradition which cannot be understood as a purely cerebral operation unrelated to the ongoing experiences of the community which carries this tradition forward."[125] What counts anywhere as reason is dependent on the plausibility structure that sustains it,[126] and reason took on historically unique characteristics in modernity. The autonomy and supremacy of Enlightenment rationality, for example, would have been unintelligible to the church fathers, to Thomas Aquinas, and to the Protestant reformers, for whom philosophy was the handmaiden of theology.[127] The indubitable "control beliefs" of classic foundationalism held

---

123. Worthen, *Apostles of Reason*.
124. Waltz, "Wesleyan Quadrilateral."
125. Newbigin, *Foolishness to the Greeks*, 58.
126. Berger and Luckmann, *Social Construction of Reality*, 92–128.
127. MacIntyre, *Whose Justice? Which Rationality?*; Taylor, *Secular Age*.

reason firmly within the bounds of religion.[128] Nevertheless, though long a vassal of the church, reason gradually ascended the throne of modern, Western Christian belief, coming to rule as the sovereign method of knowing with purportedly preeminent power to grasp truths about the world.

Modern and Postmodern

Though such observations are grounded in cultural studies and the sociology of knowledge, they are also central to the postmodern critique of modernist notions of rationality. Whereas ancient Gnosticism shunned the material realm in favor of the spiritual realm, modernism embraced the mind above all else. Descartes's renowned conclusion—"I think, therefore I am"—separated the mind from the body, and entrenched the view of humans as primarily "thinking things" or "brains on a stick."[129] It resulted in "the valorization of thinking as the core of human identity and the devaluation of embodiment as a source of deception and distress . . . [I]f the essence of the human person is thinking, then what really matters is what can be thought—and what can be thought is what can be calculated, inferred, deduced, and articulated in propositions."[130]

Like Gnosticism, this cultural privileging of the cognitive in modernity also denigrates and negates the particularities and contingencies of embodied lives (gender, race, geography, culture, language, history, and yes, religion) by implying the universality of reason, or more exactly, the pure neutrality of reason because of its impersonal and purportedly ahistoric universality. According to this modern model of reason, "any rational person may judge the worthiness of any other belief. As *universal*, every reasonable human being possesses the ability to *access* the rational grounds of belief; as *objective*, every reasonable person possesses the ability to *assess* the grounds for belief; and as *neutral*, every reasonable person possesses the *authority* to judge the merits of any belief."[131] And just as the rationalization of action leads inexorably to secularization, so too this self-assured assumption of modern rationalism leads unremittingly to secularism, via faith in the supposedly neutral, objective, unbiased knowledge that obtains from reason.[132]

---

128. Wolterstorff, *Reason Within the Bounds*.
129. Both of these phrases are used frequently by James K. A. Smith.
130. Smith, *Thinking in Tongues*, 54.
131. Penner, *End of Apologetics*, 33.
132. Taylor, *Secular Age*.

Postmodernism, in contrast, maintains that such "foundationalist epistemologies are discredited, and impersonally objective forms of human knowledge are impossible... There is for humans no 'God's eye' view 'from nowhere,'" because human cognition can only inhabit a particular world of time and space.[133] "There simply is no universal, neutral, pre-conceptual, and indubitable foundation for knowledge."[134] Moreover, human identity cannot be reduced to a disembodied mind, and reason is not the queen of human capacities. In *What is a Person?* Christian Smith identified, explored, and rank-ordered thirty specific human capacities, from existence to primary experience to secondary experience to creating to highest order capacities. Abstract reasoning and truth-seeking were sixth and fifth highest, respectively. Interpersonal communion and love was the highest.[135]

Postmodernism views human rationality as only one culturally embedded way of processing the world and developing a perspective of it, and modern Enlightenment rationality as only one conception of reason, distinct from others. Contrary to caricatures, the postmodern critique of modern rationalism is not so much anti-rational as it is anti-rational*ist*, not a rejection of reason as much as a rejection of the idolatrous construction of a reductionist model of reason. Contrary to Cartesian mind-body dualism and purely intellectual perception, humans are understood to be oriented to the world primarily through precognitive, affective, and even physical comportment. Indeed, "[c]ertain kinds of non-cognitive knowledge—such as knowing how to ride a bicycle—may not be conceptually mediated, but directly embodied."[136]

Mind and Body

In the field of philosophy, a foreshadowing of this now cultural understanding of mind-body interactivity appeared as early as seventeenth-century philosopher Baruch Spinoza, a contemporary of Descartes, who directly contested dualism and described how the human mind is affected by both mental and physical factors. Nineteenth-century philosopher Friedrich Nietzsche, in a section of "Thus Spoke Zarathustra" aptly entitled On the Despisers of the Body, asserted that "There is more reason in your body than in your best wisdom."[137] Twentieth-century philosopher Henri Berg-

---

133. Smith, *What is a Person?*, 157.
134. Smith, *What is a Person?*, 207.
135. Smith, *What is a Person?*
136. Smith, *Religion*, 9.
137. Nietzsche, "Thus Spoke Zarathustra," 146.

son argued that processes of immediate experience and intuition are more significant than abstract rationalism and science for understanding reality.

In the field of contemporary neuroscience, Antonio Damasio has presented extensive research on how emotions play a central role in social cognition, the use of reason, and the process of decision-making. In *Descartes' Error*, he demonstrated how reasoning, like almost all mental processes, is "embodied," that is, based in biological drives, body states, and emotions. Not only what people reason about, but how they reason is highly influenced by non-conscious physical factors. "This is Descartes' error: the abyssal separation between body and mind . . . the suggestion that reasoning, and moral judgment, and the suffering that comes from physical pain or emotional upheaval might exist separately from the body."[138] In *Looking for Spinoza*, Damasio suggested that Spinoza was a protobiologist, in that his thinking also foreshadowed current discoveries in biology.[139]

In the fields of the humanities and social sciences, a growing number of theories link mind to body, denying that reasoning is autonomous not just culturally, but personally. For one, embodied cognition holds that many features of cognition are shaped by the brain and other aspects of the agent's entire body. For another, affect theory, originally formulated by Spinoza and elaborated by Bergson and others, is a recent interdisciplinary field built on the concept of affect, including emotions and feelings.[140] In current theorizing, affect is "the name we give to those forces—visceral forces beneath, alongside, or generally *other than* conscious knowing, vital forces insisting beyond emotion—that can serve to drive us toward movement and extension."[141] Enthusiasm for such approaches has become a movement termed the "affective turn."[142]

In the field of literature, the novelist Milan Kundera asserted that

> *I think, therefore I am* is the statement of an intellectual who underrates toothaches. *I feel, therefore I am* is a truth much more universally valid, and it applies to everything that's alive. My self does not differ substantially from yours in terms of its thought. Many people, few ideas: we all think more or less the same, and we exchange, borrow, steal thoughts from one another. However, when someone steps on my foot, only I feel the pain. The basis of the self is not thought but suffering, which is the most

---

138. Damasio, *Descartes' Error*, 249–50.
139. Damasio, *Looking for Spinoza*.
140. Massumi, *Parables for the Virtual*.
141. Gregg and Seigworth, *Affect Theory Reader*, 1.
142. Clough and Halley, *Affective Turn*, 1.

fundamental of all feelings. While it suffers, not even a cat can doubt its unique and non-interchangeable self.[143]

In the field of psychology, modern understandings of the self have been subject to vigorous critique.

> In a real sense, Descartes' modern self was lost from the beginning. Humans were jettisoned from a meaningful world in which they had enjoyed a central place and a divine purpose, and were consigned to be isolated, free floating intellects, while their bodies were reduced to (placeless) space and (purposeless) time. In a real sense, the Cartesian self is schizophrenic—lost in thought and separated from reality.[144]

However, postmodern understandings of the self have fared no better. As remedy, a transmodern self, one that transforms, transcends, and transects the best of the premodern, modern, and postmodern self, has been proposed as a way to reclaim, reconnect, and re-stabilize the self. Notably, transmodernism includes "a concern with religions and transcendent spiritual themes; a rediscovery of the importance of truth, beauty, goodness, and harmony."[145] It recovers vertical values and adds them back into the exclusively horizontal values of postmodernism.[146] The transmodern self is still a rational subject, but it exists within a relational framework; it is affected by the individual, not constructed by the individual.[147]

Postmodernism, and certainly transmodernism, do not necessarily pit the heart against the head in some kind of anti-intellectual, purely subjective emotionalism, but they do take seriously the limited, embodied, social location and affections of finite humans whose thinking is not unaffected, and who are only capable of perspectives of truth. In the critical realist terms framing this analysis, humans are only capable of direct or indirect experience of the empirical, and are simply incapable of reasoning their way to all that is actual, much less all that is real. As will be explicated in Essay Two, acknowledging human limitations is imperative, in the realm of religion more than any other.

Yet, contrary to Jesus, who did not impose knowledge of himself upon others, Enlightenment rationalism's inclination toward imperial coercion and conquest is too often implicit in the modern Christian mantra that all

---

143. Kundera, *Immortality*, 200.
144. Hodges, "Persons as Obligated," 63–64.
145. Vitz, "Future of the University," 113–14.
146. Norwine et al., "Personal Identity."
147. Burns, "Self-Construction through Consumption."

truth is God's truth.[148] Though the phrase is best understood in Abraham Kuyper's sense of affirming common grace,[149] it is at times used to frame truth in the Enlightenment sense rather than the incarnational sense. The less triumphalist, pre-Enlightenment phrase Cervantes used in *Don Quixote* was "where truth is, there God Himself is." The post-Enlightenment claim that all truth is God's truth "reduces truth to universal, objectively neutral propositional truth rather than retaining the relational, personal, and particularistic dimensions of truth that the sense of Hebrew and Christian scriptures imparts to the idea of truth."[150] Overall, "we can summarize the differences between modernism and postmodernism by the stark difference between the modern ideal of dispassionate, disinterested objectivism and the postmodern affirmation of a passional, even confessional perspectivalism."[151]

Apologetics

Rationalism in Christian faith finds its foremost current expression in extreme forms of modern Christian apologetics, the Enlightenment project of defending Christian faith by attempting to establish rational foundations which make Christian belief believable, justifiable, or warranted.[152] *Apologia* means to give a defense, such as what Paul offered the Jews in Acts 13, the Gentiles in Acts 17, and what Jesus himself offered his disciples in Acts 1:3, giving them many convincing proofs that he had risen from the dead. Though Christian apologetics have taken at least five historical forms,[153] most take 1 Pet 3:15 as their biblical mandate: "Always be ready to make your defense to anyone who demands from you an accounting for the hope that is in you" (NRSV).[154] But as Peter Enns explained, "the persecuted readers are not being told that they need to be intellectually certain of God's existence and communicate effectively to atheists and pagans how they know they are right. Rather, in the face of persecution, Peter wants

148. Miller, "Reframing."
149. Kuyper, *Common Grace*.
150. Kuyper, *Common Grace*, 136.
151. Smith, *Thinking in Tongues*, 59.
152. Leading proponents include William Lane Craig, J. P. Moreland, and Douglas Groothuis.
153. The five approaches are Classical, Evidential, Presuppositional, Reformed Epistemology, and Cumulative Case. See Cowan, *Five Views on Apologetics*.
154. Many other, especially earlier translations use some combination of wording that includes giving an answer or explanation to those who ask for a reason, which inclines interpretation to focus more on meanings associated with rationality.

them to be prepared at any moment to bear witness to the God they trust with their very lives."[155]

Furthermore, contemporary practice of apologetics has been subject to recent critique externally by postmodernists,[156] but also internally by some of its own practitioners. According to Alister McGrath's *Mere Apologetics*, it has "neglected the relational, imaginative, and existential aspects of faith."[157] Consequently, *Christianity Today* gave its 2014 Book Awards in the category of Apologetics to two works that turned sharply away from rational argument for belief. Francis Spufford's *Unapologetic: Why, Despite Everything, Christianity Can Still Make Surprising Emotional Sense* is a profanity-laced ode to the emotional mending of Christian forgiveness, redemption, and hope, the polar opposite of rational arguments about ontology or teleology.[158] God, as the ground of being, is to be experienced emotionally, bathed in a sense of mystery and elusive presence that both frightens and comforts. Spufford thus offered "a defense of Christian emotions—of their intelligibility, of their grown-up dignity," much like Smith had earlier offered a dispassionate social scientific explanation of why Christianity works emotionally.[159]

The 2014 Apologetics Book Award of Merit was given to Myron Penner's *The End of Apologetics: Christian Witness in a Postmodern Context*, a treatise firmly "against apologetics," thoroughly anti-rationalistic, though irenically not anti-reason.[160] To begin, Penner drew approvingly on Kierkegaard's statement that whoever came up with the idea of defending Christianity rationally in modernity is a second Judas who betrayed Christ under the guise of a friendly kiss; only, Kierkegaard added, the apologist's treachery (unlike Judas's) is "the treason of stupidity." In imagining itself to be engaging in an objective rational discourse outside of political power, and dealing only with the rational justifications for objective truths, the modern apologetic paradigm, according to Penner, is itself a product of modernity. As a kind of "apologetic positivism," it is thereby incapable of defending authentic Christian faith.

Penner argued that both the liberal Christian program of accommodating to rationalism by reducing tenets of faith to the verifiable, as well

---

155. Enns, *Sin of Certainty*, 114–15.

156. Nevertheless, as oxymoronic as it may sound, there is a tepid postmodern apologetics. See Gschwandtner, *Postmodern Apologetics?*

157. McGrath, *Mere Apologetics*, 28.

158. Spufford, *Unapologetic*.

159. Smith, "Why Christianity Works."

160. Penner, *End of Apologetics*.

as the conservative Christian program of employing rationalism to defend tenets of faith as justifiable, have acquiesced to the terms of, and been formed by, the modern sense of reason. To that extent, Christian apologists and the New Atheists are mirror images of each other. Furthermore, Christian apologetic discourse is often violent "at both the personal level (when apologetic arguments are used to treat their interlocutors as the 'faceless unbeliever') and the social level (when Christian apologetic practice merely reinforces and defends a given set of power relations operative within an unjust social structure)."[161] Concurring with Jonathan Wilson's assessment that the church's Enlightenment project is "the attempt to commend the Gospel on grounds that have nothing to do with the Gospel itself,"[162] Penner's own concluding appraisals were equally strident. The rationalism of much Christian apologetics undermines, subverts, and betrays the faith it intends to defend, emptying faith of its content, and failing to edify the person. "Apologetics might be the single biggest threat to genuine Christian faith that we face today . . . It is tantamount to conceptual idolatry and methodological blasphemy."[163] If so, what might Christian faith be, if not accumulating reasons to believe?

Personal Faith

While rationalism in Christian faith is a product of social and cultural history at the macro level, it can also be a product of personal history at the micro level. The role of rationality in faith can wax and wane over the course of an individual's lifetime due to developmental psychological processes. Fowler's theory of faith, referenced earlier, is a complex model of psychological development that combines the earlier developmental models of Erik Erikson, Jean Piaget, Lawrence Kolberg, and Robert Selman, and identifies six stages of faith through which an individual may or may not evolve during their lifetime.[164] Fowler's measures of faith, which when combined, function as an operational definition of faith, include an individual's form of logic, social perspective taking, form of moral judgment, bounds of social awareness, locus of authority, form of world coherence, and role of symbols.

All these aspects of faith evolve through all six stages of faith, the middle four of which are salient here: Stage 2 Mythic-Literal Faith; Stage 3 Synthetic-Conventional Faith; Stage 4 Individuative-Reflective Faith; and

---

161. Penner, *End of Apologetics*, 18.
162. Wilson, *Living Faithfully*, 29.
163. Penner, *End of Apologetics*, 12 and 62.
164. Fowler, *Stages of Faith*.

Stage 5 Conjunctive Faith. To over-simplify using other descriptors, these stages can be understood as the Stage 2 literalist, the Stage 3 conformist, the Stage 4 rationalist, and the Stage 5 spiritualist. Our interest here of course is in Stage 4, which Fowler characterizes as the critical examination or demythologizing of commitments for the purpose of constructing a personal, explicit meaning system that is rationally defensible and exclusive. He characterizes Stage 5 as a post-critical awakening to the paradoxical nature of truth and the need to unite the seeming opposites of assertion and waiting, logic and mystery. It replaces the tribalism of the Stage 3 conformist and the ideological warfare of the Stage 4 rationalist with the epistemological humility, ironic imagination, and second or willed naïveté of the Stage 5 spiritualist who is open to the larger movement of spirit.

As a cognitive structural model of psychological developmental, Fowler observed that persons advance through the respective stages until they equilibrate at one stage or another, and then regard all further stages as heretical, to the limited extent that they can even understand them. Hence the Stage 4 rationalist will always look askance, and with grave suspicion, at the Stage 5 spiritualist. He also hastened to insist that later stages were not theologically superior to earlier stages; God is equally pleased with persons at every stage of faith, from the uneducated Stage 2 literalist to the post-rational Stage 5 spiritualist.

Among the multiple questions the model raises is whether not only individuals, but organizations, communities, and even historical eras can also be staged, that is, accurately described as holding up the faith of a certain stage to be orthodox and optimal. A historical development of enculturated faith is readily discernable in Fowler's sequence, premodern faith being conformist, modern faith being rationalist, and postmodern faith being spiritualist. But then a postmodernist who merely parrots the language of spiritualist faith without having arrived there personally through fully inhabiting each of the preceding stages for a while is actually still practicing conformist faith, as is the modernist who merely parrots the language of rationalist faith. But the point here is that faith in which rationality is paramount is for some a place where they arrive developmentally and remain for the rest of their lives, and for others a phase through which they pass on their way to more tempered, conjunctive faith.

Going Beyond

In concert with the postmodern turn toward spirituality, modern rationalism is losing its grip on Christian faith.[165] Resistance to the disenchantment of not only the world but the Word itself is growing. Rationalistic biblical hermeneutics and theology pursued within what in the end can only be a less than completely rational granting of authority to the Bible are progressively suspect and wearying for ever more of the faithful. Literalism—"text without context is pretext"[166]—was such a reading of the Bible, as was the fundamentalism that literalism spawned. Assertions of the inerrancy of the Bible were evidence of how "the rationalism of the Enlightenment infected even those who were battling against it."[167] Biblicism, which is "a theory about the Bible that emphasizes together its exclusive authority, infallibility, perspicuity, self-sufficiency, internal consistency, self-evident meaning, and universal applicability,"[168] is increasingly unconvincing. At some point the expectations placed on such a rationalistic reading of the Bible makes it "impossible," and begets the irrationality of rationality. Content exhausts itself. "There is more and more information, and less and less meaning,"[169] until it implodes. It cannibalizes itself. So *A New Evangelical Manifesto* calls conservative Christians away from their rationalist, objectified reading of the Bible, so that it may again become an enchanted, living Word not reduced to propositional truths alone.[170] Only the language of myth and metaphor has the "power to detach us from the world of facts and demonstrations and reasonings, which are excellent as tools, but are merely idols as objects of trust and reverence."[171]

Evidence of this postmodern cultural turn includes recent empirical data documenting how little interest even college-educated religious people today have in rational arguments for the existence of God.[172] In expressing their beliefs, their language is more demure than dogmatic. No longer defining themselves by what propositions or concepts they believe, or defining their faith as a system of beliefs, more and more have migrated toward

---

165. Chamberlain, *Why People Stop Believing*.

166. In biblical scholarship, the phrase has been popularized by D. A. Carson, but it has a hundred-year history in other fields as well, such as journalism and government.

167. Wright, *Simply Christian*, 183.

168. Smith, *Bible Made Impossible*, viii.

169. Baudrillard, *Simulacra and Simulation*, 79.

170. See Cheryl Bridges Johns, "A Disenchanted Text," in Gushee, *New Evangelical Manifesto*.

171. Frye, *Double Vision*, 18.

172. Wuthnow, *God Problem*.

emulating the love and compassion that Jesus taught and practiced.[173] No longer feeling obligated to appear rationally self-assured, and troubled by potentially disagreeable impressions given off if they would, Christians are increasingly unafraid to admit uncertainty about God. Faith for many today is returning to less rationalistic forms.

F. NON-RATIONALISTIC CHRISTIAN FAITH

Questions

When the actions of Christian faith are subjected to rationalization, doing so is often justified as the most efficient and responsible means of promoting the kingdom of God. Likewise, when the beliefs of Christian faith are subjected to rationalism, doing so is often justified as an innocent and noble pursuit of truth. Both claims are questionable when rationalization and rationalism are understood as products of modernity, and in light of their consequences. Rationalization of Christian faith is hardly efficient and responsible when it alienates individuals and secularizes the collective ethos. Rationalism in Christian faith is hardly innocent and noble when it is deeply political and secularizing. Yet Durkheim's scientific conceit, quoted earlier, is apparently agreeable to rationalistic Christians if applied to rationality instead: religion can affirm nothing that rationality denies, and deny nothing that rationality affirms.

Christianity has always maintained that God is transcendent and infinite, as well as immanent and self-revealing in his Word, his works, and his incarnation in Jesus. Both of these claims are metaphysical, and therefore not subject to empirical verification or falsification. Indeed, the transcendent is by definition beyond the physical, that is, beyond sense evidence. So if Christian claims are metaphysical (transcendent beyond the physical), and if God is supernatural (transcendent beyond the natural), why is Christian faith not also meta-rational or super-rational (transcendent beyond the rational, and therefore transcendent beyond the laws of logic)? Why should Christian faith be limited to the rational when it is not limited to the empirical? Why should reason remain the unbowed arbiter of ultimate truth? Why must finite human notions of the correspondence, coherence, or pragmatic tests of truth define Ultimate Truth? Even to qualify that rationality does not define truth, but merely serves as a test of Ultimate Truth, is to make truth subservient to rationality—if something does not pass muster of rationality, it cannot be true.

---

173. McLaren, *Great Spiritual Migration*.

Contradictions

Take for example the oft-referenced foundational law of non-contradiction, the second of the three classic Western laws of thought, which states that nothing can both be and not be at the same time and in the same respect.[174] Attempting to verify or falsify this law, like other laws of logic, requires appealing to the laws of logic themselves in order to reach a conclusion. The only evidence that can verify the law of non-contradiction "proves to have already been constituted and framed by the deeper belief commitments from which [it] is derived . . . beliefs that *cannot themselves be verified except by means established by the presumed beliefs themselves.*"[175] This is self-assuming, and hence effectively self-defeating, the same charge that rationalists are fond of levelling against what they critique as faulty reasoning. Furthermore, given that the law of non-contradiction holds better in the material realm than in the non-material realm, where values held by one culture and identities held by one person can readily be contradictory, it is at least limited.

Moreover, the Middle Way that is the goal of reasoning in Chinese thought is completely contrary to the third classic Western law of thought, the law of excluded middle. When comparing Western and Asian thought patterns, Richard Nisbett found that "[w]hen confronted with two apparently contradictory propositions, Americans tended to polarize their beliefs, whereas Chinese moved toward equal acceptance of the two propositions."[176] Some of the many differences between Western and Eastern religion "can be understood in terms of the 'right/wrong' mentality of the West in contrast to the 'both/and' orientation of the East. Eastern religions are characterized by tolerance and interpenetration of religious ideas."[177]

But regardless, why does God have to fit the properties to which the propositions of Western rationality refer? Why does God have to adhere to the law of non-contradiction? Whatever the theological explanation the Council of Chalcedon in 451 CE assembled and articulated for Jesus being both fully human and fully divine, on the face of it, the belief that Jesus had two such opposite natures violates the law of non-contradiction. If all humans are fallen, and Jesus was fully human, was he fallen yet fully divine? How is that not a contradiction? One leading theological account for what

---

174. Law One is the law of identity: Whatever is, is. Law Two is the law of non-contradiction: Nothing can both be and not be. Law Three is the law of excluded middle: Everything must either be or not be. See Russell, *Problems of Philosophy*.

175. Smith, *Moral, Believing Animals*, 51 and 54 (italics in original).

176. Nisbett, *Geography of Thought*, 192.

177. Nisbett, *Geography of Thought*, 199.

Catholics term the "hypostatic union" is a "kenotic Christology" based on Philippians 2, where Paul describes Jesus as having emptied himself of his divine attributes—omniscience, omnipresence, and omnipotence—and thereby become human. But here again are beliefs that cannot themselves be verified except by means established by the presumed beliefs themselves, and we are back again to contradiction, and asking again why the character of God cannot contain contradictions.[178]

Many have pointed out the many other "inconsistencies" in the Bible itself, or in Christian theology more generally. For example, the millennia-old "omnipotence paradox" arises with the assumption that an omnipotent being has no limits and is capable of even logically contradictory formulations, such as a square circle. But this is conventionally rejected by Christian theologians via debating the definition of omnipotence, usually concluding that it does not mean breaking the laws of logic. It is argued that God cannot perform self-contradictory, inherently nonsensical, logical absurdities. For example, Aquinas asserted that omnipotence is the ability to perform any real or actual thing. C. S. Lewis in turn asserted that God cannot do contradictory things "not because His power meets an obstacle, but because nonsense remains nonsense even when we talk it about God."[179] The "real" or "actual" in this sense are clearly not that of critical realism, and are in fact closer to the "empirical," which is granted the power to define "nonsense." The implied conclusion is that God obeys the laws of logic because logic is an eternal part of God's nature, and God is in fact limited in actions to God's nature. In the end, God is logic, and therefore, in effect, logic is God.

Other so-called "inconsistencies" are likewise explained away theologically, however (un)satisfactorily: God is both all-powerful and all-loving, God is three persons in one, humans have free will and God predestines them, humans are saved by faith and works, believers live between the already and the not yet, the first shall be last and the last shall be first, and so on. The nineteenth-century preacher Henry Clay Trumbull described the Christian life as made up of seeming contradictions. "[G]iving is getting; scattering is gaining; holding is losing; having nothing is possessing all things; dying is living. It is he who is weak who is strong . . . Happiness is

---

178. As Danish physicist Niels Bohr, winner of the 1922 Nobel Prize for Physics, is said to have put it, "The opposite of a correct statement is a false statement. But the opposite of a profound truth may well be another profound truth." However, this statement is a common unsourced variant. His son, Hans Bohr, wrote in an essay entitled "My Father," that "One of the favorite maxims of my father was the distinction between the two sorts of truths, profound truths recognized by the fact that the opposite is also a profound truth, in contrast to trivialities where opposites are obviously absurd." In Rozental, *Niels Bohr*, 328.

179. Lewis, *Problem of Pain*, 18.

found when it is no longer sought; the clearest sight is of the invisible; things which are not bring to naught things which are."[180] However, when seen as paradoxes instead of contradictions, they are often celebrated and embraced. The promise that apparent opposites can cohere in a life lived with a both/and perspective instead of an either/or orientation was promoted and modelled by the Catholic Thomas Merton and the Quaker Parker Palmer.[181]

Merriam-Webster defines a contradiction as "a proposition that asserts both the truth and falsity of something; a logical incongruity." A paradox is defined as "a statement that is seemingly contradictory and yet is perhaps true; an argument that apparently derives self-contradictory conclusions by valid deduction from acceptable premises." A mystery is "something not understood or beyond understanding; a religious truth that one can know only by revelation and cannot fully understand." Bruce Baugus sorts the three out well in Christian theology.

> Paradox in Christian theology is, then, a particular kind of revealed mystery . . . As such, theological paradoxes expose the limits of finite human reason *coram Deo* ["in the presence of God"] . . . When confronting paradox, however, fallen reason tends to take offense, bristling at the implications of the paradoxical point of doctrine for the presumed competency of autonomous human reason in theology. Faith, on the other hand, recognizes the limits of reason, while affirming its ministerial usefulness, as it rests in the divinely revealed paradox in awe before a transcendent and incomprehensible God . . . Theological paradox checks reason's overreach. If reason refuses to be disciplined by paradox it will find itself falling into various errors and incoherent babbling. In a reflexive, self-defensive, projection, offended reason naturally (though unjustly) suspects the paradoxical doctrine of being incoherent. Ultimately, paradox calls us to humble ourselves *coram Deo*.[182]

Who are finite humans to even imagine that they have sufficient grasp of the reality of infinite God so as to be able to assess whether any particular claim about God corresponds to the facts about the real total being of God, and thereby judge the claim to be true or false? Here again critical realism is instructive, making an important distinction between two dimensions that must not be conflated.[183] The intransitive is the world or the object of

---

180. Trumbull, *Practical Paradoxes*, 9.
181. Palmer, *Promise of Paradox*.
182. Baugus, "Paradox and Mystery," 249.
183. Bhaskar, *Realist Theory of Science*.

knowledge as it is, in this case God. The transitive is our theories about the world or the intransitive object of knowledge, in this case God, and how we go about studying that object. The transitive is a fallible social construction that changes over time without changing the intransitive object, which does not depend on the transitive for its being. As Augustine declared, "God is not what you imagine or what you think you understand. If you understand, you have failed."[184]

Alternative Faith

Alternative, more non-rational forms of Christian faith are not only surviving but thriving in the current century-old "Age of Spirit"[185] that, in the more recent turn from religiosity to spirituality, is now in full bloom. The Pentecostalism born a hundred years ago and now the largest and fastest growing form of Christian faith worldwide is likely the leading case study of literally embodying a more expansive, affective, and thicker way of knowing that cannot be translated into propositions or syllogisms. James Smith describes Pentecostalism as "a quintessentially incarnational faith and practice" which deems rationalism to be insufficiently incarnational, and therefore rejects cognitive fundamentalism.[186] Pentecostal epistemology and knowledge is narrative; the narrative *is* the knowledge.

As Christian Smith observes, humans not only make stories, but are *made by* their stories.[187] When contemporary persons are disconnected from their shared stories that ground the self, or worse, when they are oblivious to how their selves are comprised through shared stories in the first place, existential disorientation ensues.[188] And as story, knowledge is always more affective than cognitive, and by extension more experiential than cognitive. "We *feel* our way around the world more than we *think* about it, *before* we think about it."[189] Rather than being derivative of prior cognitions, as rationalists contend, emotions are irreducible, precognitive construals and interpretations that constitute the world before we think about it or perceive it.[190] Unlike Fowler's logic of rational certainty which seeks deductive certainty, or at least inductive probability, and thereby serves as the "mother

---

184. Quoted in Callen, *Discerning the Divine*, 6.
185. Cox, *Future of Faith*.
186. Smith, *Thinking in Tongues*, 61.
187. Smith, *Moral, Believing Animals*, 64.
188. Taylor, *Sources of the Self*.
189. Smith, *Thinking in Tongues*, 72.
190. Riis and Whitehead, *Sociology of Religious Emotion*.

of skepticism,"[191] this logic of conviction is capable of producing the refrain commonly heard in Pentecostal worship services of testimony and witness: "I know that I know that I know."

The recent postmodern emergent church movement[192] is only the latest to dislodge rationality from dictating the organization of action,[193] and from forming the foundation of belief. This worldwide network of thousands of congregations is a "deconstructed church," a "creative, entrepreneurial religious movement that strives to achieve social legitimacy and spiritual vitality by actively disassociating from its roots in conservative, evangelical Christianity,"[194] and even calling for a post-Christian Christianity.[195] Like postmodernism in general, it resists definition and eschews labels. One of its senior leaders, Brian McLaren, reviewed many traditions of faith and called for a radical, Christ-centered orthodoxy of faith in his book entitled A *Generous Orthodoxy*. The cover elucidated the contents as follows: Why I Am a Missional + Evangelical + Post/Protestant + Liberal/Conservative + Mystical/Poetic + Biblical + Charismatic/Contemplative + Fundamentalist/Calvinist + Anabaptist/Anglican + Methodist + Catholic + Green + Incarnational + Depressed-yet-Hopeful + Emergent + Unfinished Christian.[196] Thriving on the margins of Protestantism, the movement resists rationalization of action and institutionalization,[197] just as its "radical deliberative democrats"[198] are averse to hierarchal authority.[199] More conversational than doctrinal, the movement eschews rationalism of belief as it "embraces irony and contradiction" in both ideology and practice.[200] As C. S. Lewis advocated in his classic, *The Abolition of Man*,[201] the emergent church movement is more intent on the right affections of orthopathy—the passionate love for neighbors and hospitality for strangers—than the right doctrine of orthodoxy or the right practice of orthopraxy.[202]

191. Westphal, "Post-Kantian Reflections," 61.

192. Leading proponents include Brian McLaren, Tony Jones, Rob Bell, Peter Rollins, Phyllis Tickle, and Donald Miller.

193. Packard, *Emerging Church*.

194. Marti and Ganiel, *Deconstructed Church*, ix.

195. Rollins, *Divine Magician*.

196. McLaren, *Generous Orthodoxy*.

197. Bielo, *Emerging Evangelicals*.

198. Burge and Djupe, "Emergent Church Practices."

199. Jones, *Church is Flat*.

200. Marti and Ganiel, *Deconstructed Church*, 5.

201. Lewis, *Abolition of Man*.

202. Vacek, "Orthodoxy Requires Orthopathy."

Wholeness

Once freed from rationality alone and fully acknowledging body and spirit as well, epistemology becomes "a kind of *aesthetic*, an epistemic grammar that privileges *aisthesis* (experience) before *noesis* (intellection)."[203] Instead of allowing worldview-talk to misconstrue humans by reducing them to the stunted state of little more than thinking things, emotions and bodies come to matter equally, and to be at least as formative.[204] We become whole, embodied spirits, affective and aesthetic creatures, in reality shaped more powerfully by desires, narrative, and imagination than by propositions, beliefs, and worldview.[205]

As Daniel Taylor's title suggests, skeptical believers tell stories to their inner atheists rather than lecture them with rational arguments.[206] The story-telling arts can access truths about the human condition as actively, and on some questions perhaps more accurately, than rationality, precisely because they can hold their audience in paradoxes where seeming opposites are both true, in a way that logic would reduce paradoxes to contradictions where one negates the other. So readers can readily identify with Pi when he says that he "just wants to love God," to pursue ultimate truth and love without having to choose between religions, and without being denigrated as irrational.[207] Faith is indeed more poetry than prose, more theater than theory. "Our most primary and fundamental mode of 'understanding' is more literary than logical; we are the kind of creatures who make our way in the world more by metaphor than mathematics. The way we 'know' is more like a dance than a deduction."[208]

Be they psychological, cultural, or spiritual, there are myriad powerful, unconscious, precognitive, affective effects constantly at work on individuals of all kinds of faith. In the Holy Spirit, Christians have a catch-all category of explanation for such non-rational effects, attributable to the work of a supernatural personal agent. Yet they often ironically shackle the Spirit with the limits of rationality, saying that the Spirit would never do this or

---

203. Smith, *Thinking in Tongues*, 80–81.

204. Smith, *Desiring the Kingdom*.

205. Smith, *Imagining the Kingdom*.

206. Taylor, *Skeptical Believer*.

207. Multireligious faith is not merely the endearing fantasy of a child. The celebrated twentieth-century theologian Raimon Panikkar, born of a Spanish Catholic mother and Indian Hindu father, often said of his own identity: "I left Europe [for India] as a Christian, I discovered I was a Hindu and returned as a Buddhist without ever having ceased to be Christian" (Panikkar, *Intrareligious Dialogue*, 40).

208. Smith, *Thinking in Tongues*, 82.

allow that because of this or that property we have ascribed to the Spirit, instead of granting that the Spirit will blow wherever it chooses (John 3:8). Even leading apologist William Lane Craig, in his well-known distinction between knowing and showing, stated that, because of the work of the Holy Spirit in him, he knew Christianity was true long before he could show that it was true.[209] Furthermore, in disavowing theological rationalism and evidentialism, he avows that Christianity is true even if he could not show that it was true, and even while he devotes his enterprise to showing that Christianity is actually true. In his personal story of faith, Craig practices Fowler's non-rational logic of conviction, not the logic of rational certainty. So do the rest of us. For just as Pi observed, so it goes with God.

Rationality is a positive and valuable aspect of human life that has contributed enormously toward human self-understanding and well-being.[210] It has also contributed much to the unfolding of Christian faith in modernity.[211] Yet as rationality and Christianity characterized and shared the modern Western world, extreme social practices of rationality in Christian faith became problematic. Modernity proved no more or less problematic for Christian faith than postmodernity is now proving to be. Rationality remains a tremendously useful tool for persons of Christian faith, but as Mark Twain quipped, if the only tool you have is a hammer, everything looks like a nail. And worse, when the tool takes over the person, the person is dehumanized, becoming robotic.

Of course, this whole analysis and critique of rationality is an exercise in rationality, subject to counter-critique by rationalists that it is therefore self-defeating. But it has also been an attempt to use rationality against rationalization and rationalism, to dethrone rationality and make way for non-rationality as one legitimate way of acting and knowing among others, and thereby democratize the elements of Christian faith. Indeed, rationality remains a good servant but a bad master. The critical realism assumed by this analysis is inherently critical of the social practices it studies, and has enormous emancipatory potential, implying that those practices need not be what they are.[212]

In the lyrics of "Come Healing," songwriter Leonard Cohen "gathers up the brokenness" of multiple dichotomies such as mind-body and spirit-limb, and calls for their healing, though "none of us deserving the cruelty

---

209. Craig, "Classical Apologetics."
210. See Rodney Stark's triumphalist *The Victory of Reason*.
211. Peterson et al., *Reason and Religious Belief*.
212. Bhaskar, *Scientific Realism*.

or the grace."[213] Mercifully, we can "see the darkness yielding / that tore the light apart / Come healing of the reason / Come healing of the heart." The darkness of rationalization and rationalism has disenchanted the world, and only when reason is healed can hearts be healed too. Then, after suggesting that the heavens are also faltering, Cohen pleads "Come healing of the Altar, come healing of the Name." Altars are the way humans relate to, reach out to, the divine. The Name is our conception of, construction of, the divine. Both need healing.

---

213. Cohen, "Come Healing."

2

ESSAY TWO: HUMILITY

A. INTRODUCTION TO HUMILITY

Story

ELIE WIESEL SURVIVED THE Auschwitz-Birkenau and Buchenwald concentration camps as a teenager, and then became a celebrated international activist and Nobel Laureate author of fifty-seven books. His most notable work was his memoir *Night*, in which he wrote:

> Never shall I forget that smoke. Never shall I forget the little faces of the children, whose bodies I saw turned into wreaths of smoke beneath a silent blue sky. Never shall I forget those flames which consumed my faith forever. Never shall I forget the nocturnal silence which deprived me, for all eternity, of the desire to live. Never shall I forget those moments which murdered my God and my soul and turned my dreams to dust. Never shall I forget these things, even if I am condemned to live long as God himself. Never.[1]

Victimized by the rationalization evident in the Holocaust, as noted in Essay One, but rooted in Hasidic Judaism which is fascinated rather than repelled by paradox, Wiesel wrestled theologically with the Holocaust in much of his work.

---

1. Wiesel, *Night*, 32.

> The grim reality of the annihilation of six million Jews presents a seemingly insurmountable obstacle to further theological thought: how is it possible to believe in God after what happened? The sum of Wiesel's work is a passionate effort to break through this barrier to new understanding and faith. It is to his credit that he is unwilling to retreat into easy atheism, just as he refuses to bury his head in the sand of optimistic faith. What Wiesel calls for is a fierce, defiant struggle with the Holocaust, and his work tackles a harder question: how is it possible *not* to believe in God after what happened?[2]

Understandably, Wiesel has often been cited as an icon of a reasonable loss of faith. Yet he denied such loss, and continued praying.

I no longer ask You for either happiness or paradise;
    all I ask of You is to listen and let me be aware and worthy of Your listening.
I no longer ask You to resolve my questions,
    only to receive them and make them part of You.
I no longer ask You for either rest or wisdom, I only ask You not to close me to gratitude,
    be it of the most trivial kind, or to surprise and friendship.
Love? Love is not Yours to give.

As for my enemies, I do not ask You to punish them or even to enlighten them;
I only ask You not to lend them Your mask and Your powers.
If You must relinquish one or the other,
    give them Your powers, but not Your countenance.

They are modest, my prayers, and humble.
I ask You what I might ask a stranger met by chance at twilight in a barren land.
I ask You, God of Abraham, Isaac, and Jacob, to enable me to pronounce these words
    without betraying the child that transmitted them to me.

God of Abraham, Isaac, and Jacob,
    enable me to forgive You, and enable the child I once was to forgive me too.
I no longer ask You for the life of that child, nor even for his faith.
I only implore You to listen to him and act in such a way
    that You and I can listen to him together.[3]

---

2. Henry, "Story and Silence," para. 3.

3. Wiesel, *One Generation After*, 200. For a fuller Wiesel prayer, see "A Prayer for the Days of Awe." It begins with "Master of the Universe, let us make up. It is time. How long can we go on being angry?" It ends with "Let us make up: for the child in me, it is unbearable to be divorced from you so long."

Theory

In every era, culture, and circumstance, people have to one degree or another utilized reason to make sense of things as they consciously evaluated and weighed reasons to believe or act. As detailed in Essay One, there are various types of rationality present in and beneficial to most aspects of human life. Only when rationality becomes the master instead of a servant do particular problems arise. Critical realism, the meta-theory or philosophy of reality and human knowledge informing this analysis, adheres to judgmental rationality as one particular kind of rationality, together with two additional crucial elements. Critical realism maintains

> that much of reality exists and operates independently of our human awareness of it (ontological realism), that our human knowledge about reality is always historically and socially situated and conceptually mediated (epistemic perspectivalism), and that it is nonetheless possible for humans over time to improve their knowledge about reality, to adjudicate rival accounts, and so to make justified truth claims about what is real and how it works (judgmental rationality). All three of these beliefs must go together to promote the acquisition of human knowledge.[4]

Judgmental rationality assumes that, though humans can never know triumphally the complete truth about reality, neither are all truth claims relativistically equal and just as useful as any other. The simplicity or "parsimony" of law-like explanations of cause in human affairs, for example, are likely less accurate than explanations that incorporate causal complexity and contingency. Some ideas and explanations are actually better than others, and rationality is the judge of which ideas are best or closer to the truth of reality. "We should make reasoned judgments about which accounts seem to explain reality better than others."[5] Nevertheless, all human knowledge is fallible and subject to ongoing improvement. The process of building, revising, refining, and legitimizing what passes for knowledge in any given time and place is what "the social construction of reality" thesis describes, as overviewed in Essay One.

Sound judgment requires wise use of reason, though reason alone in the form of rationalization or rationalism is an impediment to wisdom, as argued in Essay One, and implicit in critical realism. The practice of rationality alone is insufficient for good judgment, unless it ironically employs rationality to own its own limitations. Hence the virtue of humility is also

---

4. Smith, *Religion*, 9.
5. Smith, *Religion*, 12.

required, and not even humility in general, but a particular kind of humility: intellectual humility. Indeed, as Felix Frankfurter, Associate Justice of the Supreme Court of the United States famously asserted so succinctly, "The indispensable judicial requisite is intellectual humility."[6] Even when rationality is explicitly required, such as in making sound judgments, it cannot be wise if it is not also humble and willing to suspend judgment when appropriate.[7] Whether humility is acquired by personally experiencing the utmost dehumanization, as suffered by Elie Wiesel, or by intellectually acknowledging that human knowledge is limited to the empirical, versus the actual, much less the real, as conceptualized by critical realism, or by simply unintentionally cultivating the personal virtue of humility apart from its intellectual aspects, humility is prerequisite for wisdom and other strengths of character.

Research

Perhaps spurred by public life becoming more partisan and polarized, scholarly attention to humility has grown in recent years. Questions about its character, its correlates and contraries, its function for the individual, its role in interpersonal and public life, and its intersection with religious life have been addressed by various academic disciplines, including philosophy, psychology, sociology, and religious studies.[8] As a personal virtue, general humility has long been examined by philosophy and theology, but with the recent rise of positive psychology, that subfield of study which focuses on the strengths of personhood rather than psychology's usual focus on the

---

6. "American Federation of Labor (AFL) v. American Sash & Door Co., 335 U.S. 538." US Supreme Court case, supreme.justia.com. January 3, 1949.

7. Schellenberg, *Wisdom to Doubt*.

8. The John Templeton Foundation has funded a number of projects on intellectual humility, including "The Science of Intellectual Humility" project at Fuller Graduate School of Psychology from 2012–2015, "The Philosophy and Theology of Intellectual Humility" at Saint Louis University from 2013–2015, and "The Intellectual Humility Massive Open Online Course" project at the University of Edinburgh. In 2014, the *Journal of Psychology and Theology* published a special theme issue on general humility, religion, and spirituality that gave considerable attention to intellectual humility as a subdomain. In 2016, *Logos and Episteme: An International Journal of Epistemology* published a special issue on intellectual humility. In 2017, the *Journal of Positive Psychology* compiled an entire theme issue devoted to intellectual humility composed of articles it had published previously. The Templeton Foundation also sponsored the University of Connecticut Humanities Institute workshop of sociologists on "Religious Conviction and Intellectual Humility in Public Life" (2017).

deficits and problems of personhood, the social sciences of psychology and sociology have added empirical research to the inquiry.[9]

Intellectual humility in particular is most challenged and tested in the domain of personal convictions. Convictions are not merely pedestrian beliefs about reality. Convictions are firmly held beliefs, even fixed beliefs, the state of being completely convinced, certain, and impervious to argument.[10] Convictions in the non-empirical realm of religion likely challenge intellectual humility more than in any other.[11] Of course, convictions in the empirical realm of science can also be strong and resistant to change, as Thomas Kuhn's influential theory of *The Structure of Scientific Revolutions* demonstrated.[12] Many scientists have clung to the paradigm of their science's subject matter so tenaciously that the paradigm would first have to cope with anomalies, and then with crisis, before revolution would eventually usher in a new paradigm.[13]

But by its very method of knowing, scientific matters are publicly verifiable and/or falsifiable in a way that religious matters are not, and hence science is constantly self-correcting and revisionary in a way that religion is not. Knowing this, scientific convictions are tempered and accountable in a way that religious convictions are not. By assuming that people are easily self-deceived, science is intrinsically humble in a way that religion is not.[14] The core components of the scientific attitude—curiosity, skepticism, and humility[15]—make science inherently progressive in a way that religion is not.[16] Therefore, freed from the possibility of (dis)proof, someone who is

---

9. Worthington et al., *Handbook of Humility* is a leading resource from the subfield of positive psychology. Similarly, Church and Samuelson's *Intellectual Humility* provides a broader interdisciplinary overview of a narrower specific aspect of humility.

10. Convictions are more about cognition and emotion, whereas commitments are more about volition.

11. McElroy et al., "Intellectual Humility."

12. Kuhn, *Structure of Scientific Revolutions*.

13. Paradigm shifts in physics include Newtonian physics in the eighteenth and nineteenth centuries, to relativity in the 1910s, to quantum physics in the 1920s, to chaos theory in the 1970s. But in *God's Planet*, Owen Gingerich argued that it takes about 150 years to move fully from one paradigm to another, such as from geocentrism to heliocentrism, or from de novo creation to evolution.

14. McMinn, *Science of Virtue*, 95–120.

15. See DeWall, "Fostering Intellectual Humility."

16. Nevertheless, there is a "skeptical religion" that is crafted specifically out of human curiosity, skepticism, and humility. In *The Will to Imagine: A Justification of Skeptical Religion*, John Schellenberg contends that the history of arguments for the existence of God do not work well as arguments for belief. Yet they do work better as arguments for types of faith which are closer to trust without certainty, or even belief.

otherwise characteristically humble may become aggressively dogmatic when discussing religious beliefs, especially with persons of differing religious beliefs.

The virtue of intellectual humility may be no more or less prevalent in social practices of rationality than in those of non-rationality, including those of religious rationality versus religious non-rationality. Both the rationalistic apologist and the charismatic Pentecostal may insist indubitably that "I know that I know that I know." But if the critique of rationality in Essay One holds any merit, what follows logically, and therefore ironically, is a call for intellectual humility in all people, not just "intellectuals," regardless of their intellectual (dis)ability. Hearing such a call then immediately invites reflection on the particular Christian call to intellectual humility, and an assessment of its relative presence and practice in Christian life.

B. PHILOSOPHICAL PERSPECTIVES

The study of intellectual humility is built upon recent philosophical work in virtue epistemology and virtue ethics.[17] Though virtue must first be conceived, usually through its telos—its ultimate aim, end, or purpose—virtue epistemology directs attention to the knower as agent more so than to what is known, in a manner similar to how virtue ethics focuses more on moral agents than on moral acts. "Virtue epistemology focuses on the process by which beliefs are formed, looking specifically at whether or not the belief was formed by an intellectually virtuous knower."[18] Intellectual humility is therefore firstly and simultaneously an intellectual and moral attribute of knowers. Because it develops virtue, it reflects a higher human capacity than abstract reasoning and truth seeking.[19]

Definition of General Humility

The concept of intellectual humility is also obviously built upon the general concept of humility. General humility is the "willingness to admit imperfections, a tendency to focus on others rather than the self, and the capacity to see the self realistically."[20] As such, it involves "an accurate view of one's strengths and weaknesses (including acknowledging one's limitations)

---

17. Zagzebski, *Virtues of the Mind*.
18. Church and Samuelson, *Intellectual Humility*, 5.
19. Smith, *What is a Person?*, 51–54.
20. Gregg and Mahadevan, "Intellectual Arrogance," 8.

and an interpersonal stance that is other-oriented rather than self-focused, marked by the ability to restrain egotism (i.e., self-oriented emotions such as pride or shame)."[21] June Price Tangney[22] offered perhaps the clearest set of criteria for general humility: "an ability to see the self and one's place in the world clearly, with low self-focus, openness, an appreciation for the value of all things, and a willingness to admit mistakes."[23]

Notably, general humility operates at both the intrapersonal level where it involves an accurate view of the self, and the interpersonal level where it involves "a position toward others that is other-oriented rather than self-focused, marked by respect and an ability to restrain egoistic motives."[24] Low self-focus is the point of the oft-quoted C. S. Lewis observation that "Humility is not thinking less of yourself, but thinking of yourself less."[25] Furthermore, general humility is best understood as both context-specific and ability-specific. An individual may show high levels of humility in their professional life but not in their private life, just as they may show high levels of humility in their sociability but not in their academic or athletic ability. The closest correlate of general humility is the virtue of modesty in the sense of being moderate or even understated in reporting or acknowledging one's abilities, though as an exclusively social trait, modesty is a narrower construct than general humility.[26] The near opposites of general humility are the vices of arrogance and narcissism, but also "vanity, conceit, egotism, grandiosity, pretentiousness, snobbishness, impertinence (presumption), haughtiness, self-righteousness, domination, selfish ambition, and self-complacency."[27]

Definition of Intellectual Humility

In addition to being a subdomain of general humility that refers specifically to humility regarding one's beliefs and worldview, intellectual humility is one of several intellectual virtues. Others include *studiositas*, which seeks "to understand all things as gifts to be explored in appropriate ways and to be used towards godly ends."[28] Education, for example, is itself a gift to

21. Davis et al., "Distinguishing Intellectual Humility," 215.
22. Tangney, "Humility."
23. Hopkin et al., "Intellectual Humility," 51.
24. Hook and Davis, "Humility, Religion, and Spirituality," 3.
25. Lewis, *Mere Christianity*, 109.
26. Exline et al., "Humility and Modesty."
27. Roberts and Wood, "Humility and Epistemic Goods," 258.
28. Entwistle, *Integrative Approaches*, 99.

be used toward the betterment of self, others, and society. Intellectual caution and courage are concerned with how we evaluate and respond to the real and imagined threats involved in intellectual pursuits.[29] Education that challenges long-held and cherished beliefs is not for the faint of heart or mind or faith. Intellectual integrity "is related to the pursuit of truth in at least two ways—the potential for self-deception, and the intent to deceive others."[30] Education that is manipulative and ideological—is there any other kind?—must always be exposed as such and own its character. And intellectual perseverance refers to the discipline required to attain greater knowledge. Educational achievement is usually more dependent on tenacity than ability.

As for intellectual humility, two aspects appear consistently in its definition, one pertaining to descriptions of the self, and the other pertaining to relationship with others. One definition of the intellectual virtue of intellectual humility describes it as "a) insight about the limits of one's knowledge, marked by openness to new ideas; and b) regulation of intellectual arrogance, marked by the ability to present one's ideas in a non-offensive manner and receive contrary ideas without taking offense."[31] As such, it involves "an accurate view of one's intellectual strengths and weaknesses, as well as the ability to negotiate different ideas in an interpersonally respectful manner."[32] On balance, just as general humility decreases focus on oneself and increases focus on others, so too intellectual humility is more oriented to other ideas and people than to oneself.

The closest correlate of intellectual humility is open-mindedness, which is the serious consideration of alternative beliefs and perspectives, though these two intellectual virtues remain distinct. Intellectual humility is an attribute of the person, whereas open-mindedness is a first-order attitude toward specific beliefs,[33] and therefore, again, a narrower construct. The opposite of intellectual humility is the vice of intellectual arrogance, though intellectual humility is not simply the diametric opposite of intellectual arrogance, but rather what occurs in the absence of intellectual arrogance.[34] Notably, real honest openness to new ideas does not imply automatic adoption of those new ideas without first thinking carefully and critically about them, and finding them compelling. Similarly, ultimate rejection of new

---

29. Roberts and Wood, *Intellectual Virtues*.
30. Entwistle, *Integrative Approaches*, 101.
31. McElroy et al., "Intellectual Humility," 20.
32. Johnson et al., "Intellectual Humility and Forgiveness," 255.
33. Spiegel, "Open-mindedness and Intellectual Humility."
34. Gregg and Mahadevan, "Intellectual Arrogance."

ideas as unconvincing after careful, critical consideration does not necessarily imply intellectual arrogance.

These initial understandings notwithstanding, Justin Barrett maintained that "a consensus definition of intellectual humility has not yet emerged,"[35] and identified three variants currently in play. First, Robert Roberts and Jay Wood originally stressed the interpersonal dimension of intellectual humility, and viewed it as unconcern with how one's intelligence bears upon one's social status.[36] They also posited that intellectual humility is especially important for individuals viewed by their communities as intellectually talented, accomplished, and skilled, such as community leaders. When leaders do not attribute their status to superior intelligence, they have better interpersonal relations with those whom they lead.

Second, Ian Church stressed the intrapersonal epistemic dimension of intellectual humility, and viewed it as the virtuous mean between the opposite vices of intellectual arrogance (claiming to know more than is merited) and intellectual diffidence (claiming to know less than is merited).[37] Unlike the Aristotelian notion of virtue as a point between a deficiency of a trait and an excess of that same trait, such as courage is a point between cowardice and foolhardiness, both intellectual arrogance and intellectual diffidence are dishonest, and to that extent simply contrary to the honest, virtuous mean of intellectual humility. Elsewhere, Church argued that whatever social or moral dimensions intellectual humility might have, it needs to be built upon or understood primarily within a doxastic account, meaning how one reasons about their beliefs, hence its epistemic dimension.[38] "Intellectual humility is the virtue of accurately tracking what one could non-culpably take to be the positive epistemic status of one's own beliefs."[39]

Third, Dennis Whitcomb et al. viewed the virtue of intellectual humility as having a healthy stance toward one's intellectual limitations.[40] This involves first being properly attentive to them, compared to the arrogant person who is oblivious to them, or the servile person who sees nothing else but them. More importantly, intellectual humility also involves owning one's intellectual limitations, which is evident in the cognitive, behavioral, motivational, and affective responses to the awareness of one's limitations.

---

35. Barrett, "Intellectual Humility," 1.
36. Roberts and Wood, "Humility and Epistemic Goods."
37. Church and Barrett, "Intellectual Humility."
38. Church, "Doxastic Account." See also Church and Samuelson, *Intellectual Humility*.
39. Church and Barrett, "Intellectual Humility," 75.
40. Whitcomb et al., "Intellectual Humility."

It "characteristically involves dispositions 1) to believe that one has them and to believe that their negative outcomes are due to them; 2) to admit or acknowledge them; 3) to care about them and take them seriously; and 4) to feel regret or dismay, but not hostility, about them."[41] Intellectual humility is an intellectual virtue because it appropriately motivates the pursuit of epistemic goods such as better knowledge and understanding, even while acknowledging and lamenting its own intellectual limitations over which it has no final control.

Of the three contending conceptions of intellectual humility identified by Barrett, Whitcomb et al.'s account best addresses all three of its dimensions: the intrapersonal self-oriented dimension, the interpersonal other-oriented dimension, and the epistemic dimension.[42] Owning one's limitations is at once both the most comprehensive yet parsimonious explanation of intellectual humility. And while intellectual humility alone may be insufficient to produce a morally good person, it does make for an intellectually good person, especially when combined with the other intellectual virtues.

Intellectual Arrogance

Though virtue theory in epistemology is now thriving, there still is a paucity of work on vices. Attempts to conceptualize intellectual arrogance are limited and underdeveloped, other than intellectual arrogance being the antithesis of intellectual humility. Aiden Gregg and Nikhila Mahadevan defined intellectual arrogance as "the inclination to regard a belief as true because it is one's own"[43] or is held by the group to which one belongs, and as such it constitutes the presence of ego involvement in beliefs. As noted above, intellectual humility is the absence of ego involvement in beliefs. Arrogance is excessive attentiveness to and over-owning one's strengths, concomitant with deficient attentiveness to and under-owning one's limitations. Servility, in contrast, is deficient attentiveness to and under-owning one's strengths, concomitant with excessive attentiveness to and over-owning one's limitations. Both arrogance and servility are problematic levels of ego involvement in knowing. Intellectual humility is the non-Aristotelian golden mean.[44]

---

41. Whitcomb et al., "Intellectual Humility," 21.
42. Barrett, "Intellectual Humility."
43. Gregg and Mahadevan, "Intellectual Arrogance," 8.
44. The Aristotelian golden mean is the desirable middle between the extremes of excess and deficiency. For example, courage is a virtue, but when excessive, courage manifests as recklessness, and when deficient, it manifests as cowardice. Intellectual

More insightfully, Gregg and Mahadevan described intellectual arrogance as the product of ideological territoriality, evidenced by the warfare metaphors used to characterize argumentation. "One *attacks* a weak argument, and *counters* with a stronger one. Some intellectual positions are *indefensible*, being held on *shaky* grounds, and criticism can be *on target*. One can even *take a stab* at making a case, and hope others get the *thrust* of what you are *driving at* . . . The purpose of argumentation seems often precisely to *defeat* one's opponent definitively, not to understand reality better."[45]

They also described intellectual arrogance as a form of mental materialism, because people experience their beliefs as objects they own personally. As such, "they can be *acquired*, *held*, and *discarded—clung to* or *given up*. Like physical substances, they can be *shaped*, *twisted*, and *conditioned*, as well as being *weighty*, *rock-solid*, and *well-supported*; yet they may be too *rigid* and *inflexible*, and susceptible to being *shattered* or *demolished*. They are also valued commodities, being *dearly held* and cherished; one can even try to *sell someone an idea*, although no one may *buy* it."[46]

The concept of "mansplaining" is an example of intellectual arrogance characteristic of large segments of half the humans in history—men. To mansplain is to explain something in a patronizing, oversimplified, and often inaccurate manner.[47] More specifically, according to Merriam-Webster, mansplaining is "what occurs when a man talks condescendingly to someone (especially a woman) about something he has incomplete knowledge of, with the mistaken assumption that he knows more about it than the person he's talking to does." Though it typically occurs when a man talks over, interrupts, or explains something to a woman,[48] it is not limited to male-female conversation, but can readily occur in male-male conversations as well. Yet it is most evident in not only male-female conversations, but in gender relations more broadly. Natalia Imperatori-Lee connected theological mansplaining to an "archipelago of arrogance" and an ecclesial war on women in the Catholic Church, where male religious elites react with hermeneutical violence toward women who speak with authority. "One need only look at the absence of women's voices in the theological canon or the gendered

---

humility is the antithesis of intellectual arrogance, not merely the desirable middle between arrogance and servility.

45. Gregg and Mahadevan, "Intellectual Arrogance," 10 (italics in original).
46. Gregg and Mahadevan, "Intellectual Arrogance," 11 (italics in original).
47. Mansplaining was named one of the Words of the Year by *The New York Times* in 2010, and one of the runners-up to the Word of the Year by the *Oxford English Dictionary* in 2014. See Rothman, "Cultural History of Mansplaining"; Jaschik, "Calling Out Academic 'Mansplaining.'"
48. Solnit, *Men Explain Things to Me*.

breakdown of the canon of saints to know that in the Roman Catholic Church, women have not been considered reliable witnesses to their own lives, or faith, or the faith of the church that they love."[49]

In essence, intellectual humility is both one aspect of general humility and one aspect of intellectual virtue. As the latter, it does not evade truth defensively, but rather pursues truth passionately while actively uncovering and intentionally neutralizing one's own biases as much as possible. Because of the ego involved, intellectual arrogance pursues knowledge in order to defend a belief or position it already holds, or more offensively, to win an argument by persuading the other to abandon theirs. Warfare metaphors such as these expose just how much self is at stake in intellectual arrogance. Intellectual humility, in contrast, pursues truth for its own sake, for enlightenment, content to let its effects be whatever they may, unconcerned about self. Nevertheless, even intellectual humility is not totally free from pre-commitments, as it will unavoidably entail deference to an epistemic principle or method of knowing that one subjectively regards as having legitimate authority, whether that be logic, science, revelation, or authority itself.[50] Perhaps the ultimate test of intellectual humility is to be open-minded about its own epistemology.

C. PSYCHOLOGICAL PERSPECTIVES

Philosophical and theoretical work on humility dramatically outpaced empirical work on it until the emergence of positive psychology in this century brought greater emphasis to character strengths that enable individuals and communities to thrive.[51] Positive psychology is the scientific study of human flourishing on multiple levels, including the personal, relational, institutional, and cultural dimensions of life.[52] In their foundational compendium entitled *Character Strengths and Virtues: A Handbook and Classification*,

---

49. Imperatori-Lee, "Father Knows Best," 91.

50. Entwistle, *Integrative Approaches*, 97–99. Notably, in Weberian conception (Max Weber, *Economy and Society*, 212–16), authority is control seen by those subject to it as legitimate, and is therefore granted by consent. Authority does not reside inherently in any text, person, organization, or method of knowing. For example, to say that any particular sacred text is authoritative is to say more about the one making the claim than about the text itself, because there are obviously those for whom that text is not sacred, or even authoritative. Even in theology, the authority of the biblical text is properly seen as a derivative rather than an inherent authority, as theologians such as Karl Barth and John Webster have argued. Authority is therefore a form of social control that has been granted legitimacy.

51. Becker and Marecek, "Positive Psychology."

52. Seligman and Csikszentmalyi, "Positive Psychology."

Christopher Peterson and Martin Seligman classified twenty-six specific character strengths under six core virtues that consistently emerge across history and culture: wisdom, courage, humanity, justice, temperance, and transcendence.[53] Humility is addressed as one of the character strengths under the core virtue of temperance. While positive psychology has examined the role of virtues such as gratitude, forgiveness, love, and self-control, humility, at the time, remained the "most overlooked and underappreciated virtue."[54] Yet themes such as ethics and health, embodied character, strength and resilience, communal embeddedness, meaningful purpose, and capacity for wisdom are virtues that all apply specifically to intellectual humility.[55]

The explosion of attention to general humility in positive psychology during the first two decades of this century was summarized in the *Handbook of Humility: Theory, Research, and Applications*,[56] and shown to have closed much of the gap on the scientific study of other virtues. Remarkably, "almost every scientist currently studying humility is Christian."[57] The *Handbook of Humility* defined general humility as comprised of three core aspects.

> First, humility involves an accurate assessment of self, including an awareness of one's limitations. Second, humility involves a modest self-presentation. Humble individuals are not only honest in their self-assessment, but seek to be honest in their self-presentation. Third . . . humility involves an interpersonal stance that is other-oriented rather than self-oriented.[58]

As with other personal variables such as anxiety, psychology differentiates between state and trait humility, state humility being a temporary product of the situation, and trait humility being a stable characteristic of the person. Though far from identical, state humility is in some ways similar to context-specific humility, and trait humility is in some ways similar to ability-specific humility.

---

53. See Peterson and Seligman, *Character Strengths and Virtues*.
54. Chancellor and Lyubomirsky, "Humble Beginnings," 819.
55. Hill and Sandage, "Promising but Challenging."
56. Worthington et al., "Introduction."
57. McMinn, *Science of Virtue*, 2.
58. Worthington et al., "Introduction," 4.

Psychological Definitions of Intellectual Humility

Two studies exemplify a unique approach to defining intellectual humility psychologically. On the basis that "the semantic structure of a language reflects to some extent the perceived structure of phenomena," and that "a virtue is often best understood in the context of related virtues and the vices they oppose," Markus Christen, Mark Alfano, and Brian Robinson employed a psycholexical approach that focused on both synonyms and antonyms of intellectual humility, yielding a thesaurus-based method to map the semantic space of intellectual humility.[59] Using thirty-nine synonyms for intellectual humility, they found three semantic clusters that compose intellectual humility: a) the sensible self most characterized by comprehension, sympathy, and sensitiveness, b) the discreet self most characterized by decency, demureness, and unpretentiousness, and c) the inquisitive self most characterized by inquiry, scrutiny, and learning. Using forty-six antonyms of intellectual humility, they found three clusters that compose contraries: a) the over-rated self most characterized by egocentrism, smugness, and vanity, b) the under-rated other most characterized by chauvinism, prejudice, and narrow-mindedness, and c) the under-rated self most characterized by timidity, submissiveness, and diffidence.

A second and similar study also used a semantic mapping technique to identify implicit theories of intellectual humility, or what the researchers termed a "family resemblance" or "folk understanding" of intellectual humility. As further constructs for comparison, Samuelson et al. sought to characterize not just the humble person, but the wise person and arrogant person as well.[60] The profile of a humble person revealed three clusters: intelligent/love of learning, humble/modest, and respectful/considerate. The profile of a wise person had four clusters: intelligent/learned, respectful/listens to both sides, reflective/perceptive, and experienced/rational. Finally, the profile of an arrogant person also had three clusters: educated/proud, arrogant/know-it-all, and opinionated/jerk. Considerable overlap was found between humble and wise persons, though the humble person was uniquely other-oriented and pro-social (kind, considerate, and unselfish).

In personality trait theory, humility is included in the self-reported HEXACO Personality Inventory developed by cross-cultural lexical studies, with sub-scales in each of Honesty-Humility (H), Emotionality (E), Extraversion (X), Agreeableness (A), Conscientiousness (C), and Openness to

---

59. Christen et al., "Semantic Space" 2.
60. Samuelson et al., "Implicit Theories."

Experience (O).[61] Most notably, honesty and humility are here considered to be connected constructs consisting of four facets (sincerity, fairness, greed avoidance, and modesty—the latter two comprising the humility portion) and contrasted by adjectives such as pretentious, boastful, and pompous. As one indication of its recent and growing theoretical importance, Honesty-Humility was not yet included as a separate category in the earlier "big five" OCEAN personality trait analysis—Openness, Conscientiousness, Extraversion, Agreeableness, and Neuroticism—though some of the characteristics belonging to Honesty-Humility are incorporated into the "big five's" Agreeableness factor.

Measurement Issues

Much more than defining intellectual humility or locating it in personality theory, empirical studies are challenged by measuring their validity and reliability. The measure of humility is extraordinarily complicated by the paradox of self-attribution in self-reporting, because the human tendency toward self-inflation on measures that are socially desirable compromises internal validity. "Someone who is genuinely humble is unlikely to report being humble, and someone who reports being humble is unlikely to be humble."[62] Self-reports of being humble are akin to bragging, and therefore self-contradictory.[63] Consequently the most prominent alternative methodology is the use of personality judgments from other observer raters that avoid the motivational and ego-defensive processes of self-report.[64] An approach that triangulates self-report, observer-report, and trait-relevant behavior is that much better.[65] Regarding trait-relevant behavior, humility is

---

61. Lee and Ashton, "Psychometric Properties"; Ashton et al., "Six-Factor Structure."

62. Christen et al., "Semantic Space," 2. There is seemingly a case of the self-contradiction of the self-attribution of humility in the Pentateuch, conventionally thought to be written by Moses. "Now the man Moses was very humble, more so than anyone else on the face of the earth" (Num 12:3). But redaction criticism would suggest that, though the source of the text may have been traditions concerning Moses passed from generation to generation, the third-person narration here indicates that the wording is a creation of someone other than Moses, someone in the vast company of unnamed prophetic redactors/editors.

63. The common conversation qualifier, "in my humble opinion" (IMHO), is likely an exception to the self-contradictory self-report of claiming humility. The phrase is usually intended to convey that the speaker is not claiming fact or accuracy, but only that "this is what I think, but I'm not an expert on this matter, and I could be wrong." The disclaimer is a comment on the claim, not the person making the claim.

64. Meagher et al., "Contrasting Self-Report and Consensus Ratings."

65. Hook and Davis, "Humility, Religion, and Spirituality."

also likely best assessed under strain, that is, in situations that evoke egoism and provoke intellectual arrogance.[66] Everett Worthington et al. provided helpful comparisons: "Just as courage is difficult to assess until someone is placed in danger and is fearful, and forgiveness is hard to evaluate until one is deeply hurt or offended, humility is best observed when the ego is placed under strain."[67]

Several attempts to measure intellectual humility have been generated. Don Davis et al. initially crafted a four-item, observer-rated Spiritual Humility Scale (SHS) that focused on the context of relational spirituality and forgiveness.[68] Stacey McElroy et al. then developed the first published measure of intellectual humility, the Intellectual Humility Scale (IHS), a sixteen-item, observer-rated measure comprised of an Intellectual Openness subscale and an Intellectual Arrogance subscale.[69] The two subscales were found to be highly correlated with each other, and preliminary evidence indicated that the IHS scale was psychometrically sound. Elizabeth Krumrei-Mancuso and Steven Rouse later created a twenty-two-item Comprehensive Intellectual Humility Scale (CIHS) which measured four distinct but intercorrelated aspects: independence of intellect and ego, openness to revising one's viewpoint, respect for others' viewpoints, and lack of intellectual overconfidence.[70] Despite the CIHS scale being a self-report measure, "validation data were obtained from multiple, independent samples, supporting appropriate levels of convergent, discriminant, and predictive validity."[71] Though Leary et al. later independently verified the CIHS's validity,[72] Hoyle et al. developed a Specific Intellectual Humility Scale (SIHS) on the premise that "intellectual humility with respect to a specific view is a complex function of dispositional intellectual humility, the extremity of the view, and the basis for the view."[73] Like so many psychological constructs, the challenge of measuring intellectual humility is not insignificant.

---

66. Davis et al., "Humility and the Development."
67. Worthington et al., "Introduction," 4.
68. Davis et al., "Relational Spirituality and Forgiveness."
69. McElroy et al., "Intellectual Humility."
70. Krumrei-Mancuso and Rouse, "Development and Validation."
71. Krumrei-Mancuso and Rouse, "Development and Validation," 209.
72. Leary et al., "Cognitive and Interpersonal Features."
73. Hoyle et al., "Holding Specific Views With Humility," 165.

Findings about Intellectual Humility

Research findings in psychology regarding general humility have shown it to be *negatively* correlated with certain vices, such as narcissism, Machiavellianism, psychopathy, self-absorption, narcissistic entitlement, high emotional reactivity, impression management, group dominance, right-wing authoritarianism, prejudice, antisocial behaviors, aggressive bullying, proclivity toward sexual harassment, deviant behaviors in the workplace, vengefulness, and the belief that the world is a competitive place.[74]

Research findings in psychology regarding intellectual humility in particular vary from theorizing about the source of intellectual humility to identifying the number and nature of its correlates. Gregg and Mahadevan offered an evolutionary account of intellectual arrogance and intellectual humility that perceives human cognition as both partly emancipated from evolution and partly embodied.[75] While human thought is not fully determined by evolution, they argued that embodiment clearly continues to shape thought. Humans have evolved to both compete and cooperate, therefore both egocentric/antisocial impulses and altruistic/pro-social impulses persist in embodied human life. A study by Matthew Jarvinen and Thomas Paulus investigated how an understanding of emotion, emotion regulation, and attachment are crucial to understanding intellectual humility.[76] It provided evidence that participants primed in a secure attachment condition demonstrated significantly greater cognitive openness to counterarguments with regard to (a)theistic belief than participants in an ambivalent priming condition, insecure in their attachment. Those identified as secure in their enduring dispositional attachment orientation exhibited significantly higher trait openness than those categorized as avoidant.

Intellectual humility applies not just to the person generally, but to specific domains such as politics, religion, and education, specific topics within those domains, and even specific issues within those topics.[77] For example, someone may be generally humble but not intellectually humble, or intellectually humble but not intellectually humble about religion, or humble about religion but not humble about matters of human life, or humble about medical assistance in dying but not about abortion. Intellectual humility

---

74. Worthington, et al., "Introduction," 6–7.
75. Gregg and Mahadevan, "Intellectual Arrogance."
76. Jarvinen and Paulus, "Attachment and Cognitive Openness."
77. Hoyle et al., "Holding Specific Views with Humility."

is "the recognition that a particular personal view may be fallible, accompanied by an appropriate attentiveness to limitations in the evidentiary basis of that view and to one's own limitations in obtaining and evaluating information relevant to it."[78] Furthermore, Krumrei-Mancuso found that intellectual humility is negatively correlated with characteristics harmful to relationships, such as arrogance, narcissism, entitlement, domination, and power-seeking.[79] In total, the data overwhelmingly affirm that intellectual humility makes one a better person, and the practice of intellectual humility makes for a more civil society that facilitates human flourishing for all.

D. SOCIOLOGICAL PERSPECTIVES

More than a personal attribute and virtue relatively present or absent within individuals, general humility exists between and among individuals, and therefore is also fundamentally social in nature. General humility implies the presence of at least one other person with whom one has at least some comparative relationship, and general humility is therefore by definition relational. Thus, "it is important that we think of humility as a social craft rather than a personal virtue."[80] Among the benefits of this craft are the development, maintenance, and regulation of a prosocial and communal orientation toward others, and the social bonds that accrue from it.[81] Consequently, general humility provides a buffer for competitive traits that would otherwise cause deterioration in relationships.[82] Furthermore, it has been empirically associated with "generosity, helpfulness and agreeableness, patience, empathy, interpersonal forgiveness, social justice commitment, avoidance of social duplicity, and graciousness in receiving from others."[83]

Wes Markofski compared intellectual humility in particular to an expanded concept of social reflexivity, which he defined as "people's capacity to think and interact flexibly and self-critically in relation to diverse social others and situations."[84] Supporting the context-specific and content-specific nature of intellectual humility identified earlier, he observed that the breadth of social reflexivity may range from segmented reflexivity (present in one type of social difference but not others) to transposable reflexivity

78. Hoyle et al., "Holding Specific Views with Humility," 165.
79. Krumrei-Mancuso, "We Know in Part."
80. Kennedy, "Educating Bees," 29.
81. Davis et al., "Humility and the Development."
82. Davis and Hook, "Humility, Religion, and Spirituality."
83. Wolfteich et al., "Humility," 192–93.
84. Markofski, "American Evangelicalism, Social Reflexivity."

(across multiple types of social difference), while the depth of social reflexivity may range from frozen reflexivity (self-critical modes of talk and action that are only partial and rigid) to deep reflexivity (self-critical and flexible modes of talk and action across difference). In sum, reflexivity ranges in both breadth and depth, that is, in the number of areas it is operative and in the degree to which it is operative. Deep reflexivity is "characterized by a consistent fallibilism that recognizes the unavoidable failure and limits inherent in all efforts to build bridges and practice social reflexivity across difference."[85]

Self and Identity

Both general humility and intellectual humility can also be examined across all orientations of sociology from the scientific to the interpretive to the critical,[86] as well as across all levels of sociology, from the intra- and interpersonal micro, to the organizational and institutional meso, to the cultural and systemic macro. According to interpretive, micro, symbolic interactionist sociology, both general humility and intellectual humility are aspects of self-esteem, which is both the evaluative component of the self-concept as well as the affective dimension of self-objectification. As such, self-esteem refers to "the positive or negative feelings we attach to ourselves and the judgments we make of our own worth."[87]

A person's relative self-esteem is typically manifest in how they present themselves to others, which is comprised of those processes by which individuals attempt to control the impressions that others form of them in social interaction.[88] One common tactic of impression management that bears on intellectual humility and intellectual arrogance is the use of disclaimers, those verbal assertions intended to ward off any potentially negative implications of questionable impending statements as irrelevant to one's identity.[89] Hedging ("I could be wrong, but ... "), credentialing ("Some of my best friends are _____, but ... "), cognitive disclaimers ("This may sound crazy, but ... "), and suspension of judgment ("No offense, but ... ") are examples of tactical impression management, or the staged self, not expressions of the authentic self.

---

85. Markofski, "American Evangelicalism, Social Reflexivity."
86. Habermas, *Knowledge and Human Interests*.
87. Sandstrom et al., *Symbols, Selves, and Social Reality*, 136.
88. Goffman, *Presentation of Self*.
89. Hewitt and Stokes, "Disclaimers."

In comparison, distinguished psychologist Gordon Allport reflected true intellectual humility in acknowledging that, "although much of my writing is polemic in tone, I know in my bones that my opponents are partly right."[90] However, when one's opponents do not reciprocate, genuine dialogue becomes impossible, because true dialogue requires authentic equality and openness of interactants. When no status differences such as teacher-student exist to frame the interaction, but equality and openness cannot be negotiated and achieved, it devolves into a duel, and we are once again at war, where "might makes right." In conversations, this usually takes the form of alternating monologues or duologues, where both parties talk at or past the other, each party taking turns at separate speech acts, neither party listening to nor responding to the other, with nothing either party says modifying what the other will say next. Intellectual arrogance then prevails, fostering self-delusion in the arrogant themselves, producing ignorance by silencing others,[91] and committing epistemic injustice.[92] Both self and other are left less than what they could have been.

Two simple clarifications about intellectual arrogance are warranted here. First, intellectual arrogance lies more in what is asserted than in how it is asserted, more in the substance of its content than in its manner of expression. It is entirely possible and often tactically effective to make the most arrogant assertions in the meekest manner, to say the unkindest things in the softest tones, and then to insist on the virtue of doing so by justifying the content as not harmful, or as prompted by good motives, or as appropriate in the circumstances. The scenario of "love the sinner, hate the sin," in which someone "lovingly" admonishes someone else whom they consider a sinner, is one generic example. Ironically, it frequently becomes unclear which of the two is the actual sinner, and by whose definition of which sin. Second, intellectual arrogance is entirely separate from logical fallacies in rational argumentation. For example, to commit the *ad hominem* fallacy, one form of a larger category of fallacies of irrelevance, is to criticize the arguer instead of the argument. But intellectual arrogance is in fact about the person, not the argument; it is pointedly "to the man." On the matter of intellectual arrogance, it is the argument that is irrelevant. Intellectual arrogance is a very intentional assessment of the vice of the knower, not the veracity of the known.

---

90. Allport, *Person in Psychology*, 405.
91. Tanesini, "Calm Down Dear."
92. Fricker, *Epistemic Injustice*.

Relational Dynamics

Intellectual humility, in contrast, is a necessary first step toward remedying the "undying certainty that we have nothing to learn from those who are different from us."[93] Intellectual humility involves "the ability to regulate one's need to appear 'right' or 'correct' in regard to one's beliefs or ideas."[94] The Dalai Lama got his priorities in good order when he said that "I'd rather be kind than right. You can always be kind." Moreover, the intellectually humble person inspires implicit trust. We feel that we can let our guard down around such a person, express our real opinions, and face at worst gentle and constructive criticism.[95] In addition to this greater trust, intellectual humility makes for greater likelihood of forgiveness, especially in religious conflict,[96] as well as the prosocial change in thoughts, emotions, and motivations toward an offender[97] which helps to repair relationships that have been damaged or ruptured. Intellectual humility is imperative for fostering and preserving authentic, open, vulnerable relationships, and has been empirically associated with higher levels of empathy, gratitude, altruism, and benevolence, as well as lower levels of power-seeking.[98] One study of Christian pastors found intellectual humility to be a positive predictor of religious tolerance, even when controlling for conservatism.[99] Overall, "a key function of intellectual humility is to prevent relational wear-and-tear, like oil prevents an engine from overheating."[100]

Cultural Dynamics

At the macro cultural level, general humility has been significantly devalued in Western modernity, in part because intellectual humility requires "epistemic anti-individualism,"[101] a collective knowing together that is anathema to the autonomous rationality and self of Enlightenment convictions. The modern liberal arts have "emphasized the development of the individual

---

93. Guhin, "Problem with 'Just a Theory.'"
94. Davis and Hook, "Humility, Religion, and Spirituality," 112.
95. Robinson and Alfano, "I Know You Are, But What Am I?"
96. Johnson et al., "Intellectual Humility and Forgiveness."
97. McCullough et al., *Forgiveness*.
98. Krumrei-Mancuso, "Intellectual Humility and Prosocial Values."
99. Hook, "Intellectual Humility and Religious Tolerance."
100. McElroy et al., "Intellectual Humility," 21.
101. Robinson and Alfano, "I Know You Are, But What Am I?"

critical thinker and not the art of thinking socially,"[102] generating an ethos of profound political, religious, and moral pluralism. But contrary to true pluralism which is at peace with differences of thought, contemporary diversity too often devolves into mutual antagonism. In the culture wars of the last generation,[103] much of the civil common ground of the public square has been eroded by the increasing polarization of left-wing versus right-wing political, social, and theological beliefs. Most combatants—for that is how they behave—are now "hunkered down behind barricades across from each other, firing lethal volleys at their ideological enemies, which makes survival as a moderate caught in the cross-fire all but impossible. Even moderate ideas draw immoderate fire from the blockades. Now it's either us or them, with partisan tribal loyalty, not principled conciliatory reflection, the only virtue that seemingly really matters."[104] In such a context, intellectual humility seems essential for peaceful interactions,[105] and especially for generating effective, constructive public discourse.[106] Only a politics of virtue rooted in solidarity and humility can sustain civility.[107]

The confounding conundrum is that conflicting political and religious ideologies have contrasting valuations of solidarity and humility, and what constitutes the moral good more broadly. Moral foundations theory, popularized by Jonathan Haidt's *The Righteous Mind*,[108] identifies five foundations underlying all moral virtues. Based on massive cross-cultural data and grounded in evolutionary psychology, moral foundations theory rejects rationalist theories of morality, maintaining that moral judgments are caused by quick, pre-rational, emotional intuitions. Moral reasoning, in contrast, is motivated by strategic objectives, and simply serves as post-hoc rationalization. Therefore morality is like viewing a painting that we instantly like or dislike, and then coming up with reasons why. The five foundations are:

> Care: preventing suffering by protecting others (the opposite of harm)

---

102. Kennedy, "Educating Bees," 29.

103. Hunter, *Culture Wars*; Hartman, *War for the Soul*; Hunter and Bowman, *Vanishing Center*.

104. Hiebert, "Call for Civility," 1.

105. Fisch, "Modest Proposal."

106. Johnson et al., "Intellectual Humility."

107. Wood, "Passion and Virtue." John Rawls addressed the dialectical tension between polarizing coercion and pervasive disagreement in *Justice as Fairness* and *Political Liberalism*.

108. Haidt, *Righteous Mind*. For a more academic overview, see Jesse Graham et al., "Moral Foundations Theory," 55–130. See also http://moralfoundations.org/

> Fairness: rendering justice according to shared rules (the opposite of cheating)
>
> Loyalty: thinking and acting in terms of "we" (the opposite of betrayal)
>
> Authority: submitting to hierarchy and tradition (the opposite of subversion)
>
> Sanctity/Purity: abhorring what is regarded as disgusting (the opposite of degradation)

A sixth foundation, Liberty (the opposite of oppression), was only added later in Haidt's book.

Significantly for cultural harmony, moral foundations theory also rejects "the common philosophical (and, sometimes, psychological) project of searching for a single, unified principle or psychological mechanism that, by itself, accounts for all of morality, a project that has thus far proved something of a quagmire."[109] Thus the theory's view of morality is "unabashedly pluralist," not monist, in its "pragmatic validity."[110] Lawrence Kohlberg was the first moral psychologist to argue for a single foundation of morality: justice.[111] Carol Gilligan then argued for dual, gendered foundations, maintaining that justice may be the male foundation of morality, but care was the female foundation of morality.[112] Moral foundation theory adds three more foundations to these first two.

Ideologies come into play in that liberals tend to rely more heavily on the first two foundations of care and fairness, whereas conservatives tend to rely more heavily on the additional three foundations of in-group loyalty, respect for authority, and sanctity or purity.[113] The intersection with intellectual humility is that the additional three foundations of loyalty, authority, and purity are more prone to intellectual arrogance, and have for decades been associated with the authoritarian personality by research in political psychology.[114] For example, Matthew Kugler et al. found that

> liberal-conservative differences in moral intuitions are statistically mediated by authoritarianism and social dominance orientation, so that conservatives' greater valuation of in-group,

---

109. Suhler and Churchland, "Innate, Modular 'Foundations.'"
110. Graham et al., "Moral Foundations Theory."
111. Kohlberg, "Stage and Sequence."
112. Gilligan, *In a Different Voice*.
113. Graham et al., "Liberals and Conservatives."
114. The original articulation was in the classic text by Adorno et al., *Authoritarian Personality*.

> authority, and purity concerns is attributable to higher levels of authoritarianism, whereas liberals' greater valuation of fairness and harm avoidance is attributable to lower levels of social dominance. [Furthermore], in-group, authority, and purity concerns are positively associated with intergroup hostility and support for discrimination, whereas concerns about fairness and harm avoidance are negatively associated with these variables.[115]

They go on to question the wisdom of treating preferences based on authoritarianism and social dominance as moral rather than amoral or even immoral, and thereby incorporating conservative ideology into the study of moral psychology. For example, perception of truth then has more to do with in-group loyalty than facts, because once an intuitive moral judgment has been made, motivated reasoning and confirmation bias simply seal it.

At the macro inter-cultural level, Western civilization as a whole is characterized by arrogance relative to other cultures, creating enormous challenges not just within cultures, but between cultures. Imperialism, the drive to conquer and subjugate other peoples which leads to the control of one territory and its peoples by another, is as old as history. But colonialism, the drive not only to conquer other peoples and control their territory, but to settle permanently into their territory in order to obtain cheap raw materials and labor, and new or expanded markets, is of more recent vintage. It may have peaked at the Berlin Conference of 1884–1885, during which the European powers eliminated or overrode most existing forms of African autonomy and self-governance, and divided up possession of Africa among themselves. By 1913, the "scramble for Africa" had 90 percent of the continent controlled by Europeans, having nobly taken up "The White Man's Burden" to civilize savages, as eloquently expressed by the British poet Rudyard Kipling in 1899. Despite the de-colonization of Africa and other continents in the second half of the twentieth century, globalization at the end of the century simply ushered in neo-imperialism and neo-colonialism, the maintenance of subjugation, not through military or political means, but through economic and cultural means. As Ludwell Denny, the American CEO of one transnational corporation put it, "We are not without cunning. We shall not make Britain's mistake. Too wise to govern the world, we shall simply own it."[116]

Also at the end of the twentieth century, in his seminal "clash of civilizations" thesis, Samuel Huntington's blunt assessment was that "Western belief in the universality of Western culture suffers three problems: it is false;

---

115. Kugler et al., "Another Look at Moral Foundations," 413.
116. Quoted in Idris-Soven et al., *World as a Company Town*, 20.

it is immoral; and it is dangerous."[117] In his prescient prediction two decades ago, "the dangerous clashes of the future are likely to arise from the interaction of Western arrogance, Islamic intolerance, and Sinic assertiveness."[118] Huntington also reminded us that "the West won the world not by the superiority of its ideas or values or religion . . . but rather by its superiority in applying organized violence. Westerners often forget this fact; non-Westerners never do."[119] At home, mistaking the study of their own history and culture as inherently ethnocentric, many Western universities discontinued teaching first year history courses in Western Civilization, because they came to be deemed intrinsically right-wing rationalizations "for Western hegemony and oppression."[120]

Yet culturally arrogant voices continue to clamor in the academy. For example, the universality of modern Western culture is precisely what Steven Pinker asserted recently in his weighty tome, *Enlightenment Now: The Case for Reason, Science, Humanism, and Progress*.[121] Marshaling massive amounts of quantitative data summarized in seventy-five astonishing graphs, Pinker argued that the Enlightenment, that compound of reason, science, and humanism, has led to dramatic progress in all areas of life all over the world. Fifteen separate measures were given separate chapters. His 450-page *tour de force* contended that the living conditions and prospects of modern populations, even in poorer countries, are clearly superior to those of the past. On average, people everywhere live longer, are better fed and educated, and are more secure than previous generations.

Pinker was quick to dismiss any critique of Enlightenment, such as that its rationalized economy of capitalism has turned human beings into slaves of alienated labor and victims of mindless consumerism. He refused to countenance the notion that science lacks any ethical logic of its own, as argued by James Davison Hunter and Paul Nedelisky,[122] or that modern "progress" is both liberating *and* threatening precisely *because* of how greatly it expands human power, including the power to doom humanity to ecological or nuclear self-destruction. His unrestrained contempt was for "progressophobia," leftist intellectuals, the populist right, the politically correct, postmodernists, theocrats, de-growth environmentalists, and Friedrich Nietzsche.

117. Huntington, *Clash of Civilizations*, 310.
118. Huntington, "Challenger Civilizations."
119. Huntington, *Clash of Civilizations*, 51.
120. Thornton, *Greek Ways*.
121. Pinker, *Enlightenment Now*.
122. Hunter and Nedelisky, *Science and the Good*.

Four years earlier, the rhetoric of Rodney Stark's title, *How the West Won: The Neglected Story of the Triumph of Modernity*,[123] reflected the tone of the content of the book, in which he sought to absolve Western culpability for everything from colonialism to slavery, child labor, and more.[124] In his closing sentences, Stark asserted that, "No doubt Western modernity has its limitations and discontents. Still, it is far better than the known alternatives."[125] Strikingly, though Pinker and Stark agreed on the triumphal merits of modernity in every other way, Pinker cast Christianity as the primary historical impediment to progress, whereas Stark cast Christianity as the primary impetus to progress. As for intellectual arrogance, even a like-minded conservative reviewer tellingly lamented that "I wish Rodney Stark had resisted overstatement and selective quotation. I also wish that he had been less polemical in tone and considerably more careful about details. Above all, I wish that he had acknowledged the ambivalence that any conservative is bound to feel about our modern age."[126]

Of course, the clash of civilizations, or the competition of cultures, if that is what it is, is not over. It may be justifiable to name a current leader, but it is too early to declare a final winner. Some of the limitations and discontents of Western modernity, such as its alienations (Marx), anomie (Durkheim), and disenchantment (Weber) may be relatively bearable compared to those of other eras and cultures. The meaninglessness and emptiness of life within a purely materialistic worldview, as portrayed by T. S. Eliot in "The Waste Land," may not be the harshest circumstance in human history.[127] The inauthentic individualism of what Charles Taylor termed "the malaise of modernity" may even be preferable to inhabitants of bleaker social environments.[128] Taylor identified three aspects of the malaise: "The first fear is about what we might call a loss of meaning, the fading of moral horizons. The second concerns the eclipse of ends, in the face of rampant instrumental reason. And the third is about a loss of freedom."[129] As stark as

---

123. Stark, *How the West Won*.

124. Other titles with similar tones in Stark's corpus include *The Victory of Reason: How Christianity Led to Freedom, Capitalism, and Western Success* (2005); *Cities of God: The Real Story of How Christianity Became an Urban Movement and Conquered Rome* (2006); *God's Battalions: The Case for the Crusades* (2009); *The Triumph of Christianity: How the Jesus Movement Became the World's Largest Religion* (2011).

125. Stark, *How the West Won*, 370.

126. Young, "Stark Truth," 67.

127. In Eliot, *Waste Land*.

128. Taylor, *Malaise of Modernity*.

129. Taylor, *Malaise of Modernity*, 10.

segments and aspects of pre-modernity were, modernity dare not be mistaken for utopia.

Furthermore, some potential deliverances of Western modernity may not even be survivable, such as the slow, ominous advance of climate change, or the sudden, catastrophic explosion of nuclear war. And what of the reconfigurations of biomedical technology, the reconstructions of genetic engineering, the invasion of artificial intelligence, or the march of robotics?[130] (To his credit, Pinker addressed all these concerns, though rather dismissively.) The technological, economic, social scientific, and political advances generated by Western modernity have by no means necessarily been ecological, moral, social, or aesthetic advances. For all the creature comforts it has delivered, industrialization was hardly an ecological advance. For all the wealth it has generated, capitalism was hardly a moral advance.[131] For all the self-actualization it has facilitated, egoism is hardly a social advance.[132] Truth be told, Western modernity is a "suicide machine" comprised of interlocking systems of prosperity, equity, security, and spirituality, each in crisis, and together terminal, if not deconstructed and reconstructed.[133]

Instead of profound Western hubris, intellectual humility seems essential for responding critically and constructively to all levels of human social life, from short-term interpersonal relationships to long-term sociopolitical dynamics,[134] and in all aspects of human social life, from religion to science. Some scientists do live out an authentic intellectual humility. Said Erwin

---

130. In "Is AI a Threat to Christianity?" Jonathan Merritt identified fundamental questions for Christianity raised by the rapid current advance of AI and robotics. For example, can we ask Siri to pray for us? Does God hear prayers spoken by any intelligent being, robot, or phone, or just prayers uttered by humans? What if robots develop the ability to make ethical decisions? And what if robots become fully sentient, rational agents—beings with emotions, consciousness, and self-awareness? Would they also be in need of salvation? Could they too establish a relationship with God? In *The Inevitable: Understanding the 12 Technological Forces That Will Shape Our Future*, Kevin Kelly argued that there will soon be a spiritual dimension to AI and robotics.

131. Hiebert, "Mechanisms and Morality."

132. Vitz, *Psychology as Religion*. Note the striking difference between American humanist psychologist Abraham Maslow's identification of self-actualization as the highest human need (see *Motivation and Personality*) compared to Austrian Holocaust survivor Victor Frankl's identification of self-transcendence as the highest human need (see *Man's Search for Meaning*).

133. McLaren, *Everything Must Change*. Allen Ginsberg's "Howl" is a powerful, prophetic, poetic rejoinder to the triumphalism of modernity, a denunciation of the failings of American society, and a literary classic (https://www.poetryfoundation.org/poems/49303/howl). See also Ginsberg, *Howl and Other Poems*.

134. Wender, "Learning through Upheaval."

Schrödinger, one of the founders of quantum theory, founder of wave mechanics, and winner of the 1933 Nobel Prize in Physics:

> I am very astonished that the scientific picture of the real world around me is very deficient. It gives a lot of factual information, puts all our experience in a magnificently consistent order, but is ghastly silent about all that is really near to our heart, that really matters to us. It cannot tell us a word about red and blue, bitter and sweet, physical pain and physical delight; it knows nothing of beautiful and ugly, good or bad, God and eternity. Science sometimes pretends to answer questions in these domains, but the answers are very often so silly that we are not inclined to take them seriously.[135]

E. PERSPECTIVES FROM RELIGIOUS STUDIES

All the great religious traditions have condemned arrogance as a vice and extolled humility as a virtue (for example, Bhagavad Gita 13:7–8; New Testament Matt 18:4; Qur'an 23:1–2).[136]

> From the religious perspective, the virtue of humility is necessarily grounded in a transcendent reality, something that stands outside of and gives ultimate meaning to the universe to which one owes deference. The religious transcendent not only puts human selves in perspective, but for each religion, transcendent reality is the on-going source of existence such that humility requires an on-going response of dependence and submission.[137]

Moreover, according to Confucius, humility is the foundation of all other virtues.

Yet as we have already observed, inasmuch as both general humility and intellectual humility are best understood as context- and content-specific, intellectual humility is challenged and tested most in the domain of strong, especially religious convictions. "[W]hether it's Christian fundamentalism, Islamic jihadism, or militant atheism, religious dialogue often remains tinted by a terrifying and dehumanizing arrogance, dogma, and ignorance."[138] Hence the paradox that, though most world religions advocate humility as a virtue, maintaining humility about one's religious convictions often

---

135. Schrödinger, *Nature and the Greeks*, 95.
136. Bollinger and Hill, "Humility."
137. Porter, "Religious Perspectives on Humility," 59–60.
138. Church and Samuelson, *Intellectual Humility*, 287.

proves extremely difficult.[139] We have defined intellectual humility here as acknowledgment of the limits of one's knowledge, an accurate view of one's intellectual strengths and weakness, an ability to present one's ideas in a non-offensive manner, and an openness to new ideas. Intellectual humility regarding religious beliefs in particular is characterized, at least in part, by "an awareness of the fallibility of one's religious beliefs, discretion in asserting those beliefs, comfort keeping one's religious beliefs private, and respect for others' religious beliefs."[140]

Theologies of Religion

The issue of intellectual humility in the context of religious conviction is enormously complicated by various and usually discrepant religious beliefs about other religions. For the most part, different religions view other religions differently, each having their own, unique, pre-dominant theology of religions. Yet variance is as readily evident within a single religion as it is between religions. Christianity, for one, contains within its spectrum all three of the general models of how religions view other religions, as first articulated by Alan Race.[141] The first model, *pluralism*, maintains that all world religions are true and equally valid in their communication of the truth about God; all religions lead to the same God, and all religious ways lead to heaven.[142] The second model, *inclusivism*, maintains that God is also present in non-Christian religions in order to save their adherents through Christ; "anonymous Christians" are thereby saved through Christ without their allegiance or even awareness.[143] The third model, *exclusivism*, maintains that there is no salvation in non-Christian religions; all other religious claims are invalid and false, based on the Aristotelian concept of truth as one and not many.[144] To evangelical Christians, both pluralism and inclusivism are enemies of Christian truth, as they eliminate the *kerygmatic* mission to evangelize the world.

---

139. Woodruff et al., "Humility and Religion."
140. Hopkin et al., "Intellectual Humility," 58.
141. Race, *Christians and Religious Pluralism*.
142. John Hick made a case for Christian pluralism in *God and the Universe of Faiths*.
143. Bernd Irlenborn made a case for Christian inclusivism in "Religious Diversity: A Philosophical Defense of Religious Inclusivism."
144. Alvin Plantinga made a case for Christian exclusivism in "Pluralism: A Defense of Religious Exclusivism."

The historic Abrahamic faiths of Judaism, Christianity, and Islam are each monotheistic, and therefore typically exclusive, and therefore also normally proselytizing (in the case of the latter two). Their exclusive proclivities have caused great conflict between individuals and groups, with their multiple denominational schisms and religious wars being the best evidence. Other historic world religions are polytheistic, such as Hinduism, or atheistic, such as Buddhism, and therefore generally more inclusive of the beliefs of other faiths, and therefore mostly non-proselytizing. Non-proselytizing religions like Hinduism embrace religious pluralism as part of their belief system, and thus have an openness built into their religious worldview that monotheistic, exclusive religions do not. With its prominent and persistent teachings about minimizing self-focus, Buddhism is in principle generally more open-minded than adherents of monotheistic faiths, though many Buddhist sects are not in practice.[145]

Therefore it could be argued that a certain intellectual arrogance is built into the worldview of monotheistic, exclusive religions. However, if their religious beliefs do in fact align with reality and are in fact true, and all other religious beliefs are false, then their exclusive devotion to their God is justified, and not arrogant. Certainly most monotheists do not see their beliefs as arrogant, and can hardly conceive of them as such. In fact, rejection of their God would then be the ultimate arrogance, elevating human reasoning and will above their God. Likewise, if those beliefs are in fact true, and someone is ideologically opposed to considering them because they are a pluralist, then from a religious perspective such ideologically committed pluralism is itself inherently arrogant and closed-minded. The key difference is not so much between the intellectual humility or intellectual arrogance of the individual religious believer, but between inclusive religious belief systems which embrace pluralism itself, and exclusive religious belief systems which reject pluralism.

Accordingly, intellectual humility cannot simply be conflated with a pluralistic or inclusivistic acceptance of and agreement with the religious "other." Intellectual humility can in fact be exemplified by religious exclusivists as well. It is entirely possible to hold beliefs in "the one true God" while maintaining awareness of their fallibility, showing discretion in asserting them, being comfortable in keeping them private when appropriate, and respecting the religious beliefs of others. However, though "it's possible to be intellectually humble and at the same time hold strong religious beliefs, there is a real worry that *everyone* with firm religious beliefs will just assume

---

145. Bollinger and Hill, "Humility."

that *their* strong convictions are the actualization of that possibility."[146] So it is that, while intellectual humility is an aid to negotiating debates over pluralism, inclusivism, and exclusivism with greater civility, it cannot alone resolve them.[147]

Intrapersonal Effects

At the intrapersonal level, faith, whether religious or not, is a form of knowing that includes but is not limited to beliefs. In James Fowler's complex theory of faith development overviewed in Essay One, faith is a combination of the logic of rational certainty and the logic of conviction, and a relationship of trust and loyalty between the self and some other, all in the context of what is deemed to be of super-ordinate value and power.[148] It is relational, not merely cognitive, yet the cognitive aspect of faith often overshadows the relational, frequently due to sheer unawareness of the subliminal relational. And when the religious ideal of a highly confident faith is understood only in terms of great weight given to cognitive claims, the door is opened to intellectual arrogance. Understanding religious faith as primarily belief in specified truth claims rather than trust in the undefinable divine encourages intellectual arrogance to creep in the door. "If we understand confidence in terms of the quality of assent to faith claims, it is difficult to reconcile a high degree of confidence with intellectual virtue."[149] However, faith as trust "leaves room for the recognition of epistemic risk needed for intellectual humility as well as for the kind of openness to revising the content of faith in the light of relevant evidential considerations that intellectual integrity demands."[150]

Confidence in religious truth claims is usually a matter of degree, with certainty being the impossible ideal. As noted in Essay One, even if the object of religious faith cannot be made deductively certain due to its supernatural qualities, it can at least be made inductively as probable as possible, so as to reduce the span of the inevitable "leap of faith" that remains necessary after reason has had its say. Some branches of some religions are more intent than others on accumulating evidence for their claims, with what counts as evidence itself being part of the debate. Reason, history, tradition, sense evidence, social practice, and non-rational experience all vie not only to

---

146. Church and Samuelson, *Intellectual Humility*, 317.
147. Schillinger, "Intellectual Humility."
148. Fowler, *Stages of Faith*.
149. Holley, "Confident Religious Faith," 211.
150. Holley, "Confident Religious Faith," 211.

count, but to count most authoritatively. Contemporary Western religions, most notably some expressions of Christianity, encourage an evidentialism that insists no belief should be held unless it is supported by Enlightenment-style evidence. Since the key claim of Christian faith, that Christ rose bodily from the dead, is a claim about something said to have occurred within history, Christians have always sought to defend their faith from attacks on its credibility with various forms of evidence, from the simple bearing of credible witness in the early church, to the Enlightenment-style reason of apologetics in the twentieth century, to N. T. Wright's historical defense in his massive *The Resurrection of the Son of God*.[151] In contrast, various practices of fideism maintain that faith is independent of Enlightenment rationality, frequently hostile to it, and often superior to it in arriving at particular religious truths.

What degree of confidence in religious truth claims constitutes intellectual humility versus intellectual arrogance remains an open question, but when certainty is avowed, fallibility is denied, and intellectual arrogance is present. At that point, the saying attributed to Bertrand Russell applies: "The whole problem with the world is that fools and fanatics are always so certain of themselves, and wiser people so full of doubts." Ironically, certainty undermines faith—"The quest for certainty is the mother of skepticism"[152]—and even eradicates the very need for the trust inherent in faith—"The opposite of faith is not doubt, but certainty."[153] Lesslie Newbigin even traced how the modern search for absolute certainty led to nihilism.[154] At the very least, "the pursuit of certitude is not genuinely religious, but a temptation constantly besetting religious institutions and people. Indeed, the direct seeking of certitude corrupts religion."[155] Eliminating an essential element of religion and assuming certainty is clearly problematic above and beyond the issue of intellectual arrogance.

Interpersonal Effects

At the interpersonal level, the interaction of deeply-held personal religious beliefs and a lack of humility about those beliefs frequently fosters relational conflict. Typically, people draw on religion when they engage in power struggles and arguments, battling for the moral high ground, seeking to be

151. Wright, *Resurrection*.
152. Westphal, "Post-Kantian Reflections," 61.
153. Lamott, *Plan B*, 256–57.
154. Newbigin, *Proper Confidence*.
155. Davis, *Temptations of Religion*, 2.

seen by others as more right and righteous.[156] As observed in moral foundations theory, virtues other than humility, such as group loyalty, respect for authority, and other markers of commitment, readily override humility, especially in religious perspectives that are highly invested in being "right" or "pursuing truth," usually defined as "correct belief."[157] Deficits in intellectual humility, one manifestation of which is constant attempts to convince and convert others to one's beliefs via the simple intellectual arrogance of aggressive proselytizing, function to polarize most people who are already adherents of other religions.[158] Furthermore, the more extreme the religious beliefs, the lower the religious intellectual humility tends to be, and conversely, the higher the religious intellectual humility, the less extreme the religious beliefs tend to be.[159] Empirical evidence suggests that humility in general and intellectual humility in particular "attenuates negative attitudes, behavioral intentions, and behaviors toward religious out-group members."[160] And in situations of religious hurt or conflict, intellectual humility remains a strong positive predictor of forgiveness, regardless of one's level of religious commitment.[161]

Intercultural Effects

At the inter-cultural level, intellectual arrogance is often manifest in the religious triumphalism closely interwoven with Western cultural arrogance. In *Embracing Epistemic Humility: Confronting Triumphalism in Three Abrahamic Religions*, Donald Borchert posits that all religious worldviews incorporate a degree of uncertainty while simultaneously viewing all other religious worldviews as false, and thus to be eliminated by conversion or violence.[162] Questioning how finite human beings can make definitive statements about the character of an infinite God, Borchert calls for intellectual humility in the form of a revised and redeemed view of the other not as competitor, but rather as colleague in search of the better world that is God's. Indeed, without intellectual humility, inter-faith dialogue is a sham. When Klaus

---

156. Johnson et al., "Intellectual Humility and Forgiveness," 256.
157. Hook and Davis, "Humility, Religion, and Spirituality."
158. Hopkin et al., "Intellectual Humility."
159. Hopkin et al., "Intellectual Humility."
160. Van Tongeren et al., "Humility Attenuates Negative Attitudes," 199.
161. Johnson et al., "Intellectual Humility and Forgiveness."
162. Borchert, *Embracing Epistemic Humility*. This claim is rather overstated. Even within evangelical Christianity, religious exclusivists, inclusivists, and even qualified (i.e., Christocentric) universalists (e.g., Barthians) can be found.

Klostermaier became a member of a group of devotees of different Indian traditions, he developed intimate spiritual relationships with them at fundamental levels. In the process, he not only found his understanding of Christ strangely deepened, but observed how the living Christ manifests himself in a strange culture. "In the encounter with Hinduism I have begun to understand how Christ meets the Hindu—not from the outside, but within his own thought and faith."[163]

On the world stage currently, the Christian struggle with Islam is foremost in Western consciousness, though likely not unique to Christianity.[164] Yet there is an underlying structure common to both Christian and Muslim conceptions of reality, monotheism being just one aspect. For a Christian or Muslim to say to the other "I'm right, you're wrong, go to hell" is at least comprehensible to the other, whereas it would be incomprehensible to a Buddhist.[165] And despite some differences of emphases, there is an underlying structure common to both Christian and Muslim accounts of humility which could play a reconciling role in Christian-Muslim dialogue. There is in fact a millennia-old tradition in the Abrahamic faiths of "learned ignorance," knowing that we do not know, though the inability to understand fully does not necessarily mean understanding nothing at all.

> Intellectual humility describes the attitude of a thinker. Learned ignorance, on the other hand, is the acknowledgment of religious believers that what they try to understand—namely, God, and the ways of God—constantly transcends their ability to grasp fully and articulate adequately what they have experienced. In other words, learned ignorance has more to do with a realization arrived at after thinking carefully about the focus of one's intellectual efforts—God—than it is a description of an attitude, appropriate as it is, of persons who know that their knowledge is limited.[166]

All major religions have branches in which doctrine morphs into dogma, generating fundamentalisms of the right and left that teach didactically some sort of creed purportedly received by revelation, and to which many adherents defer. Yet many religions also emphasize the ineffable nature of the divine that is impossible for mortal minds to fathom fully. In the end, their god remains elusive, which generates the mystic spiritual traditions in which ideas *about* the divine ultimately prove an impediment to union

---

163. Klostermaier, *Hindu and Christian in Vrindaban*, 117.
164. Hartley, "Bounded Intellectual Humility."
165. Lewis, "I'm Right, You're Wrong."
166. Heft et al., *Learned Ignorance*, 4.

with the divine, as will be explored in Essay Three. Divine essence is then understood to transcend rational thought and empirical evidence, without necessarily being contrary to it. After all, some level of reliable knowledge of the divine remains necessary for union and relationship with the divine. Claiming to have communion with an entirely elusive spirit is to be vulnerable to that spirit being merely the product and projection of one's own mind.

Intellectual humility in the religious realm is simply owning the limitations of human knowledge about that which is by definition beyond human knowledge, as critical realism assumes. As the devout Puritan Oliver Cromwell famously wrote in his 1650 letter to the Assembly of the Church of Scotland, "I beseech you, in the bowels of Christ, think it possible you may be mistaken." Yet literary expressions of intellectual humility often serve better than analytic assertions or earnest pleas. Said Pulitzer-Prize-winning novelist Marilynne Robinson, "The primary intuition of the strangeness of it all, of our single selves as unspeakably fragile and brilliant observers of a grandeur for which we have tried through all our generations to find words, this is the experience that seems to me to underlie religion."[167] So it was that, after devoting most of his days to writing weighty tomes of systematic theology, Thomas Aquinas ceased doing so toward the end of his life, sensing that his mystical experience rendered such work redundant.[168]

F. THE CHRISTIAN VIRTUE OF INTELLECTUAL HUMILITY

Biblical Passages

The biblical text is repeatedly emphatic: pride is a vice condemned by God, while humility is a virtue commended by God. "God opposes the proud, but gives grace to the humble" (Prov 29:23, repeated in Jas 4:6 and 1 Pet 5:5). Christ-followers are called to humility (Eph 4:1,2) to the extent of clothing themselves with humility (Col 3:12; 1 Pet 5:5). Relationally, they are instructed to, "in humility, regard others as better than yourselves" (Phil 2:3). The Greek word *tapeinophrosune* in Eph 4:2 and Phil 2:3 is best translated as "humblethink," a recognition that most knowledge is at once both intellectual and social.[169] Jesus is represented as humble (Matt 11:29), and his humility of mind specifically is held up as the Christian attitude toward others (Phil 2:5–11). "The doctrine of kenosis—the self-emptying incarnation

---

167. Robinson, "Credo," 29.
168. Pieper, *Silence of St. Thomas*.
169. Kennedy, "Educating Bees."

of God in the person of Jesus—calls Christ-followers to renounce privilege, practice humility, prioritize others' interests and perspectives, and reach across difference with love in the manner of their incarnate and crucified God."[170]

Scriptural themes related more indirectly to intellectual humility include that, in the divine realm, some of God's truths, particularly those that bear on God's self-disclosure in Christ, remain unknown.[171] "No one knows the Son except the Father, and no one knows the Father except the Son" (Matt 11:27). In the human realm, "all have sinned and fall short" (Rom 3:23), "the heart is deceitful above all things" (Jer 17:9), and we only "see through a glass dimly" (1 Cor 13:12). Human finiteness and fallenness requires that we acknowledge that even our rational and empirical knowledge is incomplete and/or corrupt—the resonance here with the critical realist perspective is palpable.

Prudence therefore necessitates that we be slow to trust ourselves, our motivations, and our understandings. There is no excuse for the kind of arrogance that Christians sometimes evince as the privileged recipients of divine knowledge.[172] From Parker Palmer's vantage point, "[n]ext to a Christian eclipsed by theological arrogance, an honest atheist shines like the sun."[173] We and all our social constructions are earthen vessels, clay pots prone to crack and leak, break and crumble, that make clear that extraordinary power belongs to God and does not come from us (2 Cor 4:7). "And that's a good thing because it reminds us we are embedded in a truth so vast that our mental constructs can never comprehend it; because it cultivates the humility required to look at that mystery through other people's eyes, giving us a chance to learn more about it; because it keeps us from becoming theological fascists."[174] Ironically, Christian intellectual humility can actually be derived from confidence in the Truth that will ultimately prevail, by recognizing that we are deeply fallible with limited access to truth. All our knowledge is partial and incomplete; now we know only in part, but one day we will know fully (1 Cor 13:12). Biblical wisdom would have us be content with fragmentary knowledge in the present, and live freely and honestly owning the limits of our knowledge.[175]

---

170. Markofski, "American Evangelicalism, Social Reflexivity."

171. Macaskill, "Humility for Creatures and Sinners."

172. Anne Lamott posed an old riddle: "What's the difference between you and God? God never thinks he's you." In Lamott, *Help, Thanks, Wow*, 36.

173. Palmer, *Promise of Paradox*, xxii.

174. Palmer, *Promise of Paradox*, xxvi.

175. Krumrei-Mancuso, "We Know in Part."

Conversely, "all those who are arrogant are an abomination to the LORD; be assured, they will not go unpunished" (Prov 16:5). Jesus equated the evil of pride with murder and sexual immorality (Mark 7:21–2), and located its origins in self-righteousness (Luke 18:11–2). Paul instructed Christians "not to think of yourself more highly than you ought to think" (Rom 12:3). In Christian tradition, pride is the first of the seven deadly sins, and Aquinas maintained that it was the root of all other sins, mirroring the Confucian insight that humility is the root of all other virtues. C. S. Lewis described pride as "the essential vice, the utmost evil . . . the complete anti-God state of mind."[176] Indeed, the sin of Sodom was rooted in arrogance, not homosexuality. Though many Christians appeal to the Sodom account to condemn homosexuality, none of the subsequent biblical figures who reference Sodom—Ezekiel, Isaiah, and Jesus—mention homosexuality. Instead, "this was the sin of your sister Sodom: She and her daughters were arrogant, overfed, and unconcerned" (Ezek 16:49). In all, arrogance, or its close correlates, is mentioned and condemned over two hundred times in the biblical text.

Translation and Interpretation

Beyond the contents of the biblical text itself are issues of its revelation, inspiration, translation, and interpretation, each their own ground for Christian intellectual humility. The challenge of translation alone reveals the ambiguity of the texts, due in part to the semantic range of words in both the original languages and the target language into which the text is translated. The translator receives the text in its original language, and is forced by the constraints of the target language to choose one word or another to re-present the meaning of the original text, as the translator understands it. In doing so, the translator will draw on their personal and cultural understanding of the intent and meaning of the text.

The translation process therefore unavoidably brings with it systemic biases that determine word choices, privileges one part of the semantic range, and thereby narrows the text to culturally preferred meanings. Whatever a word meant in the original language to the original audience—it may itself contain an ambiguous semantic range—then gets overlain with the meaning of the word chosen by the translator to re-present the original word for a subsequent audience. How readers of the translated text receive that wording in subsequent generations and in other cultures adds a third level of complexity, or compromise, to the original intent and wording of

---

176. Lewis, *Mere Christianity*, 109.

the text. But at the center of the process lies the Italian expression: *Traduttore, traditore* ("translator, traitor").

And it begins right *bereshit*, "in the beginning." This oft-repeated opening phrase of the biblical text is found in almost all English translations of Genesis, and skews the creation versus evolution debate. Though it contains a significant semantic range, and its meaning is tied to the grammatical relationship between verses 1 and 2, the Hebrew preposition *bet* is generally translated as "in"—"at" would also be appropriate—which suggests a moment in time. Such a historical moment in turn suggests, or at least lends credence to, a strict literalism in which creation days were 24-hours, producing a young universe that is only 6,000 years old, and thereby rendering macro-evolution impossible.

But the range of translations proposed by Hebrew scholars, both ancient and modern, for the opening words of Genesis, *bereshit bara elohim*, suggest that it can be translated with equal validity as "at the beginning," or "when God began to create."[177] Compared to "in" or "at," "when" does not suggest a moment in time, and allows for the possibility that God used evolution as the method of creating the universe. The NRSV opens with "In the beginning when God created," but then in a footnote adds the option of "when God began to create." Perhaps for marketing reasons, due to deep traditional religious sensibilities about the text, the NRSV conceded to the convention of "in the beginning" but inserted "when" in order to represent the complexity of the grammatical construction.[178]

Later in the Old Testament, the word *barak* appears, and its primary definition in Hebrew is "to bless." However, when used with reference to God, some scholars argue that it should be treated as a euphemism and thus translated as "to curse." But it can be translated with equal validity as either "bless" or "curse." Though the counsel of Job's wife has been understood historically as "curse God and die" (Job 2:9), an equally valid and grammatically correct translation into English is "bless God and die."[179] That it is conventionally translated as "curse" reflects a historical sexism inclined to belittle and stigmatize women.

Elsewhere, the Hebrew conjunction *waw* can be translated with equal validity as "and," "but," or "or." So the lover in Song 1:5 has been understood historically as avowing that "I am black but beautiful," whereas in

---

177. Hamilton, *Book of Genesis*, 104; Wenham, *Genesis 1–15*, 11–14. The Living Bible opens with "When God began creating," whereas the Common English Bible opens with "When God began to create."

178. In *Genesis: Translation and Commentary*, 3, Robert Alter also renders the opening "When God began to create," as does the Jewish Publication Society's *Tanakh*.

179. Linafelt, "Undecidability of *barak*."

contemporary translations sensitive to racism, she simply describes herself as "black and beautiful." She is not beautiful despite her black color; her black color is one aspect of her beauty.[180] The issue with *barak* is clearly one of translation, whereas the issue with *waw* is one of reader reception.

In the New Testament, the Greek word *dikaiosune* can be translated with equal validity as either "righteousness" or "justice." Yet in the context of Western pietistic individualism, of the two hundred times it appears in the New Testament, only once is it conventionally translated into English as justice (Col 4:1), while in Plato's *Republic* it is routinely translated as justice. Hence, the rendering of Matt 5:6 could just as justifiably be "blessed are those who hunger and thirst for justice, for they will be filled."

Beyond issues of translation, the realm of biblical hermeneutics has produced what Christian Smith termed "pervasive interpretive pluralism," the reality that "on important matters the Bible apparently is not clear, consistent, and univocal enough to enable the best-intentioned, most highly skilled, believing readers to come to agreement as to what it teaches."[181] Contrary to biblicism, which is "a theory about the Bible that emphasizes together its exclusive authority, infallibility, perspicuity, self-sufficiency, internal consistency, self-evident meaning, and universal applicability," the Bible is actually multivocal, polysemous, and multivalent in nature.[182] It contains many voices, multiple meanings, and manifold values. As evidence, Smith lists thirty-four books outlining multiple Christian views on various doctrinal and ethical issues, plus fifty-seven separate, profound disagreements about truth within evangelicalism alone, creating tens of millions of possible unique combinations. But Smith's primary criticism is directed toward the implied intellectual arrogance of autonomous individual Christians claiming interpretive authority for themselves because they take the "Bible alone" to be unproblematically clear about everything.[183] Plainly, the hermeneutical complexity and ambiguity of their sacred text also calls Christians to intellectual humility.

Christian Practices

Christian intellectual humility in the early modern era was exemplified well by the Jesuits, who, as pioneer globalizers, "combined a deep religious

---

180. Barton, "I am Black and Beautiful." See also Moore, *God's Beauty Parlor*.
181. Smith, *Bible Made Impossible*, 25.
182. Smith, *Bible Made Impossible*, viii.
183. For an evangelical critique of Smith's critique of biblicism, see DeYoung, "Christian Smith Makes the Bible Impossible."

conviction as global missionaries with a peculiar openness, controversial at their time, to accommodate other cultures and to enter into deep intercultural encounters."[184] Nevertheless, the Jesuits were equally capable of intellectual arrogance, as demonstrated in their less than accommodating, indeed quite intolerant, attitude and actions toward Protestants. Christian intellectual arrogance in the modern era was perhaps best exemplified by historic fundamentalist distrust of science because it did not hold a biblical worldview.[185] Only what was held as the inerrant biblical text was deemed sound and irrefutable, what nineteenth-century theologian Charles Hodge regarded as a "storehouse of facts." Accepting evidence only when it affirms non-negotiable presuppositions is what philosophy terms "pre-suppositional evidentialism," and psychology terms "confirmation bias." As practiced today, many evangelicals reject evolution and climate change as myths, embrace capitalism as God's ideal for society, and assume Jesus would have voted Republican. But "the religious tradition of fact denial long predates the rise of the culture wars, social media, or President Trump."[186] At the same time, many currently leading evangelical scientists, pastors, biblical scholars, theologians, and philosophers have practiced true intellectual humility in changing their minds about evolution. Twenty-five tell their own story in *How I Changed My Mind about Evolution: Evangelicals Reflect on Faith and Science*.[187] Others have also changed their minds about sexual orientation due to some combination of scientific evidence and the love ethic.[188]

Therein lies the first necessary level of qualification to such generalizations about fundamentalists and evangelicals: some of their leaders are more intellectually humble when exposed to new ideas or data than average, ordinary, everyday adherents are. Their scholars who engage in more informed and refined arguments frequently demonstrate more intellectual humility than the majority who do not grapple deeply with the complexity of issues. For example, fundamentalist scholars and intellectuals, being saturated in Baconian inductivism and Scottish common sense realism as their reigning philosophy of science, may contest how "real" science should be done "properly," but the average fundamentalist is simply resistant to science. Ironically, average fundamentalist commoners are in this sense more intellectually arrogant than fundamentalist intellectual elites. As contemporary flat earth societies exemplify, neither intellectual humility nor intellectual

---

184. Casanova, "Religious Conviction and Intellectual Humility."
185. Worthen, "Evangelical Roots."
186. Worthen, "Evangelical Roots."
187. Applegate, *How I Changed My Mind*.
188. Gushee, *Changing Our Mind*; Reitan, *Triumph of Love*.

arrogance are the preserve of intellectual elites. As for evangelicals, James K. A. Smith noted in *The State of the Evangelical Mind* that

> scholarly, intellectual endeavors are flourishing in evangelical institutions . . . But we simply have to recognize and confess how utterly disconnected all of this is from the vast majority of evangelical congregations . . . The voices that command evangelical attention are often horrendously unreflective, parading their anti-intellectualism as a badge of being "real Americans" and fomenting the worst of evangelicalism's populist impulses . . . Because of this continued disconnect between the work of evangelical reflection and the paucity of careful, nuanced thought in evangelical congregations . . . evangeli*calism* is a mission field for evangelical scholarship.[189]

Intellectual humility's openness to new ideas and willingness to change its mind in response to compelling new evidence, arguments, or scientific facts is a challenge for all people, not only those with certain traditional convictions. In selecting a title for his book explicating moral foundations theory, Jonathan Haidt deliberately chose the "righteous" mind instead of the "moral" mind in order "to convey the sense that human nature is not just intrinsically moral, it's also intrinsically moralistic, critical, and judgmental."[190] For example, research in moral foundations theory has documented how both conservatives and liberals stereotype and exaggerate their political and moral differences.[191] Hence, the percentage of Republicans who had "very unfavorable" attitudes toward Democrats nearly tripled from 21 percent in 1994 to 58 percent in 2016, while the percentage of Democrats who had equally unfavorable attitudes toward Republicans more than tripled from 17 percent in 1994 to 55 percent in 2016.[192] Evidently, the natural disposition of convictions across all spectrums is toward self-righteous intellectual arrogance.

While evangelicals do feel called by their sacred text to general humility, apparently not all feel likewise called to intellectual humility. Like most religious believers, evangelicals do think they are right, at least more right than anyone else. Therefore intellectual humility is evidently not a virtue of foremost value for the overwhelming majority of white American evangelicals who have supported the current public face of intellectual arrogance, President Trump, "an individual who arguably represents the embodied

---

189. Smith, "Future is Catholic," 142–48 (italics in original).
190. Haidt, *Righteous Mind*, xix.
191. Graham, "Moral Stereotypes."
192. Doherty and Kiley, "Key Facts about Partisanship."

antithesis of intellectual humility, responsiveness to facts, and openness to the Other."[193] Presumably, their support has been based on other positions and policies he has espoused that they deem more important. This lesser regard for intellectual humility, properly understood, "stems more from a lack of effective religious conviction among evangelicals, rather than from its surplus. The problem is not necessarily that evangelicals are 'too evangelical' or too deeply committed to particularistic religious convictions to practice intellectual humility in public life. Rather, the problem is often that they are not evangelical enough . . . [The idea that] increasing strength of religious convictions moves in lockstep with increasing dogmatism, tribalism, and intellectual unreasonableness"[194] is flatly unbiblical.

At the same time, Pope Francis, the foremost Christian world leader currently, has exhibited a greater intellectual humility, "a greater communicative openness to controversial church and societal debates that affirms diversity of opinion and lived experience, and the importance of honest dialogue with difference."[195] Examples of his papal commentary with this character include the topics of economic inequality, climate change, gay rights, and divorce. Granted, he has not to this point altered the content of traditional Catholic teaching, much less rescinded the Catholic doctrine of papal infallibility, but his tone and openness undeniably show a greater intellectual humility than customary from the Bishop of Rome. However, reception has been mixed. For some Catholics it serves an emancipatory function, while others resist it and continue to advance partisan convictions of both the right and the left. Nonetheless, intellectual humility is in tune with expectations of mutual respect for both religious and secular convictions.

Open-mindedness, Apologetics, and Integration

Among Christian scholars, discussion of the intellectual virtue of intellectual humility is rare, partially because disagreement about how to characterize it masks deeper disagreement about its telos, the ends the intellectual virtues are meant to serve. Some suspect that any such discussion is driven by liberal political commitments,[196] just as others suspect that avoidance of such discussion is driven by conservative political commitments. For the

---

193. Markofski, "American Evangelicalism, Social Reflexivity." See also Bruni, "Commander in Chief."

194. Markofski, "American Evangelicalism, Social Reflexivity."

195. Dillon, "Humility Regained."

196. Dunnington, "Intellectual Humility."

purpose of reconciliation, it is helpful to distinguish between two types of open-mindedness. Personal open-mindedness, the willingness to reconsider revising one's evaluations of other people, is practically beneficial, biblically endorsed, and positively advantageous to Christian flourishing intellectually, morally, and socially.[197] Propositional open-mindedness is the willingness to reconsider one's views, which in turn is largely dependent on Christian ways of relating to God.

Though intellectual arrogance is never explicitly named in their pages, both *The Myth of Certainty: The Reflective Christian and the Risk of Commitment*[198] and *The Sin of Certainty: Why God Desires Our Trust More than Our "Correct Beliefs"*[199] call for faith that is more than its intellectual content, more than dogmatic ideas *about* God.[200] Here again, faith is a verb, something we do, not a noun, or an object we possess. Faith is the act of practicing trust and loyalty, not a form of mental materialism. As noted in Essay One, to believe in God is not merely to weigh the rational or empirical evidence for the existence of God, but to trust and take refuge in the holy, Wholly Other.

Yet sectors of conservative Christianity in the last century have been preoccupied with the apologetic project of defending Christian truth claims by practicing Enlightenment rationalism, as detailed in Essay One. It has been employed both defensively to marshal maximal evidence for one's own convictions, as well as offensively to persuade others of the same firm beliefs. The potential intellectual arrogance of the latter inclination toward convincing others can become as coercive cognitively, emotionally, and socially as old-time tent meeting altar calls, and not unlike neo-imperial conquest. Yet commitments won via argument, and conversions compelled via pressure, like information extracted via torture, can be profoundly unreliable and counterproductive. Mark McMinn has suggested that someone with doubts about God may receive more effective ministry from a humble person than from an apologist who offers cognitive arguments for God. "The humble person may have less certainty to offer the quester, but the humility will likely rub off in some winsome sorts of ways, and with humility the divine struggle may subside."[201]

---

197. Spiegel, "Open-mindedness and Christian Flourishing."
198. Taylor, *Myth of Certainty*.
199. Enns, *Sin of Certainty*.
200. Bass, *Christianity after Religion*.
201. McMinn, *Science of Virtue*, 118.

Cognizant of the capability of apologetic hubris to alienate as readily as attract—"new evidence that demands a verdict"[202]—John Stackhouse for one acknowledged that Christian belief cannot be compelled, and called for a *Humble Apologetics* that was not merely intent on winning interpersonal arguments or staged public debates.[203] Too much of contemporary apologetics, according to Stackhouse, is self-centered and uninterested in real, whole, other persons, seeing them only as threats to fend off or as opportunities to exploit by practicing the art of making them sorry they inquired about Christianity. Ironically, according to Craig Boyd, Christian apologists and the New Atheists mirror each other's intellectual arrogance.[204] Neither has the virtue epistemology or necessary habits of thought to make a careful and thoughtful consideration of evidence. And in the rub of everyday life, "how good faith Christians engage in relationships says more about the truth of what we believe than all our well-argued apologetics."[205]

Apart from traditional professional apologists who too often engage other scholarly disciplines at a surface level in order to win an argument, a more humble form of apologetics is practiced more quietly by a growing number of natural scientists who are Christians, and see themselves as doing implicit or indirect apologetics, instead of the explicit and direct variety. They are not interested in confrontational debates or heated arguments. They humbly want to help others to consider equally humbly the rational credibility of Christian claims, and they do so by simply contributing to their respective scientific disciplines while bearing witness to their Christian faith, and raising questions of the deeper meanings and implications of their work. They trust truth to prevail in its own time, and feel little need to defend it argumentively. The American Scientific Affiliation, Biologos, and the Veritas Forum exemplify this kind of irenic and amicable "apologetics."

In the bigger picture, intellectual arrogance is in fact lurking in the entire faith-learning integration paradigm of Christian higher education when in practice traffic actually flows only in one direction,[206] and "faith has the right, and indeed the duty, to critique learning but learning has no authority to critique faith."[207] What is then needed is "more epistemological humility in allowing a mutually enriching conversation between faith and learning rather than insisting that our current understanding of the

---

202. McDowell, *New Evidence*.
203. Stackhouse, *Humble Apologetics*.
204. Boyd, "Humility, Virtue Epistemology."
205. Kinnaman and Lyons, *Good Faith*, 154.
206. Moroney, "Where Faith and Learning Intersect."
207. Jacobsen and Jacobsen, *Scholarship and Christian Faith*, 23.

faith always trump our current scholarly ideas."[208] And research shows that professors who excel most at the integration of faith and learning are most markedly characterized by intellectual humility.[209] Conversely, worldview analysis that does not "make us better believers and doers of the truth . . . becomes a mental exercise that breeds arrogance and shores up the false security of intellectual elites."[210]

Poetic Prayers

Known for writing in multiple genres, C. S. Lewis was also thrust into the public spotlight, somewhat reluctantly, as a Christian apologist, due to broadcast talks he delivered on the BBC that eventually became the text of *Mere Christianity*. Able to deliver incisive reasons for the Christian faith, Lewis was also very wary of the spiritual danger of the pride naturally infecting those who merely seek to win rational arguments for Christian faith. Fittingly, he used poetry to admonish his own pride in his own reasoning.

"The Apologist's Evening Prayer"—C. S. Lewis[211]

From all my lame defeats and oh! much more
From all the victories that I seemed to score;
From cleverness shot forth on Thy behalf
At which, while angels weep, the audience laugh;
From all my proofs of Thy divinity,
Thou, who wouldst give no sign, deliver me.

Thoughts are but coins. Let me not trust, instead
Of Thee, their thin-worn image of Thy head.
From all my thoughts, even from my thoughts of Thee,
O thou fair Silence, fall, and set me free.
Lord of the narrow gate and the needle's eye,
Take from me all my trumpery lest I die.

Lewis also recognized that he did not fully know whom he was defending to others, or addressing in person.[212] He did, however, fully understand

---

208. Moroney, "Where Faith and Learning Intersect," 143–44.
209. Matthias, "Professors Who Walk Humbly."
210. Bertrand, *(Re)Thinking Worldview*, 13–14.
211. Lewis, "Apologist's Evening Prayer," 129.
212. Though the language in the following poem suggests that Lewis took the divine to be male, Lewis would likely have acknowledged that too to be a feeble human symbolic construction.

and own the limits of his own understanding, and the nature and necessity of mere symbols to ponder the imponderable. He therefore qualified his perceptions and words as being just that in the following footnote to the previous poem,[213] and to all his other prayers.

"Footnote to All Prayers"—C. S. Lewis[214]

> He whom I bow to only knows to whom I bow
> When I attempt the ineffable Name, murmuring *Thou*,
> And dream of Pheidian fancies and embrace in heart
> Symbols (I know) which cannot be the thing Thou art.
> Thus always, taken at their word, all prayers blaspheme
> Worshipping with frail images a folk-lore dream,
> And all men in their praying, self-deceived, address
> The coinage of their own unquiet thoughts, unless
> Thou in magnetic mercy to Thyself divert
> Our arrows, aimed unskillfully, beyond desert;
> And all men are idolaters, crying unheard
> To a deaf idol, if Thou take them at their word.
> Take not, oh Lord, our literal sense. Lord, in Thy great,
> Unbroken speech our limping metaphor translate.

Lewis's self-effacing admissions, like Elie Wiesel's tortured bewilderment, are respectively wise and broken expressions of intellectual humility, the polar opposite of the smug hubris of intellectual arrogance. When it comes to the transcendent divine, nothing is more necessary. When it comes to human relationships, nothing is more virtuous. When it comes to the personal self, nothing is more honest. As Brian McLaren put it,

> [W]hoever and whatever God is, our best imagery can only point toward God like a finger. We can never capture God in our concepts like a fist. In fact, the more we know about God, the more we have to acknowledge we don't know. The bigger our understanding about God, the bigger the mystery that we must acknowledge. Our faith must always be open to correction, enhancement, and new insight. That's why humility is so essential for all who speak of God.[215]

---

213. "Footnote to All Prayers" appears as the very next poem to "The Apologists Evening Prayer" on the very same page in Walter Hooper's collection of Lewis's poems.
214. Lewis, "Footnote to All Prayers," 129.
215. McLaren, *We Make the Road by Walking*, 2.

Gandhi is frequently quoted as lamenting that "I like your Christ. I do not like your Christians. Your Christians are so unlike your Christ." Lack of intellectual humility was no doubt part of his dislike. It fits best in the third of his seminal Seven Social Sins: knowledge without character.[216] Thankfully, the postmodern turn away from religion toward spirituality[217] has included a Christian turn away from intellectual arrogance toward intellectual humility, with its concomitant softening of how more and more Christians today present themselves to non-Christians.[218] Far from being feeble-minded, weak-willed, left-leaning, doubting Thomases, "intellectually humble people are able to constrain their need for being 'right' and are open-minded towards new information, even when it differs from their original position."[219] And they are able to place the relationality of their love ahead of the rationality of their truth.[220] "While we may long for our world to reflect our own Christian values, without intellectual humility we run the risk of damaging our overall witness and greatly hurting our cause . . . The gospel itself is offensive, but that doesn't mean that our attitude toward others should heighten the offense."[221]

Yet the ultimate audience and receptor of our intellectual humility is not our human neighbors. Our ultimate audience is God, as the prayers of Lewis and Wiesel so poignantly demonstrate. In the end, our intellectually humility is not about our understandings *of* God, as we may speak of them to others. It is about our intellectual humility *before* God. Equipped with mere finite reason and physical senses in the face of unfathomable divine mystery, the only appropriate response is to bow in awe and not speak at all. As noted in Essay One, the immanence of God notwithstanding, the complete transcendence and final incomprehensibility of God "calls us to humble ourselves *coram Deo* [in the presence of God]."[222]

---

216. Gandhi's Seven Social Sins are wealth without work, pleasure without conscience, knowledge without character, commerce without morality, science without humanity, religion without sacrifice, and politics without principle.
217. Cox, *Future of Faith*.
218. Wuthnow, *God Problem*.
219. Johnson et al., "Intellectual Humility and Forgiveness," 256.
220. Hiebert, "Truth and Love in Christian Life."
221. Branum, "Journal of Psychology and Theology 43," 99.
222. Baugus, "Paradox and Mystery," 249.

3

ESSAY THREE: SPIRITUALITY

A. INTRODUCTION TO SPIRITUALITY

Story

SALVATION ON SAND MOUNTAIN is Dennis Covington's first-person memoir of being drawn to the people and practices of the snake-handling churches of the southern Appalachian Mountains.[1] Assigned by *The New York Times* to cover the trial and conviction of one of the snake handlers for attempting to murder his wife with rattlesnakes, Covington becomes increasingly intrigued by the mystics of the religious sub-culture who, taking Mark 16:17–18 literally,[2] drink strychnine and drape themselves with rattlesnakes as they worship. As he studies the socio-economic and cultural history of these Scottish-Irish hillbillies,[3] Covington discovers they are his own ances-

---

1. Covington, *Salvation on Sand Mountain*. The book was a finalist for the National Book Award for nonfiction, and is often compared to the writings of Flannery O'Connor.

2. "And these signs shall follow them that believe; In my name shall they cast out devils; they shall speak with new tongues; They shall take up serpents; and if they drink any deadly thing, it shall not hurt them; they shall lay hands on the sick, and they shall recover" (KJV). Most biblical scholars maintain that verses 9–20 were not in Mark's original manuscript, the earliest of the Synoptic Gospels, but were fragments from the resurrection narratives of Matthew and Luke that were added later.

3. The #1 *New York Times* bestseller by J. D. Vance, *Hillbilly Elegy: A Memoir of a Family and Culture in Crisis*, traces the updated fate of these hillbillies who moved north to the Rust Belt.

try and lineage. They are his people. He soon joins the Church of Jesus With Signs Following in Alabama, and experiences both a descent into himself and an ascent into the sublime as he eventually speaks in tongues and takes up snakes, enthralled.[4] By doing so, Covington crosses over from impartial observer and journalist to devout convert, what social scientists call "going native." The story becomes less about snake handlers, and more about his own spiritual quest. When he observes someone handling a snake,

> It occurred to me then that seeing a handler in the ecstasy of an anointing is not like seeing religious ecstasy at all. The expression seems to have more to do with Eros than with God, in the same way that sex often seems to have more to do with death than with pleasure. The similarity is more than coincidence, I thought. In both sexual and religious ecstasy, the first thing that goes is self. The entrance into ecstasy is surrender . . . The paradox of Christianity, one of many of which Jesus speaks, is that only in losing ourselves do we find ourselves, and perhaps that's why photos of the handlers so often seem to be portraits of loss.[5]

When Covington himself takes up his first rattlesnake,

> Nothing was required except obedience. Nothing had to be given up except my own will. This was the moment. I didn't stop to think about it. I just gave in . . . I felt no fear. The snake seemed to be an extension of myself. And suddenly there seemed to be nothing in the room but me and the snake. Everything else had disappeared . . . And I realized that I, too, was fading into white. I was losing myself by degrees . . . There is power in the act of disappearing; there is victory in the loss of self.[6]

When he ponders the serene, solitary suicide of his Baptist minister uncle, "My uncle's death confirmed a suspicion of mine that madness and religion were a hair's breadth away . . . Feeling after God is dangerous business. And Christianity without passion, danger, and mystery may not really be Christianity at all."[7] When he contemplates chance versus providence in his life, it occurs to him that "[m]ystery, I'd read somewhere, is not the absence of meaning, but the presence of more meaning than we can comprehend."[8]

---

4. "Descent into himself" is from the quote taken from Flannery O'Connor's *Mystery and Manners* that serves as the epigraph in Covington's book.
5. Covington, *Salvation on Sand Mountain*, 99.
6. Covington, *Salvation on Sand Mountain*, 169–70.
7. Covington, *Salvation on Sand Mountain*, 177.
8. Covington, *Salvation on Sand Mountain*, 204.

While Covington is being increasingly integrated into the snake handler community, he is also feeling increasingly conflicted internally, and doubtful. He eventually comes into open disagreement with them about their interpretation of Scripture regarding gender inequality, and ultimately about the nature of God. "I had found my people. But I had also discovered that I couldn't be one of them, after all. Knowing where you come from is one thing, but it's suicide to stay there . . . I refuse to be a witness to suicide, particularly my own."[9] So Covington leaves, rather abruptly, and for good, skeptical of what he has experienced, but ever the spiritual seeker.[10]

Questions

Of course, Covington's non-rational experience leaves many questions. Was it madness or religion? Was it psychological, sub-cultural, or spiritual?[11] After all, he had acknowledged repeatedly that, as a former war correspondent, he had always been drawn to the thrill of danger. And he had explained with great insight the cultural history of why his disenfranchised, disinherited, and disillusioned people had taken up snakes beginning in the early 1900s. Exactly what is the human spirit that can soar or plummet, compared to human spirituality that seeks the non-empirical sacred, compared to the presence of the Spirit that will blow wherever it chooses without being fully

---

9. Covington, *Salvation on Sand Mountain*, 236 and 238.

10. A few years after Covington wrote his book, but before I read it, I attended a Saturday evening snake handler service near Sand Mountain, one of the most unforgettable experiences of my life. I met Brother Carl Porter, Aunt Daisy the prophetess, and other characters I later heard described and saw pictured in Covington's book. And I could not identify with Covington more, from his initial impartial observations and perspectives, to his desire to immerse himself in the spiritual quest, to his disagreement, disappointment, and exit from the religious group, to the first name he and I share. I am struck by the oxymoronic embodied spirituality of the snake handlers—the snakes, the strychnine, the speaking in tongues. It reminded me of the Sunday morning service I attended in rural Uganda, where there would be no musical prelude to the songs. Instead, the worship leaders would first start to sway, seeking a body rhythm in common, then fumble for a shared key for the music, not always successfully, and finally add some words—embodiment first, melody second, lyrics a distant third. It also reminded me of the charismatic worshipers I witnessed at a Friday evening service during the "Toronto Blessing," that charismatic revival of the 1990s characterized by unusual physical manifestations, including one celebrant slain in the spirit and holding a supine, meditative posture on the floor that is otherwise physically impossible—embodiment first, spirituality second, rationality a distant third.

11. The most authoritative academic analysis of snake-handling is by Hood and Williamson, in *Them That Believe*. A moving, pictorial account is provided by Lauren Pond, in *Test of Faith*.

known by humans?[12] Can some combination of personality, temperament, circumstance, and collective ethos produce extraordinary experiences on its own, apart from the spiritual? Is there an identifiable and verifiable dimension of individual personhood separate from and beyond the physical, emotional, and mental? How might the Spirit manifest itself in different social contexts? What is spirituality, really?

Whatever spirituality may be, most would suppose initially that it is likely not limited to the rational. There may be a certain degree of rationality within spirituality, a certain degree to which it is reason-able, but it is likely not confined to the rational. Presumably spirituality is also not merely irrational or anti-rational, but something simply other than the rational, that is, by definition non-rational in the sense discussed in Essay One. Likewise, most would suppose initially that the parameters of spirituality, if such there be, are by definition not all knowable. We may not even be able to "know it when we see it." Or we may not even be able to see it when it is present. Therefore the only appropriate posture toward spirituality is one of both general humility and intellectual humility as discussed in Essay Two.

And in the terms of the meta-theoretical position of critical realism framing this analysis, spirituality is presumably a real mechanism with its own causal capacities that exists independently from human awareness of it. When it is activated, or perhaps because it is constantly activated, it is also actual, producing events in time and space, whether observed by humans or not. When it is sensed by humans through direct or indirect experience, it also becomes empirical and to that extent knowable and known. As already quoted in the introduction to this book, critical realism posits that "what we observe (the empirical) is not identical to all that happens (the actual), and neither is identical to that which is (the real)."[13] Spirituality presumably and by definition takes us beyond the empirical.

Given the critique of rationalization and rationalism in Christianity in Essay One, and the call for intellectual humility in Christians in Essay Two, a non-rational, humble spirituality would presumably be an imperative aspect of Christian life. But again, what might Christian spirituality in particular all entail? What of spirituality can be understood, experienced, or even practiced, and at least to that extent known? To borrow, ironically, the famous phrase from the apologist Francis Schaeffer, how should we then live?[14] Unlike the literature on intellectual humility which is relatively new

12. "The wind blows where it chooses, and you hear the sound of it, but you do not know where it comes from or where it goes. So it is with everyone who is born of the Spirit" John 3:8 (NRSV).

13. Smith, *What is a Person?*, 93.

14. Schaeffer, *How Should We Then Live?*

and still emerging, the vast literature on Christian spirituality reaches back through all Christian history. But before the emic approach of the "subjective," native, religious insider is taken, the etic approach of the "objective," non-native, social scientific outsider will be overviewed.

Yet even the emic-etic distinction must be qualified. Max Weber was the first to insist that social science attempt as much as possible to be value-free or at least value neutral, an endeavor, radical in his day, that his later critics viewed as overly optimistic and simply naïve.[15] Contrary to David Hume and Enlightenment thought, fact and value, is and ought, description and prescription, positive and normative are never entirely separable, especially in the social sciences, and even more so in the humanities. Yet Weber readily acknowledged that almost all social science is value-relevant in the sense that what social scientists choose to study is always relevant to their values.[16] As Andrew Ross put it later, "I don't believe that anyone undertakes any kind of cultural study . . . that one is not personally invested in."[17] This is true of why I am writing these words about spirituality, and why you are reading them. And it exemplifies again that human beings are enormously complicated enmeshments, incapable of purely rational, neutral objectivity. Recognizing as much is the intellectual humility necessary for pondering spirituality honestly and well.

B. DEFINITIONS OF SPIRITUALITY

Sociological Perspectives

The editors of *A Sociology of Spirituality* explicitly stated that their choice of the indefinite article "a" in their title, in contrast to the definite article "the," reflected an intentional, self-conscious hesitancy about how to characterize the elusive phenomenon addressed in their compendium.[18] How can the preverbal and unfathomable even be theorized, much less subjected to empirical inquiry? How can what is by definition indeterminate be measured with any degree of validity and reliability even indirectly, much less directly? How can it be measured even qualitatively, much less quantitatively? Naturally, such formidable theoretical and methodological challenges have made the social sciences cautious and at times seemingly reluctant to address the

---

15. Weber, *Methodology*.

16. The same has been argued for the natural or hard sciences. See Putnam, "Perceiving Facts and Values."

17. Ross, "New Age Technoculture," 554.

18. Flanagan and Jupp, *Sociology of Spirituality*.

topic, until recently. When claims of spirituality became common in Euro-American culture, the sheer prevalence of such claims begged and even demanded scrutiny and at least some analysis, tentative and tepid as it may be. This is the honest current state and stage of "the" social science of spirituality, especially when separated out from the social science of religion.

If the aforementioned *Sociology of Spirituality* anthology is authoritative by virtue of combining the views of multiple international scholars on the topic, its joint working definition of spirituality should be a worthy starting point. However, one searches the text in vain for a straightforward definition. In the introduction, Kieran Flanagan offers many eloquent rhetorical flourishes describing what *characterizes* spirituality, and what spirituality *does*.

> [S]pirituality does not only relate to supernatural forces; it bears on the recognition and pursuit of matters of ultimate concern that lie beyond the limits of the corporeal and the social . . . Spirituality is not only about what is beyond human limits; it is the sensibility of incompleteness in the journeying . . . Those with spiritual powers know what it is to be touched by them. Yet, oddly, those who come closest to the realms of spirituality seem to be struck dumb in articulating adequately what they feel they discerned . . . [I]s its authentic location in the hinterland of the individual where the self finds its ultimate destination, its own unique source of transcendence? . . . As a phenomenon, spirituality is something subjective, experiential, non-rational, unverifiable, and serendipitous in its eruptions . . . Spirituality partly overlaps with theology . . . it relates to what is proper to metaphysics . . . it realizes emotions . . . it inheres in the social . . . it is available to some but then decidedly unavailable to others.[19]

But Flanagan never explicitly delineates what exactly spirituality *is* apart from what it *does* and what characterizes it. In the perennial debate between functional and substantive definitions, his is a functional definition of spirituality, not a substantive one, much like Durkheim's classic definition of religion quoted in Essay One. Functional definitions of religion identify functions such as the provision of meaning and belonging, social control and social cohesion, without suggesting a distinctive element of religion that distinguishes it from other phenomena. Substantively, Flanagan leaves the reader with only the understanding that spirituality is rife with "paradoxes, mysteries, and conundrums,"[20] and that "the trouble with spirituality

---

19. Flanagan, "Introduction," 1–2.
20. Flanagan, "Introduction," 2.

is that its opacity admits too much but precludes too little."[21] We seemingly must then add spirituality to authority, the sacred, beauty, and all else that is in the eye of the beholder; it too is a social construct.

Other scholars have been somewhat more definitive and delimiting in conceptualizing spirituality. As noted earlier in Essay One, Donald Swenson summarized spirituality as the sacred *within*, in contrast to religion which is the sacred *between* or *among*.[22] Durkheim provided the seminal definition of the sacred, differentiating it from the profane.[23] The sacred is that which is set apart from everyday life to be honored beyond questioning and defended above all, calling out reverence, awe, and obligation. The profane is everything else, that is, the ordinary, mundane, and merely instrumental. While the sacred usually implies the higher powers of the divine or transcendent, virtually anything can be deemed worthy of veneration or reverence, including what is material as readily as what is non-material. "[B]y sacred things one must not understand simply those personal beings which are called Gods or Spirits; a rock, a tree, a spring, a pebble, a piece of wood, a house, in a word, anything can be sacred."[24]

Equating spirituality with religiousness, as do others,[25] Swenson defined and elaborated spirituality under the broader category of individual religious experience.[26] Spirituality "refers to those aspects of religion and religiosity or religiousness that have an internal presence to the individual. It includes such elements as feelings, moods, attitudes, beliefs, attributions, and the like."[27] Spirituality is thus internal to the individual, whereas religion is external, the latter residing in social institutions. But even this is a statement more about the location of spirituality than about its essence. William James, Durkheim's contemporary a century ago, concurred with its location and its characteristics: "In the more personal branch of religion, it is on the contrary the inner dispositions of man himself which form the center of interest, his conscience, his deserts, his helplessness, and his incompleteness."[28]

---

21. Flanagan, "Introduction," 11.
22. Swenson, *Society, Spirituality, and the Sacred*.
23. Durkheim, *Elementary Forms*.
24. Durkheim, *Elementary Forms*, 52.
25. See Swatos, "Religiosity"; Yamane, "Spirituality"; Smith, *Religion*.
26. Forms of religious experience other than spirituality include rituals, behaviors, and practices more generally, as practices have been defined in this analysis.
27. Swenson, *Society, Spirituality, and the Sacred*, 43.
28. James, *Varieties of Religious Experience*, 29.

If Flanagan's introduction to "a" sociology of spirituality was too avoidant of definition, an equally authoritative summative source, venturing the definite article in "The Sociology of Spirituality," posed the opposite problem of a definition reduced to a single word. Matthew Wood defined spirituality simply as self-authority. Underlying the various sociological definitions of spirituality, Wood noted, was the commonality of people exercising their own authority.[29] Here again is the problem of characterizing a phenomenon without actually stating what it is. Ignoring the possibility that a higher power beyond the self might actually be operative authoritatively on or in the self, self-authority may be one aspect of spirituality, but there are surely many other forms of self-authority that have nothing to do with and make no claim to anything spiritual. The arrogance and narcissism discussed in Essay Two are good candidates. Wood was also highly critical of such a conception of spirituality on the grounds that it presented people as autonomous individuals, not as social actors, and therefore failed to address the social practices, social interaction, and social contexts of spirituality. Christian Smith's sociological description, if not definition of spirituality, serves well as summary.

> By spirituality I mean that dimension of human life that concerns the most profound, meaningful, and transcendent visions of human existence, feeling, and desires. Spiritual matters . . . concern . . . the greatest and highest good, truth, rightness, value, vitality, meaning, and beauty . . . Things spiritual of this nature have a quality that transcends instrumental means-ends rationality. They sustain and guide people . . . in ways that actually pre-rationally and a-rationally govern, rather than are governed by, preferences, rationality, and calculated choices.[30]

Psychological Perspectives

Despite perhaps more extensive efforts than in sociology, the psychology of religion and spirituality also lacks "any consensual definition of the numinous," and therefore also lacks "connection, convergence, and cumulativeness across studies."[31] Both terms are frequently viewed as prototype or family resemblance concepts, thereby allowing for the pragmatics of definition to determine "how a particular definition performs in a particular

---

29. Wood, "Sociology of Spirituality."
30. Smith, *Sacred Project of American Sociology*, 2.
31. Piedmont, "Looking Back," 265.

context."[32] At times the psychological literature still conflates religion and spirituality because they have in common the search for a coherent and well-functioning meaning system involving the sacred. Yet even when they are distinguished, they are still viewed as complementary, with religion intended to foster spirituality. Hence, for example, "the field of religion is to spirituality as the field of medicine is to health."[33]

Furthermore, when distinguished, one consistency with perspectives from other disciplines is that religion connotes the organized and institutional components of faith traditions, whereas spirituality connotes the more inward and personal side of faith, whether that be inside a formal religious tradition or outside any tradition. Another consistency is their implicit but at times explicit unequal valuation. Bradford Verter even argued that institutions have become largely irrelevant to spirituality. Spirituality "generally connotes an extra-institutional, resolutely individualistic, and often highly eclectic personal theology self-consciously resistant to dogma."[34] Brian Zinnbauer and Kenneth Pargament describe the difference as follows:

> With the emergence of spirituality, a tension appears to have risen between the constructs of religiousness and spirituality. In its most extreme form, the two terms are defined in a rigidly dualistic framework. The most egregious examples are those that place a substantive, static, institutional, objective, belief-based, "bad" religiousness in opposition to a functional, dynamic, personal, subjective, experience-based, "good" spirituality.[35]

However, Zinnbauer and Pargament then promptly provide convincing critiques of each of these polarizations. Indeed, extreme spiritual practices can lead to self-destructive asceticism, self-absorbed narcissism, and self-aggrandizing arrogance as readily as religious practices can. Nevertheless, spirituality is often seen as the intrinsic human capacity, not always actualized, for self-transcendence, not merely self-indulgence. On balance, "different forms of 'spirituality' can lead to either self-indulgence or a deepened social engagement, but so can institutional religion."[36]

Oman summarized ten considerations for the pragmatics of definition,[37] several of which are salient here. One is whether a definition is sufficiently sensitive and specific; definitions should be neither too narrow

---

32. Oman, "Defining Religion and Spirituality," 31.
33. Miller and Thoresen, "Spirituality, Religion, and Health," 28.
34. Verter, "Spiritual Capital," 158.
35. Zinnbauer and Pargament, "Religiousness and Spirituality," 24.
36. Cox, *Future of Faith*, 11–12.
37. Oman, "Defining Religion and Spirituality."

nor too broad. Another is the distinctive feature that distinguishes religion and spirituality from other phenomena: the construct of the sacred. A third is whether a definition can articulate the relation between extrinsic engagement as a means to an end versus intrinsic engagement as an end in itself. The excessive polarization of means-oriented religion from ends-oriented religion, originally articulated by Gordon Allport,[38] is unhelpful, because "lived" religion is usually a complex interplay of both profane "means" motives and sacred "ends" motives. Notably, Pargament singled out spirituality as designating that which seeks the sacred as an end.[39]

Levels of Analysis

When attempting to grasp all that is experienced as spirituality, it is imperative to bear in mind that all phenomena occur at multiple levels of reality, perhaps none more so than spirituality. As the saying goes, reality is not flat. In the human realm alone, reality exists as subatomic particles, atoms, molecules, organelles, cells, tissues, organ systems, person, family, community, culture/subculture, society/nation, and biosphere.[40] As levels, each stratum is described as lower or higher, though this by no means implies evaluative judgments of better or worse. Each is also intricately connected to the level below and above it. Therefore,

> each increasing level includes and transcends the previous level, and displays emergent phenomenon appearing at each novel level that are non-reducible to previous levels. Fundamental levels are necessary but not sufficient for the organization of higher levels. Thus, [for example] . . . groups are composed of individuals, but group processes and behavior are not captured in the study of any single person in the group. Causality can move up and down the levels of analysis, and a phenomenon at one level may have correlates at different levels.[41]

Well-developed separate sciences are by now devoted to examining each level of reality. The challenge of the sciences is to avoid the reductionism that says to humans, as did Francis Crick, co-discoverer of DNA structure, "You're nothing but a pack of neurons."[42] Known colloquially as

---

38. Allport, "Religious Context of Prejudice."
39. Pargament, "Of Means and Ends."
40. Wilber, *Sex, Ecology, Spirituality*.
41. Zinnbauer and Pargament, "Religiousness and Spirituality," 31.
42. Crick, *Astonishing Hypothesis*, 3.

"nothing buttery," reductionism is the claim "that some property observed at one level can be fully accounted for and explained by properties, structures, or dynamics operating at a lower level."[43] The truth is that human phenomena are operative at more than one level, and they cannot be reduced completely to presumably more fundamental processes. "One can no more invalidate an experience because its physiology is known than one can invalidate physiology because its biochemistry has been identified."[44] Therefore mystical experiences of oneness with the universe cannot be reduced to changes in neurotransmitter levels in the brain. Instead, something like the ecstasy of snake-handling can be understood at multiple levels: "cellular changes, brain system changes, cognitive-affect-behavioral changes, social changes, cultural changes and global changes."[45]

Anything less than a multi-level analysis of spirituality is clearly less than the total picture, the present inquiry included. The three levels of sociological analysis, as already employed in Essay Two, are the personal and interpersonal micro level, the organizational and institutional meso level, and the cultural and societal macro level. The three levels of psychological analysis are the biological, which examines physical aspects of the brain, the cognitive, which examines the cognitive processes of the brain, and the socio-cultural, which examines the effect of the social environment on behavior. Overlap between the sociological and psychological analysis occurs at all three levels, perhaps most unexpectedly at the third, cultural level. But as psychologists themselves recognize,

> to conceptualize spirituality as a solely personal phenomenon is to ignore the cultural context in which this construct has emerged. Spirituality as an individual expression is not culture-free; it is neither interpreted nor expressed in a social vacuum. As a movement toward individualism, a rebellion against tradition, or a reaction to hierarchically arranged social organizations, spirituality is still embedded within a cultural context.[46]

From the perspective of psychology alone, "religiousness is not just beliefs about God. Spirituality is not just oneness with life. Both constructs contain multiple dimensions including, but not limited to, biology, sensation, affect, cognition, behavior, identity, meaning, morality, relationships, roles, creativity, personality, self-awareness, and salience."[47] Yet even a cross-disciplinary

---

43. Smith, *What is a Person?*, 36.
44. Hood and Chen, "Mystical, Spiritual, and Religious Experiences," 428.
45. Zinnbauer and Pargament, "Religiousness and Spirituality," 31.
46. Zinnbauer and Pargament, "Religiousness and Spirituality," 27.
47. Zinnbauer and Pargament, "Religiousness and Spirituality," 32.

scientific examination of the multidimensionality of spirituality cannot account for the metaphysical, spiritual dynamics that may also be operative.

In sum, Zinnbauer and Pargament's overview of cross-disciplinary definitions of both religiousness and spirituality identified three critical terms common to all definitions: "significance," "search," and "sacred."[48] The substantive core of spirituality is whatever is deemed sacred, the sacred determines whatever is deemed ultimately significant, and spirituality is the search for that sacred significance.

C. TYPES OF SPIRITUALITY

Talk about spirituality in the streets, workplaces, playgrounds, media—everywhere—has spiked in the last generation, and whenever it is discussed, it is typically understood, explicitly or implicitly, in the context of or in contrast to religion. The two appear to be permanently tethered. Traditionally, spirituality was presumed to occur within religious parameters, but increasingly it is as readily pursued and experienced outside religion. This creates a fourfold matrix of self-identification—religious, spiritual, both, or neither. Comparative American[49] and Canadian[50] national percentages of self-identification are as follows:

Religious and/or Spiritual Self-Identification

	Americans in 2017	Canadians in 2015
Both religious and spiritual	48%	24%
Spiritual but not religious	27%	39%
Religious but not spiritual	6%	10%
Neither religious nor spiritual	18%	27%

Apart from those who self-identify as traditionally religious, three categories of the irreligious have been labelled and researched by social science.

---

48. Zinnbauer and Pargament, "Religiousness and Spirituality."
49. Lipka and Gecewicz, "More Americans."
50. "Religion and Faith in Canada Today."

Nones

First, the rapid recent rise of religious "nones," those atheists, agnostics, humanists, and others who claim no religion or religious affiliation, is well-documented and well-known. In America, they rose from 16 percent of the population in 2007 to 23 percent in 2014, an increase of 7 percent in 7 years.[51] In Canada, they rose from 4 percent in 1971 to 26 percent in 2015, an increase of 22 percent in 44 years.[52] And in Britain, they rose from 48 percent in 2015 to 53 percent in 2017, an increase of 5 percent in just 2 years.[53] Nones are "the fastest growing 'religious' group in much of the modern Western world,"[54] and have been described as "The World's Newest Major Religion."[55] Fully one quarter to one half of Euro-Americans now reject religion, or are at best indifferent to it.

But it's not that simple or clear-cut. Just as in the realm of politics, where the term "none" originated and signified no political party affiliation but not necessarily political apathy or inactivity, so too in the realm of religion. For example, on several common measures such as prayer and belief in God, nones in the United States exhibit nearly equal levels of spirituality to self-identifying Christians in Western Europe.[56] In *Choosing our Religion: The Spiritual Lives of America's Nones*, Elizabeth Drescher documented how, in their everyday lives, many nones are not substantially different from "somes," those with some affiliation with traditional religion. Most nones also believe in a higher power, pray in order to connect with transcendence and the sacred, engage in rituals that mark sacred space and time, and ground ethical action in Good Samaritan care for others. However, they take interpersonal relational intimacy to be the starting point of spiritual life, maintaining that caring compassion, not ideology or theology, is the core of meaningful spiritual life. Spirituality for them is less about believing, behaving, and belonging, in whatever order, and more about being and becoming. "In contrast to the thin, internalized, self-referential quality that is often ascribed to spiritualities pursued outside institutional contexts, a spirituality of being and becoming includes a number of robust practices that unfold in the context of everyday life."[57]

---

51. "America's Changing Religious Landscape."
52. "Religion and Faith in Canada Today."
53. "British Social Attitudes."
54. Thiessen and Wilkins-Laflamme, "Becoming a Religious None," 64.
55. Bullard, "World's Newest Major Religion."
56. "Being Christian in Western Europe."
57. Drescher, *Choosing Our Religion*, 14.

Throughout the process of her qualitative research via focus groups and personal interviews, Drescher refined a compilation of the twenty-five most spiritually meaningful practices of nones, ranked according to survey results. The top four were what she termed and elaborated as the "Four Fs:" enjoying time with family, friends, food, and fido (pets). Other activities included specific ways of enjoying nature, art, physical activity, reflection, and service, as well as traditional religious activities such as praying, studying sacred texts, and attending worship. Notably, the data showed little difference between the nones and the somes, suggesting that both experience spirituality similarly in everyday life, much like Nancey Ammerman documented the "sacred consciousness" in the stories Americans use to narrate their lives, and the Golden Rule ethic they use to live them.[58] Drescher concluded that the construct of spirituality is more fluid than fuzzy, and more horizontal than vertical. But "the boundaries between the affiliated and the unaffiliated are remarkably porous . . . the spiritual paths of the Nones and Somes parallel and intersect on a regular basis."[59]

Dones

Second, the "dones" are a more recent category of people more reactive to religion. They are persons of deep Christian faith who have reluctantly despaired of the organized church and become de-churched. They are simply done with church, but not their faith. Josh Packard and Ashleigh Hope coined the term "church refugees" to describe those

> who've been forced from their homes—where they'd prefer to stay—for fear of persecution . . . [who] tell stories of frustration, humiliation, judgment, embarrassment, and fear that caused them to leave . . . [who] worked diligently for reform within the church but felt the church was exclusively focused on its own survival and resistant to change . . . They're people who've made an explicit and intentional decision to leave organized religion. They didn't drift away casually.[60]

Nonetheless, Packard and Hope found that the dones were mostly not angry with the church. Instead, most were just bored and feeling stunted spiritually, convinced that they had to get out if they were to survive spiritually. Church refugees wanted the interpersonal relationality of community, but

---

58. Ammerman, *Sacred Stories, Spiritual Tribes.*
59. Drescher, *Choosing Our Religion,* 10.
60. Packard and Hope, *Church Refugees,* 15–16.

got judgment instead. They wanted meaningful activity in the life of the church, but got bureaucracy instead. They wanted authentic conversation, but got didactic doctrine instead. They wanted meaningful engagement with the world, but got moral prescriptions instead. When dones leave churches, they take with them their often freed and deepened belief in God, their love of community, and their need to be actively engaged in community. "We expected to find a lot of overworked, stressed-out people opting out of leadership responsibilities so they could take a break. This could not be further from the truth. The de-churched are, as a general rule, leaving to do more, not less."[61]

The Barna Group numbered those who "love Jesus but not the church," at 10 percent of Americans in 2017, up from 7 percent in 2004. The biggest differences from evangelicals in spiritual practices were that 32 percent spent time in nature for reflection compared to 13 percent of evangelicals, 26 percent read Scripture compared to 82 percent of evangelicals, 20 percent practiced meditation compared to 5 percent of evangelicals, 10 percent practiced yoga compared to 1 percent of evangelicals, 9 percent read books on spiritual topics compared to 35 percent of evangelicals, and 0 percent attended groups or retreats compared to 31 percent of evangelicals.[62]

SBNRs

A third category of religiously unaffiliated persons, likely the most claimed and controversial on the irreligious end of the spectrum, is more accurately understood as a sub-category of the nones. It is also even more recently emergent than the nones as a whole, and rising more rapidly. The "spiritual but not religious" are rooted in the early-nineteenth-century theology of Friedrich Schleiermacher, the early-twentieth-century psychology of William James, the counterculture of the 1960s, and the New Age movement of the 1980s. First named in 2000,[63] they are by now simply identified by their initials: SBNR.[64] In America, they rose from 19 percent of the population in 2012 to 27 percent in 2017, an increase of 8 percent in 5 years.[65] Characterized as cultural progressives driven by frustration with the institutional and hunger for the mystical,[66] they have also been criticized as superficial

61. Packard and Hope, *Church Refugees*, 133.
62. "Meet Those Who 'Love Jesus but Not the Church.'"
63. Erlandson, *Spiritual but Not Religious*.
64. Alternately, "spiritual but not affiliated"—SBNA.
65. Lipka and Gecewicz, "More Americans Now Say They're Spiritual."
66. Fuller, *Spiritual but Not Religious*.

patrons of consumer culture,[67] disinterested in and probably incapable of the sustained dedication and asceticism of classical mysticism. They have been caricatured as casual dabblers in feel-good practices that do not challenge their self-interested priorities. And they have been castigated as narcissists who have descended into spiritual navel-gazing. From his overview of quantitative data, Reginald Bibby concluded that "many SBNRs are more religious than they think. They are also frequently not as spiritual as they think."[68]

Yet Linda Mercadante's qualitative research into the minds of the SBNRs in turn contests such superficial critique with a more nuanced, sympathetic, and even-handed corrective.[69] For one, she differentiates five sub-types of SBNRs. First, "dissenters" take issue with the theology of organized religion, intentionally embrace contrary positions, and are comprised of three further sub-sub-types. "Protesting dissenters" have been turned off by negative personal experiences, "drifted dissenters" have simply fallen out of touch, while "conscientious objector dissenters" are overtly skeptical of all religious institutions. Second, "casuals" engage in spiritual practices occasionally and functionally for therapeutic benefits in times of trouble, or for meaningful leisure activities. Spirituality neither captures their attention nor organizes their lives. Third, "explorers" are "spiritual tourists" with a strong "spiritual wanderlust" and an "unsatisfied curiosity" about the diversity of options in the religious marketplace. Seeking novelty and new experiences, they find fulfillment in the journey, and have no intention to commit to a home destination. Fourth, "seekers" are eager to find a completely new religious identity or alternative spiritual group to which they can commit. They actively pursue a new spiritual home. Finally, "immigrants" are "trying on" a radically new spiritual home, but are still adjusting to their new environment, and often struggling with its demands.

At the same time, Mercadante teases out a common, emerging set of beliefs and even latent theologies of SBNRs concerning transcendence, human nature, community, and the afterlife, though they are often unaware of the commonalities they share. Framing it all is a firm rejection of religious exclusivism and a warm acceptance of religious syncretism, reaching toward what Wayne Teasdale termed the "interspirituality" that could potentially result from interfaith dialogue, and be approached through mystical experience.[70]

67. Martin, *Capitalizing Religion*.
68. Bibby, *Resilient Gods*, 154.
69. Mercandante, *Belief Without Borders*.
70. Teasdale, *Mystic Heart*.

As the data show, half of Americans identify as both religious and spiritual, and presumably sense no tension between the two. Their spirituality is experienced within traditional religion. But more than one quarter of Americans, and significantly higher percentages in other Western nations, identify as spiritual but not religious, sensing clear conflict between the two, and siding with the former. Their spirituality is experienced outside traditional religion. The fundamental facts then are that, for the general population, the two are separable and one is preferable. Neuroscientist Sam Harris, one of the four horsemen of the New Atheism, is a high-profile example of someone evangelistically opposed to religion, yet paradoxically a practitioner of spirituality. In *Waking Up: A Guide to Spirituality Without Religion*,[71] he adopted a "rational approach to spirituality" and reported on his own spiritual quest, advocating for meditation and mindfulness in Buddhist forms. Though consciousness is real, the self, he asserted, is an illusion that can be extinguished through meditation, leading to compassionate and ethical behaviors toward others. Attempting to find a middle way between the pseudo-scientific and the pseudo-spiritual, he inexplicably legitimated his own spiritual experience even as he de-legitimated spiritual experience that is religiously informed and framed.

One other survey serves well as summary. Claiming no scientific rigor, church historian Diana Butler Bass asked various focus groups comprised of clergy and active church members across North America to "play a word association game" with the words "spirituality" and "religion."[72] Though different in order and emotional connotation, the lists generated were remarkably similar in content to distinctions drawn above. Her summary list is as follows:

Words Associated with Spirituality and Religion

SPIRITUALITY	RELIGION
experience	institution
connection	organization
transcendence	rules
searching	order
intuition	dogma
prayer	authority
meditation	beliefs

71. Harris, *Waking Up*.
72. Bass, *Christianity After Religion*, 69.

nature	buildings
energy	structure
open	defined
wisdom	principles
inner life	hierarchy
12-steps	orthodoxy
inclusive	boundaries
doubt	certainty

This word association is some empirical evidence that over the course of the twentieth century, "the word spirituality gradually came to be associated with the private realm of thought and experience, while the word religious came to be connected with the public realm of membership in religious institutions, participation in formal ritual, and adherence to official denominational doctrines."[73]

As all the foregoing qualitative social scientific research demonstrates, it is imperative that, whatever scholars conclude spirituality is or is not, they first listen to the meanings given to spirituality by those who claim and practice it. Observing actions and practices is an important means of comprehending spirituality, but observation alone is inadequate. Until the meanings of actions are accessed, understanding is shallow, and the only means of accessing meanings is through the words of practitioners themselves. Collective actions and meanings can then no doubt be interpreted, assessed, and systematized by scholarship, but the reality of subjective experience dare not be trampled. Social science itself is called to humility, because it is probable that

> any scientific operational definition of spirituality is likely to differ from what a believer means when speaking of the spiritual. Scientists study beliefs or feelings or perceptions about spirituality, or they study behavioral practices and effects related to religion, all of which, from the believer's perspective, are essentially physical manifestations that fall far short of representing or comprehending the real thing, the essence of what is experienced as spirituality. Although scientists frequently conceptualize and are interested in that which is not directly observable, scientific constructs are generally assumed to correspond, albeit imperfectly, to physically real entities. The believer, on the other hand, is surely not meaning anything like an underlying neurobiological event or structure when speaking of what is spiritual.

---

73. Fuller, *Spiritual but Not Religious*, 6.

This difference of meaning creates an inherent definitional if not a procedural tension in the study of spirituality.[74]

Hence the loudening call for a new multilevel interdisciplinary paradigm in the study of spirituality.[75] With this caution fully in mind, social scientific perspectives of spirituality are nevertheless able to provide further insight.

D. PSYCHOLOGICAL PERSPECTIVES

History of Psychology

Like religion, spirituality came a long way toward respectability in psychology as the young field grew and branched throughout the twentieth century. In Freudian psychoanalytic psychology at the beginning of the century, spirituality was seen as "a manifestation of poor psychological health; something defensive which should be analyzed away."[76] When based on wishful thinking, it could be used as an escape from reality or intimacy, a means of repressing, denying, or avoiding psychological problems.[77] Spirituality, it was assumed, could be used defensively by the believer "for any affect or ideation that for dynamic reasons needs to be displaced without delay."[78] Certain forms of Christianity, for example, were seen as pathological distortions which created "God images which are all in different ways defenses designed to freeze, misrepresent, or obliterate aspects of reality."[79] In its break with Freudian psychology, Jungian psychology was a notable exception that foreshadowed future developments.

In the middle of the century, a second force within psychology shifted from pathologizing spirituality to dismissing it, as behavioral psychology took a sharp naturalistic turn. The foremost radical representative of behaviorism, B. F. Skinner, "took his naturalistic assumptions so much to heart that he rejected not only spiritual and supernatural entities as inherently unscientific but also mental and emotional constructs"[80] as well. Albert Bandura's more moderate cognitive behaviorism, while allowing for non-observable entities such as the mind, still maintained "that control and interpretation

---

74. Miller and Thoresen, "Spirituality, Religion, and Health," 27.
75. Paloutzian and Park, "Recent Progress and Core Issues."
76. Izzard, "Holding Contradictions Together," 3.
77. Vaughan, "Spiritual Issues in Psychotherapy."
78. Rizzuto, "Exploring Sacred Landscapes," 25.
79. MacKenna, "Self Images and God Images," 7.
80. Slife, "Religious Implications of Western Personality," 802.

of the human mind was naturalistically determined."[81] Therefore, Bandura did "not think twice about omitting spiritual and supernatural concerns and explanations from his work . . . considering them irrational or problematic cognitive interpretations of the real world. In this sense, Bandura clearly continues behaviorism's naturalistic bent away from spiritual and religious worldviews."[82]

Beginning in the second half of the century, a third force arose in psychology that questioned naturalistic assumptions and shifted from dismissing spirituality to validating it. Psychological humanism, first put forward by Abraham Maslow, was a reaction to Freud's psychoanalytic theory and Skinner's behaviorism. Believing humans to be inherently good, and focusing on self-exploration, self-awareness, and self-actualization via holistic mindfulness, humanistic psychology was open to all aspects of humanness—behavior, cognition, even spirituality. Psychologically healthy spirituality involved personal responsibility and autonomy, taking responsibility for one's beliefs, values, attitudes, and spiritual assumptions, what Wood termed self-authority. It supported and encouraged personal freedom, self-esteem, and social responsibility.[83] From a wide range of humanistic psychology sources, Elkins et al. compiled a definition and description of spirituality rendered in nine key components:

- an acceptance of a transcendent dimension to life;
- a belief that life is meaningful and has purpose;
- a sense of vocation in one's life;
- the acceptance of the sacredness of all life;
- the priority of spiritual values over material values;
- a capacity to be touched by the pain of others;
- a commitment to the betterment of the world;
- an awareness of the tragic reality of human existence—pain, suffering and death;
- the realization that one's spirituality has a discernible effect on one's relationship to self, others, nature, life, and the Ultimate.[84]

---

81. Slife, "Religious Implications of Western Personality," 802.
82. Slife, "Religious Implications of Western Personality," 803.
83. Vaughan, "Spiritual Issues in Psychotherapy."
84. Elkins et al., "Towards a Humanistic-Phenomenological Spirituality."

Yet Maslow himself became dissatisfied and disaffected with humanistic psychology, and in the late 1960s founded the fourth force of transpersonal psychology that not only validated spirituality, but pursued it.[85] With origins in nineteenth-century transcendentalism, William James, and Carl Jung, it was also driven by "the profound philosophical implications of quantum-relativistic physics forever changing our understanding of physical reality . . . Quantum-relativistic physics has shown that matter is essentially empty and that all boundaries in the universe are illusionary."[86] Transpersonal psychology therefore addressed two shortcomings of mainstream psychology.[87] First, the ethnocentrism promoted by Western science took matter as primary, and Western culture was urged to move beyond its materialist metaphysical model toward a post-materialist science.[88] Second, the cognicentrism of mainstream psychology took ordinary states of consciousness as normal and healthy, rendering non-ordinary states of consciousness as abnormal and unhealthy. The latter were deemed to be altered states instead of alternative states, and thereby pathologized, when persons who actually experienced them frequently found them to be heuristic, healing, and transformative.

Three themes were distilled from a review of 160 definitions of transpersonal psychology: it is 1) the content of psychology beyond ego, 2) the context for integrative psychology of the whole person, and 3) the catalyst for human transformation.[89] In short, transpersonal psychology investigates transcendence, wholeness, and transformation. It examines both the experience of the immanent divine, which is the subtly but profoundly transformed perception of everyday reality, as well as the transcendent divine, which is unavailable to perception in the everyday state of consciousness.[90] It probes phenomena ranging from simple inner states of peace to non-ordinary experiences that transcend time, space, identity, and physical reality. More specifically, for example, it explores the triggers, characteristics, duration, and after effects of spiritual awakening experiences.[91] However,

> the new field represented such a radical departure from academic thinking in professional circles that it could not be reconciled with either traditional psychology and psychiatry

---

85. Hastings, "Transpersonal Psychology."
86. Grof, "Brief History of Transpersonal Psychology," 51 and 49.
87. Harner, *Way of the Shaman*.
88. Taylor, "Moving Beyond Materialism."
89. Hartelius et al., "Transpersonal Psychology."
90. Grof, "Brief History of Transpersonal Psychology."
91. Taylor and Egeto-Szabo, "Exploring Awakening Experiences."

or the [seventeenth century] Newtonian-Cartesian paradigm of Western science. As a result, transpersonal psychology was extremely vulnerable to accusations of being "irrational," "unscientific," and even "flakey," particularly by scientists who were not aware of the vast body of observations and data on which the new movement was based.[92]

Most recently and contrastingly, at the material, lower, biological level of the spectrum that is psychology, neuroscience has explored brain mechanisms that explain the neurocognitive basis of spirituality. In developing an integrated predictive processing framework, which simply means that "humans use prior cognitive models to predict and perceive the world,"[93] Michiel van Elk and Andre Aleman provided insight into four different proximate mechanisms that support supernatural beliefs and experiences, as substantiated by empirical findings. "The proposed predictive processing framework has the potential to account for the emergence of 1) religious visions and hallucinations, 2) mystical experiences, 3) personal experiences of God, and 4) the acceptance and maintenance of religious beliefs."[94] Nevertheless, they acknowledged that all the studies they overviewed provided anecdotal evidence at best and suffered from methodological problems, and therefore did not meet current standards of research practice. They stated emphatically that their findings "in no way provide a defeater for religious beliefs," and claimed only that neurocognitive processes *play a role* in different aspects of spirituality.[95] Interestingly, they suggested that neuroscientific findings could be compatible with a theistic view, in that a Creator could have used these processes to enable human beings to endorse supernatural beliefs and experience the supernatural, as Alvin Plantinga argued.[96]

From this exceedingly brief overview of spirituality in the history of psychology, it is evident that the rise of awareness and pursuit of spirituality in the everyday life of persons in Western culture is mirrored in the rise of scientific study of it. Social science itself responds to cultural change, as it should.

---

92. Grof, "Brief History of Transpersonal Psychology," 50.
93. Van Elk and Aleman, "Brain Mechanisms in Religion," 361.
94. Van Elk and Aleman, "Brain Mechanisms in Religion," 362.
95. Van Elk and Aleman, "Brain Mechanisms in Religion," 374.
96. Plantinga, *Where the Conflict Really Lies*.

Spiritual Experience

If spirituality is more Frankl's self-transcendence than Maslow's self-actualization as noted in Essay Two, and if spirituality is more than self-indulgence as noted above, a refining question is whether the self-transcendence of spirituality is vertical or horizontal. Spirituality within a religious tradition usually entails reaching only upward beyond oneself for a higher, usually divine power, and is usually a largely experiential component of religious faith.[97] Spiritual experiences must then be defined

> within the linguistic forms of the particular faith tradition . . . [and the] normative constraints and social support that legitimate particular religious experiences . . . For many Pentecostals, the experience of the paranormal is normal. However, even among religious groups that accept paranormal claims, like apparitions, they must conform to a particular meaning system to be deemed religious.[98]

Spirituality outside any religious tradition usually entails reaching both upward and outward, seeking connection not only with a higher power, but also with other humans, the universe at large, and ultimately, paradoxically, oneself. Such a spirituality that is both vertical and horizontal is typically both experiential and cognitive, lacking as it does the linguistic forms, normative constraints, and social supports of a religious tradition. The third type of spirituality, a purely horizontal spirituality, contains no concept of the supernatural, and finds expression in the lateral transcendence of oneself, the getting beyond oneself in this world only.

Nonetheless, the interpretation of spiritual experience is constantly contested by the various groups. As overviewed above, the empirical record has long shown that "nones" report at much the same rate comparable mystical and paranormal experiences that SBNRs define as spiritual, and that the religious define as religious. Nevertheless, despite the perhaps innate ability of humans to experience the mystical and paranormal, without religious and cultural support, such experiences are likely to decline in the future.

Ralph Hood Jr. and Zhuo Chen have drawn a careful, neutral distinction between numinous experience and mystical experience. Clearly a vertical form of self-transcendence, "a numinous experience is an awareness of a holy other beyond nature with which one is felt to be in communion."[99]

---

97. Zinnbauer et al., "Emerging Meanings."
98. Hood and Chen, "Mystical, Spiritual, and Religious Experiences," 423 and 426.
99. Hood and Chen, "Mystical, Spiritual, and Religious Experiences," 431.

Conceptually, this definition is built on the *"mysterium tremendum et fascinosum"* in Rudolph Otto's classic *The Idea of the Holy*,[100] described in Essay One. Understandably, religious traditions that assert some concept of the holy promote such numinous experience, and reject all interpretations that reduce it to something else and less.

Mystical experience, in contrast, is equally and understandably not promoted as ardently by especially theistic religions, because it is a broader category involving "introvertive factors [of] experiencing an undifferentiated unity through dissolution of selfhood, extrovertive factors [of] achieving a unified vision of the multiplicity of the world, and [the unavoidable] interpretive factors."[101] Conceptually, this definition is built on William James's classic criteria of mystical experience: 1) ineffable in that it cannot be described or communicated, and remains at its core inexpressible; 2) noetic in that it imparts a state of knowledge previously unreached; 3) transient in that it cannot be maintained indefinitely; and 4) passive in that the subject feels more acted upon, than acting.[102] Accordingly, Covington's personal experience of taking up snakes was more mystical than numinous. Because these criteria imply an extraordinary, delimited spiritual experience instead of everyday spirituality, others have added the criteria of consciousness of the oneness of everything, a sense of timelessness, and the conviction that the ego as experienced is not the real I.[103]

Given its elusive character, the challenge of measuring spirituality psychologically is daunting to say the least, because it requires not just a valid conceptual definition, but a valid and reliable operational definition as well. Doing so is substantially more difficult than the problems and complications of measuring humility discussed in Essay Two.[104] In providing a critical review of the current status of psychological measures of spirituality, Afton Kapuscinski and Kevin Masters first acknowledged the disciplinary disagreement regarding the nature of spirituality per se, and its relationship to religiousness.[105] Nevertheless, they assessed twenty-four scales that measure spirituality, granted the grave limitations of quantitative measures, lamented the lack of qualitative measures, and identified the most robust scales available.[106]

---

100. Otto, *Idea of the Holy*.
101. Hood and Chen, "Mystical, Spiritual, and Religious Experiences," 433.
102. James, *Varieties of Religious Experience*, 302–3.
103. See Happold, *Mysticism*.
104. Zinnbauer et al., "Emerging Meanings."
105. Kapuscinski and Masters, "Current Status of Measures."
106. The Daily Spiritual Experiences Scale, the Spiritual Transcendence Scale, the

In sum, several aspects of the psychology of spirituality are apparent. Spirituality is difficult to define and measure, spirituality has progressed from disfavor to favor, and spirituality is a positive aspect of personal well-being. As summary evidence for the latter, in the field of cognitive behavioral therapy, the majority of studies show that spirituality is in general good for mental health.[107] And in positive psychology, spirituality has been shown to contribute to positive functioning and subjective well-being across different cultures and religions around the world.[108] No longer disdainful or dismissive of spirituality, there is a certain exemplary intellectual humility in the science regarding what lies beyond the rational and the empirical.

Susannah Izzard elaborated one particular aspect of mature, psychologically healthy spirituality, ironically from a neo-Freudian object-relations approach, one that is relevant to our larger project here. It holds together opposites that feel like contradictory truths, what therapists call tolerance of ambivalence,[109] which is a key hallmark of psychologically healthy spirituality.[110] Izzard pointed to the paradoxical experience of mystics in which the inconceivable is encountered, and argued that mature spirituality accepts the inconceivability of God.

> [I]t is not simply God's capacity to contain opposing and contradictory material which defines the God of mature spirituality: this God also holds in his or her being something of the inconceivable contradictions themselves . . . The God of the spiritually healthy individual contains *and* transcends the contradictions of our existence and in so doing makes it more possible to face them. This God is *of his/her essence* a God who *is* both light and shade, love and hate, creation and destruction. A God expressed in myths that do not seem to worry too much about conscious logic and contradiction, but are held together by the kind of logic we see in the workings of the unconscious mind.[111]

Thus a characteristic of psychologically healthy spirituality is a tolerance of truth which is itself tolerant of opposed truths. Rodney Bomford flatly asserted that truths that are not this kind "are not revelations of God at

---

Theistic Spiritual Outcome Survey, and the FACIT-Spiritual Well-Being Scale.
107. Koenig, "Religion, Spirituality, and Health."
108. Kim-Prieto, *Religion and Spirituality across Cultures*.
109. Izzard, "Holding Contradictions Together."
110. Bomford, *Symmetry of God*.
111. Izzard, "Holding Contradictions Together," 6.

all."[112] Indeed, he averred that "There is no truth which must not at once be balanced by its opposite—except perhaps the truth that there is no truth."[113]

E. SOCIOLOGICAL PERSPECTIVES

The Kendal Project

Perhaps the most significant recent sociological field study of spirituality was conducted by Paul Heelas and Linda Woodhead and reported in *The Spiritual Revolution: Why Religion is Giving Way to Spirituality*.[114] Referenced earlier in Essay One, this landmark study has provided guiding concepts subsequently employed in the sociology of spirituality, although their particular terms, while descriptive, remained rather awkward. Their hypothesis was that traditional religion has suffered secularization, and has been eclipsed by a new spirituality enjoying sacralization in a "holistic milieu." As Carl Jung declared earlier, "We are only at the threshold of a new spiritual epoch."[115] To make sense of both the decline of religion and the rise of spirituality, Heelas and Woodhead offered a "subjectivization thesis" that resonates with what Charles Taylor called "the massive subjective turn of modern culture."[116] This is "a turn away from life lived in terms of external or 'objective' roles, duties, and obligations, and a turn towards life lived by reference to one's own subjective experiences."[117] In the terms that Heelas and Woodhead generated, it is a turn away from "life-as" in which

> people think of themselves first and foremost as belonging to established and 'given' orders of things which are transmitted from the past ... What matters is obeying, heeding, pursuing ways of life which stand over and above the individual self and bestow meaning upon life ... The most extreme examples of 'life-as' can be found in military contexts (where, to quote Tennyson in 'The Charge of the Light Brigade', it is 'Theirs not to make reply / Theirs not to reason why / Theirs but to do and die'), or in the religious life (where, to quote the Constitutions of the Society of

---

112. Bomford, "God and the Unconscious," 10.
113. Bomford, "God and the Unconscious," 9.
114. Heelas and Woodhead, *Spiritual Revolution*.
115. Jung, "Spiritual Problem of Modern Man," 229.
116. Taylor, *Ethics of Authenticity*, 26.
117. Heelas and Woodhead, *Spiritual Revolution*, 2.

> Jesus, the Jesuit should become 'a corpse which suffers itself to be borne and handled in any way whatsoever').[118]

The corresponding turn toward "subjective-life" is toward finding one's own unique source of significance, meaning, and authority in

> states of consciousness, states of mind, memories, emotions, passions, sensations, bodily experiences, dreams, feelings, inner conscience, and sentiments—including moral sentiments like compassion . . . Thus the key value for the mode of 'life-as' is conformity to external authority, whilst the key value for the mode of 'subjective-life' is authentic connection with the inner depths of one's unique life-in-relation. Each mode has its own satisfactions, but each finds only danger in the other, and there is a deep incompatibility between them.[119]

Heelas and Woodhead referenced marriage to illustrate such incompatibility. Seeing marriage as a sacred institution, a "life-as" spouse is called to sacrifice personal happiness for marital duty. Seeing marriage as "subjective-life" prevents undermining and potentially damaging the inner realities of who spouses are as persons in themselves.

The application to religion and spirituality is obvious; religion sacralizes "life-as," while spirituality sacralizes "subjective-life." The research hypothesis which Heelas and Woodhead tested empirically, both qualitatively and quantitatively, and verified in what has come to be known as the Kendal Project because of the small city in northwest England in which it was conducted, was as follows:

1. Life-as forms of the sacred, which emphasize a transcendent source of significance and authority to which individuals must conform at the expense of the cultivation of their unique subjective-lives, are most likely to be in decline;

2. Subjective-life forms of the sacred, which emphasize inner sources of significance and authority and the cultivation or sacralization of unique subjective-lives, are most likely to be growing.[120]

In assessing "the winners and losers in the contemporary spiritual marketplace,"[121] Heelas and Woodhead brought to light the central importance of culture on matters of religion, faith, and spirituality. While expressly

---

118. Heelas and Woodhead, *Spiritual Revolution*, 3.
119. Heelas and Woodhead, *Spiritual Revolution*, 3–4.
120. Heelas and Woodhead, *Spiritual Revolution*, 6.
121. Heelas and Woodhead, *Spiritual Revolution*, 10.

avoiding "some sort of paean of praise for the self-centered self,"[122] they did describe in detail the holistic nature of "subjective-life" spirituality that involves self-in-relation rather than self-in-isolation.

Of course, not all were convinced by Heelas and Woodhead's analysis. For example, David Voas and Steve Bruce criticized the conflation of leisure and therapeutic activities with the sacred, disputed the significance of the "holistic milieu," and concluded that its flourishing confirms rather than challenges secularization.[123] Assessing the "spiritual revolution" as another false dawn for the sacred, they maintained that "unconventional spirituality is a symptom of secularization, not a durable counterforce to it."[124] They also questioned how a distinctively spiritual element can be isolated and identified in therapeutic activities such as yoga, massage, Reiki, or acupuncture. Overall, they questioned the magnitude, depth, and staying power of the spirituality Heelas and Woodhead observed, and suggested that the significance of the phenomenon had been exaggerated. "[E]vidence that holistic concepts are becoming part of the culture do not show that a spiritual revolution is coming, any more than the strength of the Christian heritage shows that a religious revival is just around the corner."[125]

Theories of Culture

The shift from "life-as" to "subjective-life" is but one characterization and labelling of a change from a former cultural ethos to the current Western cultural ethos, one that many theorists have observed and attempted to describe, label, and explain. Few would dispute that significant cultural change has transpired in Western societies in the last fifty years. Fewer would dispute that momentous cultural change has transpired in Western societies in the last two millennia.

Whenever cultural change occurs at the macro, societal level, the task of social science is to ascertain first if it has indeed occurred, and if so, to

---

122. Heelas and Woodhead, *Spiritual Revolution*, 11.

123. Voas and Bruce, "Spiritual Revolution."

124. Voas and Bruce, "Spiritual Revolution," 43.

125. Voas and Bruce, "Spiritual Revolution," 59. In "A Phoney Holy War," William Keenan was bellicose and verbose in dismissing the notion of a current spiritual revolution as myth. Judging it to be "implicitly ideological" and "fatally flawed" due to "self-inflicted mortal wounds," he identified nine fallacies regarding religion and spirituality, including the assumptions of concreteness, separateness, conflict, and the superiority of spirituality. "Consequently, to speak of spiritual revolution is, at best, make-believe, pseudo-scientific hyperbole" (157). As a more constructive framework, Keenan suggested spirituality be understood as "implicit religion."

identify its components, aspects, and dimensions.[126] The first component of change is its identity. Is the whole culture changing, or is only one specific phenomenon within culture changing? For example, is Euro-American culture becoming more subjective as a whole, or is it only the religion and/or spirituality within it? The second component is level. Is culture changing at the micro, meso, or macro level, or all three? Is religion changing at the individual level, the organizational level, or the societal level, or all three? Third is the duration or lifespan of change. Is it short-term, middle-term, or long-term? Is current change in religion a temporary response to transitory social conditions, an alteration that will continue for the foreseeable future, or a permanent transformation from which there can be no return?

The fourth component of cultural change is its magnitude. Is the change incremental, comprehensive, or revolutionary? Does the turn from religion to spirituality constitute a small, medium, or large change in how Christianity has been practiced by everyday people for the last two millennia? Fifth is the rate or speed of change. Is the shift fast or slow, constant or spasmodic, orderly or erratic? Is current change in religious practices more or less rapid or uniform compared to other changes in religious history? Sixth is intentionality. Is particular cultural change deliberate or unplanned? Is current change in religious practices something culture is doing to religion, something religion is doing to itself, or something fortuitous? Seventh, and finally, are the consequences of change. Will the outcomes of cultural change be the realization of some anticipated and desired goals, or will they be unexpected happenstance that leave bewilderment and a whole new set of challenges? Will the turn from religion to spirituality be functional or dysfunctional? For whom? To address adequately all these questions about the turn from religion to spirituality, even within Christianity alone, would obviously require more space than is available here.[127]

It is currently conventional to distinguish eras of human history in terms of premodern, modern, and postmodern cultures, as already employed in Essay One, though their character, time-span, and very existence are constantly debated. One summary characterized pre-modernity as comprised of knowledge that was predominantly religious, a structure of consciousness that was dualistic in believing in both this-worldly and other-worldly reality, and collective interests that were focused on security, solidarity, and acceptance in both realities.[128] In modernity, knowledge was predominantly rational, the structure of consciousness denied

---

126. Vago, *Social Change*.
127. Huss, "Spirituality."
128. Flint, "Critical Sociology."

other-worldly reality and adhered only to a master narrative of logocentrism and enlightenment, and collective interests were focused on controlling and manipulating environments through physical and social technologies. In postmodernity, knowledge is predominantly critical, understanding society and social reality as the creation of social relations, the structure of consciousness is alternately pessimistic and optimistic, and collective interests are focused on communication and action to create community.

The three aspects of the three historical eras perhaps most pertinent to the analysis of spirituality are that, first, discrepant realities were deemed to be mysteries in premodernity, but were deemed to be contradictions in modernity, and are deemed to be paradoxes in today's postmodernity. Second, religion and God were deemed to be authoritative in premodernity, whereas logic and science were deemed to be authoritative in modernity, and the self or group in postmodernity. Third, the nature of the self was deemed to be embedded and unseen in premodernity, autonomous and fixed in modernity, and relational and adaptable in postmodernity. Intriguingly, advocates of transpersonal psychology have suggested that "the driving force behind a transition to transmodernism is spirituality."[129]

In *A Secular Age* (note again the indefinite article), Charles Taylor described the three distinct historical epochs as nonetheless having in common a desire for connection with the transcendent.[130] In the *ancien régime* (pre-modernity), relation to the transcendent came via a pre-ordained cosmic order. In the *age of mobilization* (early modernity), that relation came via engagement with the social institutions and practices in which the transcendent had been subsumed. Humans were then tasked with realizing the divine plan in their everyday activities and relations of mutual obligation in what Weber termed the new "this-worldly" reorientation of religion.

Today in the *age of authenticity* (1960s—present), expressive individualism and authentic selfhood are given preeminence as means of connection with the transcendent. An outgrowth of nineteenth-century romanticism, this focus on the individual leads to conflict with traditional, institutional forms of religion, and with the needs of religious communities. Some individuals then leave religion while others reinvent it, seeking new ways to find meaning in the transcendent. As Taylor opined, "[I]f we don't accept the view that the human aspiration to religion will flag, and I do not, then where will the access lie to practice of and deeper engagement with religion? The answer is the various forms of spiritual practice to which each is drawn

---

129. Burns, "Self-Construction through Consumption," 166.
130. Taylor, *Secular Age*.

in his/her own spiritual life."[131] Nevertheless, Taylor argued that the collective dimension of religion that Durkheim emphasized, and the component of collective effervescence in particular, remains important. "Thus, Taylor concludes that while the new frame for religious practice is individualistic, it is not necessarily individuating. People still seek others with whom to pursue their chosen belief in the transcendent."[132]

Just prior to the phrase "spiritual but not religious" entering popular parlance, the famous case of Sheila Larson became iconic in literature on religion. Sheila was a pseudonym for one of the interviewees in the chapter on religion in Robert Bellah et al.'s landmark *Habits of the Heart*.[133] She was presented as an exemplar of the privatization of religion, and what the research team conceptualized as expressive individualism, in contrast to instrumental individualism.

> Sheila Larson is a young nurse who has received a good deal of therapy and who describes her faith as "Sheilaism." "I believe in God. I'm not a religious fanatic. I can't remember the last time I went to church. My faith has carried me a long way. It's Sheilasim. Just my own little voice . . . It's just try to love yourself and be gentle with yourself. You know, I guess, take care of each other. I think He would want us to take care of each other." Like many others, Sheila would be willing to endorse few more specific injunctions.[134]

Though Bellah and his colleagues speculated on the subsequent possibility of each person then having their own religion, today Sheila would likely have described her personal faith, however vague and vacuous, as spirituality, not religion.

To Taylor's point, Sheilaism may well have been individualistic, but it would prove to be less than individuating by the turn of the twenty-first century. Twenty years after Bellah's work, in the massive National Study of Youth and Religion, Christian Smith and Melinda Lundquist Denton distilled the *de facto* creed of what they termed "moralistic therapeutic deism" which had become the *de facto* faith of most American youth.

- A God exists who created and orders the world and watches over human life on earth.

---

131. Taylor, *Secular Age*, 515.
132. Ritzer and Stepnisky, *Sociological Theory*, 554.
133. Bellah et al., *Habits of the Heart*.
134. Bellah et al., *Habits of the Heart*, 221.

- God wants people to be good, nice, and fair to each other, as taught in the Bible and most world religions.
- The central goal of life is to be happy and to feel good about oneself.
- God does not need to be particularly involved in one's life except when God is needed to resolve a problem.
- Good people go to heaven when they die.[135]

Scarcely more substantive than Sheilaism, moralistic therapeutic deism nevertheless includes a moral dimension traditionally associated with, if not derived from religion, a therapeutic dimension currently more coupled with spirituality, and a theological dimension inherited from Christianity, the deism of a transcendent (versus immanent) distant divine. Thus it contains the primary ingredients of the *de facto* spirituality of many who would not identify as religious.

Two twentieth-century sociologists developed theories of culture that offer insight into the twenty-first-century turn from religion to spirituality without necessarily addressing it directly. Though most known as a microsociologist, Georg Simmel also focused extensively on the cultural level of social reality, what he termed "objective culture." Culture is clearly created and constantly re-created by people, taking on a life of its own, becoming reified, growing ever larger, more elaborated, more intertwined, and more powerful, and exerting ever more coercive force on the lives of individual actors, what Simmel termed "subjective culture." Thus the growth of collective, objective culture threatens the growth of individual, subjective culture. According to one of Simmel's general principles, "The total value of something increases to the same extent as the value of its individual parts declines."[136] This impoverishment of subjective culture by the expansion of objective culture is what he termed "the tragedy of culture." As culture gets thicker, individuals get thinner, leading them to alienation, cynicism, blasé attitudes, impersonal relations, and cultural malaise.

Religion, according to Simmel, is part of objective culture, and the recent rise of spirituality can be understood in part as pushback from subjective culture against objective culture, attempting to reverse and rectify the tragedy of culture. "In his assessment of modern culture, Simmel points out that there is an overarching struggle between life and form, and says that one 'can find the same tendency in contemporary religion.'"[137] He states that "mystical tendencies suggest that life's longing may be frustrated by

---

135. Smith and Denton, *Soul Searching*.
136. Simmel, *Philosophy of Money*, 199.
137. Varga, "Georg Simmel," 157.

objective forms in themselves . . . Mysticism aspires toward a deity which transcends every personal and particular form; it seeks an undetermined expanse of religious feeling which does not conflict with any dogmatic barrier, a deepening into formless infinity, a mode of expression based only on the powerful longing of the soul."[138] Simmel postulated that the more traditional religions are rigidified, the greater the emergent need for spirituality to transcend them would become, and the greater the likelihood that spirituality would revitalize religion.

The possibility of revitalization is also germane to Pitirim Sorokin's theory of cultural change, in which change is seen as cyclical, or more accurately pendular, instead of linear in the pre-modernity-modernity-postmodernity sense. All cultures tend to swing back and forth between the opposite extremes of what Sorokin termed "sensate" periods and "ideational" periods.[139] Sensate periods are materialistic, viewing true reality as sensory—only the material world is real. The dominant values are wealth, health, bodily comfort, sensual pleasures, power, and fame, most of which are pursued via science and technology. Religion is considered a relic of the past, with what remains of it tending toward either fundamentalism or fideism. At the other end of the pendulum, ideational periods are spiritualistic, viewing true reality as super-sensory and transcendent. Mysticism and revelation are considered valid sources of truth and morality, leading to asceticism and moralism. Even economics is conditioned by religious and moral commandments, such as laws against usury, and religious art flourishes, such as Gothic cathedrals. However, each extreme carries the seeds of its own decay, neither is sustainable indefinitely, and both reverse into the other.

As the cultural pendulum swings from one extreme to the other, cultures pass through an integral period which Sorokin termed "idealistic" culture, and which he described as a harmonious balance between sensate and ideational tendencies. Desirable as it may be, it is nonetheless seemingly impossible for cultures to maintain the ideal balance. As for Sorokin's assessment of the culture of his day, mid-twentieth-century Western culture was, in his detailed historical comparisons, the third and most sensate in history, and "overripe" for reversal. Employing Sorokin's concepts and confirming Sorokin's theory in his own overview of Western history since 800 BCE, Frederic Baue argued that twenty-first-century Western culture is now transitioning from that overripe sensate mode back to an ideational mode,

---

138. Simmel, "Conflict in Modern Culture," 23.

139. Sorokin, *Social and Cultural Dynamics*. For a good summary, see http://www.john-uebersax.com/pdf/SorokinCulturalOrientations.pdf.

resulting in another spiritual revolution.[140] Furthermore, Baue argued that Christianity is a paradoxical blend of the spiritual and the material, an integral, idealistic balance of sensate and ideational tendencies, in contrast to what he critiqued as the vague and vacuous postmodern spirituality "lurking" in the current swing back toward an ideational culture. "An ideational culture can be spiritual without being Christian. In fact, it can be positively antagonistic toward Christianity."[141]

Contrasting Spiritualities

Based on in-depth interviews of people across the religious spectrum as well as large-scale surveys, Robert Wuthnow brought finer distinctions to the spirituality that arose in the second half of the twentieth century in America.[142] Like Sorokin, Wuthnow identified two dysfunctional extremes, with a potentially more functional, integral combination centered in between. The conservative 1950s were characterized by a "spirituality of dwelling" that "inhabited" the sacred places and spaces of established religious institutions. Since then, this spirituality has become a refuge for fundamentalism's crusade against the secular. Its failing was that it fostered dependence on communities that were inherently undependable, and encouraged idolization of particular places.

The radical 1960s and following were characterized by a "spirituality of seeking" that "negotiated" movement beyond religious institutions. The journey became more important than arriving at or staying in any one place, the spiritual quest more meaningful than the religious community. Vacating traditional religious establishments, the sacred took up residence in the inner self, as the boundary between religion and therapy become ever more porous. Wuthnow highlighted the obsession with angels in the 1990s as one exemplification. When angels visit, they do not demand church attendance, lasting spiritual commitments, or change in behavior, and encounters with them are brief, subjective, and almost always therapeutic, like much spirituality of the 1990s. The failing of this spirituality of seeking was that it was too unstable to provide social support, or to nurture growth into spiritual maturity. Recognizing the opportunity, established religious organizations adopted seeker-sensitive programming in an attempt to win people back.

As a middle way forward, Wuthnow advocated an alternative "spirituality of practice" for those who want more than endless seeking. Involving

---

140. Baue, *Spiritual Society*.
141. Baue, *Spiritual Society*, 54.
142. Wuthnow, *After Heaven*.

both individual and communal dimensions, it included prayer, devotional reading, service to others, contact with the divine, discernment, orderly ritual, sharing experiences and stories with others, and attention to ethics, among other practices. Such a spirituality, he suggested, is best fostered by practice-oriented religious organizations that both ground their members in the essentials of their tradition, and yet at the same time encourage an open, holistic spirituality. They pay attention to "specific spiritual practices by those who desire to live their whole lives as practice . . . the point of spiritual practice is not to elevate an isolated set of activities over the rest of life, but to electrify the spiritual impulse that animates all of life."[143] This may be the best that organized religion can do or hope for currently, though it is surely less organizationally advantageous than the spirituality of dwelling of the 1950s.

But could a spirituality of practice fostered by practice-oriented religious organizations be healthiest for all individuals, especially those who are no longer interested in being, or even capable of being either spiritual dwellers or spiritual seekers? Why must it be either/or? Why must spirituality be pitted against religion? Have modern religious organizations really driven authentic spirituality out of their midst? Have the prescribed practices that constitute religion, according to Smith's definition cited earlier, really nullified a spirituality of practice? Surely an authentic spirituality can flourish as readily within a religious tradition as it can outside of a religious tradition.

Christian Cultural Theories

The emic perspective of the subjective religious insider sees cultural change pertaining to religion differently than the etic perspective of the objective social scientific outsider described above. Indeed, adherents of a religion do not see their worldview, beliefs, and prescribed practices as religion at all. Theirs is simply the truth of reality; it is all other worldviews, beliefs, and resultant prescribed practices that are mere religion. In a sense, the very concept of religion arises only in pluralist contexts where more than one are present to each other. Only when confronted with an "other" is there need for an overarching term describing alternatives. Yet when Christian insiders track the turn from religion to spirituality, the analysis sounds remarkably similar in the dispassionate details. But of course the tone takes on a passion that social scientific outsiders lack, because the insider's collective self is at stake. The insider is invested in ways that the outsider is not, which typically colors the analysis with a decidedly evaluative hue. Some are unabashedly

---

143. Wuthnow, *After Heaven*, 198.

explicit about their assessment of the cultural turn as positive or negative, progressive or regressive, optimistic or pessimistic, triumph or disaster.

James Herrick is representative of evangelical Christian scholars who view the turn from religion to spirituality critically, even alarmingly, and at times disdainfully. In his polemic against what he termed the "New Religious Synthesis" that has displaced the "Revealed Word" tradition, he surveyed an impressive array of disparate movements and advocates that have arisen in the wake of the Enlightenment, and together conspired against Christianity, colonizing Western religious consciousness.[144] Herrick spelled out seven components of the New Religious Synthesis, summarized by Baer as follows:

> 1) an ahistorical spirituality that denies the necessity and value of grounding religion in actual time and space, 2) the spiritual centrality and indeed divinity or potential divinity of human reason (or mind, consciousness, imagination, or intellect), 3) a pantheistic infusing of nature with divinity or a life force that animates all matter with "divine energy or soul," thus warranting its "study by science as a source of spiritual knowledge"; 4) the consequent "spiritualization of science" in a monistic universe; 5) a Gnostic focus on secret or occult knowledge as the key to spiritual enlightenment and human progress; 6) spiritual evolution leading to individual human divinity; and 7) mystical experience as the universal bedrock of human religiosity, thus uniting all religious expressions in shared mystical wisdom, validating religious pluralism, and undermining Christian exclusivity (Herrick, p. 33–35).[145]

In his conclusion, Herrick emphasized that the New Religious Synthesis "promises to secure the soul's triumph over external restraints including time, space, evil, other people, conventional morality, and especially religious tradition."[146] As such, Herrick denounced all that he took as other than strict historical orthodoxy. His was certainly a staunch defense of defined Christian tradition (which he also summarized in seven points) against the heresy of everything other.

On the other hand, Phyllis Tickle is representative of Christian scholars who view the turn from religion to spirituality approvingly.[147] Whereas Herrick's attention was focused more on the Western cultural context of

---

144. Herrick, *Making of the New Spirituality*.
145. Baer, "Making of the New Spirituality."
146. Herrick, *Making of the New Spirituality*, 279.
147. Tickle, *Great Emergence*.

Christianity, Tickle's attention was more on what has evolved within Christianity itself. Yet as she recognized and overviewed, movements toward spirituality within the church have been impelled by the monumental cultural disruptions of the twentieth century, exacerbated now by postmodernity and its economic, political, technological, and scientific correlates that have brought into question basic presuppositions. She conceptualized spirituality, simply defined as "experiences and values that are internal to the individual,"[148] to be braided together with corporeality and morality to form religion—further evidence that orthodoxy has given way to orthopraxy and orthopathy.

Tickle's "big theory" is that about every five hundred years the church feels compelled to clean out its attic and hold a giant rummage sale of worn-out items. Old dogmas and practices are cast off to make room for teachings and practices that speak more directly to the new age, as Christianity renews itself in 500-year cycles. In the sixth century, following the fall of the Roman Empire, Gregory the Great guided Christianity into the monasticism that would protect and preserve it through the five hundred years of Dark Ages to come. In the Great Schism of 1054, Rome and Constantinople exchanged their anathemas and bulls of excommunications and split Christianity into its Western and Eastern brands. In the Great Reformation of the sixteenth century, Protestants and Catholics did much the same. Today, in the Great Emergence, the emergent church movement summarized in Essay Two is forging a way forward, as a renewed cultural imagination takes hold. The question underlying every reformation is about the location of authority, the most recent being the Reformation's understanding of Scripture. Though it may be premature and rather presumptuous to grant it such historical significance, Tickle is effusive in her praise and enthusiasm for a vibrant, reconstituted Christianity. "If . . . the Great Emergence really does what most of its observers think it will, it will rewrite Christian theology—and thereby North American culture—into something far more Jewish, more paradoxical, more narrative, and more mystical than anything the Church has had for the last seventeen or eighteen hundred years."[149]

Of the seven components of cultural change identified earlier, the two most pressing questions about the turn away from religion toward spirituality concern its magnitude and its consequences. Perhaps only the first can be answered with any accuracy and confidence at this point in history. If we are in fact in the midst of a full-blown spiritual revolution, the magnitude can hardly be overstated. Second, what the consequences will be cannot yet

---

148. Tickle, *Great Emergence*, 36.
149. Tickle, *Great Emergence*, 162.

be fully determined, as most of those effects still lie mostly in the future. What will Christianity in particular look like when the loss of basic biblical literacy, theological acumen, and institutional authority is more acute than what is already evident? One could argue that such conditions have already existed in previous historical eras, and that lack of biblical literacy, theological acumen, and institutional authority has in fact long characterized the personal Christian faith of the average feudal serf working the fields, the average industrial laborer working the mills, and even the average self-taught clergyman working the pulpit.[150] But though they may share some similar characteristics, practicing that kind of Christian faith in pre-modern, pre-Christendom cultural conditions, where the biblical text has never been read by the average adherent, theological doctrine has never been understood by the average believer, and church authority has never been decisive for the average follower, is nonetheless a profoundly different experience than doing so in post-modern, post-Christendom conditions where those practices are relics of the past now spurned.

Two additional questions are also pressing. Third, and more interpretively, what does the turn toward spirituality mean? Is it another stage of religious evolution, another manifestation of secularization, or a counterforce to secularization? Were he updating his account of his five historical stages of religious evolution outlined in Essay One, Robert Bellah may simply cast the present age as the next, sixth, postmodern stage of religion. Yet others see it not as benign religious transformation, but rather as malignant religious decline, now in its terminal stage. Steve Bruce,[151] for one, sees the displacement of institutional dogma with individual subjectivity or self-authority as the basis for religious legitimacy as "the last gasp and whimper of concern with the sacred in the West, an inconsequential dabbling that is doomed to disappear almost as quickly as it appeared."[152]

Fourth, and more evaluatively, is this turn toward spirituality a positive development or a negative development, a good thing or a bad thing? For whom? According to whom? And by what criteria and measurements? Just as a correlation coefficient indicates both the magnitude and direction of relationship between two variables, is this cultural turn a +.1 or +.9, a -.1 or -.9? Whereas "value-free" social scientists writing from an etic perspective aspire to avoid e-value-ation, Christian scholars writing from an emic perspective aspire to no such aversion. Of the latter already reviewed here, Herrick was thoroughly critical of the turn, as implied by his title: *The*

---

150. Stark, "Secularization, R.I.P."
151. Bruce, *God is Dead*.
152. Heelas and Woodhead, *Spiritual Revolution*, 2.

Making of the New Spirituality: The Eclipse of the Western Religious Tradition. In contrast, both Tickle and Bass were enthusiastically affirming of the turn, as trumpeted in Bass's title: *Christianity After Religion: The End of Church and the Birth of a New Spiritual Awakening*. Canadian pastor Bruxy Cavey's title, *The End of Religion: Encountering the Subversive Spirituality of Jesus*,[153] is equally emphatic and blunt.

Regardless of its consequences, its meaning, or its evaluation rendered by Christians, the magnitude of the turn away from religion toward spirituality is as massive as Taylor's "subjective turn of modern culture." Tickle equated it with only three other great movements in Christian history: Gregory the Great, the Great Schism, and the Great Reformation. As outlined in Essay One, Harvey Cox equated it with only one other age transition, the first being from the Age of Faith to the Age of Belief, and now from the Age of Belief to the Age of Spirit. The widespread appeal of spirituality "constitutes a sign of the jarring transition through which we are now passing from an expiring Age of Belief into a new but not yet fully realized Age of the Spirit."[154] In Christian history, it is the "most momentous transformation since its transition in the fourth century CE from what had begun as a tiny Jewish sect into the religious ideology of the Roman Empire."[155]

Seen in this fuller historical trajectory, the rise of snake handling among isolated twentieth-century hillbillies is actually not that anomalous or idiosyncratic. It may indeed be psychological, sub-cultural, *and* spiritual, but it is certainly part of a larger movement, to the extent that it is social, and a larger awakening, to the extent that it is spiritual. As detailed above, "[s]piritual experiences involve the experience of a transcendent reality, and are often characterized by a sense of 'awe', feeling of oneness, loss of sense of space and time, and the blurring of the boundaries between self and others."[156] So it was that when Covington took up the snake, he felt the power and victory of "losing himself." He later concluded his book with an allegory from his childhood about what in hindsight was a numinous experience, in contrast to the mystical experience of snake handling. He recalled how his boyhood friends were summoned home for supper by their parents calling out from their porches, or clanging the bells bolted to their doorframes. But he was not. Instead, his father would always come looking for him. "This is how he got me to come home. He always came to the

---

153. Cavey, *End of Religion*.
154. Cox, *Future of Faith*, 14.
155. Cox, *Future of Faith*, 2.
156. Hood and Chen, "Social Scientific Study," 361.

place where I was before he called my name."[157] So too, religion stands at a distance and calls to all equally, but the Spirit comes to wherever we are and invites us personally by name.

F. CHRISTIAN PERSPECTIVES

Dennis Covington's childhood experience of his father regularly coming to look for him and calling him by name to get him to come home contains core allegoric elements of Christian conceptions of spirituality. In Evan Howard's comprehensive, interdisciplinary, ecumenical, academic textbook on Christian spirituality written from an evangelical perspective, he defined spirituality in general as "human interaction with the transcendent or divine. Within the Christian tradition, it refers specifically to relationship with God though Jesus Christ."[158] Covington was clearly in relationship with his father who regularly came looking for him, just as in Christian spirituality the God who first conceived and created humans then also constantly comes back looking for each of them, all of whom God knows by name. What sets Christianity apart from other religious mythologies is that most others consist of human ascent and divine response, in which the human seeker struggles via their own efforts to ascend to the divine realm in hopes that the divine will then look upon them with favor and reward them accordingly. Christianity, in contrast, consists of divine descent and human response, in which God descends and incarnates into the human condition as Jesus, and invites a simple human response of trust.[159] Like Covington's father, God takes the initiative, and has the power to bridge the chasm.

Covington's father was also not looking for just anyone, but looking specifically for Dennis Covington, calling him by name in the way that Christian spirituality is personal and individual without necessarily being idiosyncratic. As Taylor concluded, it is individualistic without necessarily being individuating. It remains grounded in the time and place which the individual inhabits, and hence in their socially constructed reality. It is the subjective, internal experience of being identified, valued, connected, and called. It is non-creedal and to that extent non-religious, that is, not subject to theological correctness and codified normativities. And if the individual responds positively to the call, it elicits a profound sense of homecoming. These indeed are the most common elements of Christian spirituality.

---

157. Covington, *Salvation on Sand Mountain*, 240.
158. Howard, *Brazos Introduction to Christian Spirituality*, 16.
159. Swenson, *Society, Spirituality, and the Sacred*, 102–6.

In the social scientific descriptors overviewed earlier, Christian spirituality paradoxically and extraordinarily includes both opposites of multiple contraries. It is both vertical and horizontal, in that it loves both the transcendent divine and the immanent neighbor. It is both subjective and objective, in that it is a subjective experience of an objective reality: God. It is both internal and external, in that spirituality is by definition internal to the individual, whereas religion is external to the individual, residing in social institutions. As such, Christian spirituality is by definition also both spiritual and religious. According to Heelas and Woodhead, spirituality sacralizes "subjective-life" while religion sacralizes "life-as," yet they were careful to nuance their conceptual distinction when it comes to Christianity.

> [S]pirituality is often used in Christian circles to express devotion to God or Christ—as when spirituality is thought of as 'obedience to the will of God' with the believer entering into an intense relationship (involving self-surrender) with the divine. Such spirituality is subjective in the sense that it involves often intense experiences (of joy awe, sorrow, gratitude, etc.), but objective in the sense that it is focused on something which is and remains external to and higher than the self. This is experience of the sacred as transcendent, higher life—whether directly by way of the inspiration of the Holy Spirit, or indirectly by way of the scripture and tradition. It is not an experience of the sacred as integral to, inseparable from, and flowing through one's own 'subjective-life.' As such, it might be called 'life-as spirituality.'[160]

History

Christian spirituality has, of course, a rich, thick, two-thousand-year history. It understandably flourished most among ordinary Christians in pre-canonical, pre-creedal, pre-Constantinian Christianity before Christianity was institutionalized, but it continued to flourish in the medieval period when most Christians were still beyond the reach and control of the organized church, and unable to access its Scriptures directly themselves. However, it then understandably flagged in many ways under the rationalized and rationalistic strictures of the modernized church. Today, "a defining characteristic of our restless times is that spirituality is back with a vengeance,"[161] though the resurgent, robust interest in Christian spiritual-

---

160. Heelas and Woodhead, *Spiritual Revolution*, 5–6.
161. Demarest, *Four Views on Christian Spirituality*, 11.

ity of the last few decades[162] is in many ways more a rediscovery of classic Christian spiritual texts, practices, and lifestyles than a new vision and experience of Christian spirituality.

Alister McGrath, in his introductory textbook on Christian spirituality, summarized in three pages each the classic texts and thought of Gregory of Nyssa (c. 330–c. 395), Augustine of Hippo (354–430), Anselm of Canterbury (c. 1033–1109), Frances of Assisi (1182–1226), Hugh of Balma, Ludolf of Saxony (c. 1300–1378), Julian of Norwich (c. 1342–after 1416), Martin Luther (1483–1546), Ignatius Loyola (c. 1491–1556), Teresa of Avila (1515–1582), Charles Wesley (1707–1788), John Henry Newman (1801–1890), and James I. Packer (1926–). The most influential Catholic spiritual writers in the English-speaking world of the last hundred years include Thomas Merton (1915–1968), Henri Nouwen (1932–1996), Richard Rohr (1943–), and Ronald Rolheiser (1947–). The most influential Protestant spiritual writers include Frederick Buechner (1926–), Anne Lamott (1954–), Brian McLaren (1956–), and Donald Miller (1971–).[163] Here again is the problem of characterizing spirituality according to texts written by the elite minority, leaving open the question of the actual lived spirituality of the silent majority.

One manifestation of contemporary Christian spiritual practices being mostly a revival of classic spirituality is *The Ancient Practices Series*. After Brian McLaren introduced the series in *Finding Our Way Again: The Return of the Ancient Practices*,[164] in which he noted Christian commonalities with the two other Abrahamic faiths of Judaism and Islam, seven separate books were devoted to prayer,[165] Sabbath,[166] the liturgical year,[167] the sacred meal,[168] fasting,[169] tithing,[170] and the sacred journey.[171]

These spiritual practices are closer to the conscious, deliberate activities more associated with sacraments, rites, and liturgies than they are to the sociological concept of social practices explicated in Essay One. Social

---

162. As one form of evidence, there is now an 850-page *Dictionary of Christian Spirituality* edited by Glen Scorgie, plus another 700-page *New Westminster Dictionary of Christian Spirituality* edited by Philip Sheldrake.

163. McGrath, *Christian Spirituality*.

164. McLaren, *Finding Our Way Again*.

165. Benson, *In Constant Prayer*.

166. Allender, *Sabbath*.

167. Chittister, *Liturgical Year*.

168. Gallagher, *Sacred Meal*.

169. McKnight, *Fasting*.

170. Leblanc, *Tithing*.

171. Foster, *Sacred Journey*.

practices are the pre-theoretical assumptions of taken-for-granted beliefs and routinized actions which constitute religion. Spiritual practices are more specific activities.

As for spiritual lifestyle, traditional Catholic monasticism has been reformed and renewed in contemporary evangelicalism's "new monasticism" or "intentional Christian communities" based on the writings of Dietrich Bonhoeffer, Alasdair MacIntyre, and Jonathan R. Wilson.[172] This new monasticism retains traditional commitment to a contemplative life and "holistic communitarianism"—political, social, and theological—over against theological individualism, and refuses to prioritize personal evangelism over social activism. However, the new monasticism, along with the emergent church and the progressive left, remains a "dominated" movement within the diverse evangelical subculture, overshadowed by the "dominant" Christian Right and megachurch movements.[173] On the opposite, conservative wing of the evangelical spectrum, Rod Dreher's more recent "Benedict option" is to disengage from society in protest and self-protection, rather than attempt to reform it,[174] similar to some communal Anabaptist withdrawals of the past.[175] Likewise drawing on MacIntyre's *After Virtue*,[176] the Benedict option also seeks radical and countercultural ways to live in spiritual community. Just as Benedictine retreat into monastic life enabled Christianity to survive the collapse of the Roman Empire, so too, it is argued, will it enable Christianity to survive the current crisis of Western culture.

Together, the new monasticism and the Benedict option make clear that evangelicalism is no conservative monolith, as its understandings of spiritually healthy living continue to innovate and evolve from within. Nevertheless, that they both seek a vibrant, shared spirituality, though defined differently, is indisputable. They both seek "to develop a more densely textured religious life, in which regular patterns of communal prayer and intellectual and spiritual development will keep alive the possibility of inhabiting a nourishing, morally rich tradition."[177]

As described earlier, Wuthnow tracked the cultural progression in the second half of the twentieth century from the extremes of a "spirituality of dwelling" to a "spirituality of seeking," and advocated for a more functional,

---

172. Leading proponents include Shane Claiborne and Jonathan Wilson-Hartgrove. See Carter, "New Monasticism."

173. Markofski, *New Monasticism*.

174. Dreher, *Benedict Option*.

175. Hunter, *To Change the World*.

176. MacIntyre, *After Virtue*.

177. Williams, "New Monasticism," 39.

centered "spirituality of practice."[178] He suggested that such a spirituality was best fostered by practice-oriented religion which both grounds its adherents in the essentials of its tradition and at the same time encourages an open, holistic spirituality. The entire history of Christian spirituality attests to the rich legacy of dweller spirituality within traditional, institutionalized Christianity. The texts, practices, and lifestyles overviewed above are all primarily forms of Christian dweller spirituality. But can there also be a Christian seeker spirituality outside of traditional, institutionalized Christianity that nevertheless remains authentically, essentially Christian? Do the failings of the spirituality of dwelling (dependence on undependable communities) and the failings of the spirituality of seeking (social instability and spiritual immaturity) identified by Wuthnow mean that some Christians are better off with some alternative spirituality of practice? How can Christianity allow for and foster such an alternative spirituality of practice, without requiring a spirituality of dwelling, or condemning a spirituality of seeking?

From the perspective of cultural analysis, the contemporary revival of interest in Christian spirituality, whether conservative or progressive, whether in texts, practices, or lifestyle, is also a postmodern return to a premodern spirituality, in reaction to a rationalized and rationalistic modern religiosity. For example, Robert Webber's *Ancient-Future Faith: Rethinking Evangelicalism for a Postmodern World,* and the Ancient-Future Faith movement it spawned, was an attempt "to restore and then adapt classical Christianity to the postmodern cultural situation."[179] As Bruce Demarest explained, "Of particular relevance for postmodern spirituality is concern for spiritual experience and human connectedness, disillusionment with material possessions, and distrust of the institutional church . . . Sculpted as *imago Dei*, humans instinctively search for the transcendent 'who' and 'why' in a [modern] world of the scientific 'what' and 'how.'"[180] Cultural analysis aside, turning from the etic approach of the "objective," non-native, social scientific outsider to the emic approach of the "subjective," native, religious insider reveals almost as much variance within Christian spirituality as within social scientific descriptions of it.

Views and Streams

Christian spirituality is far from uniform or isomorphic, largely due to Christianity as a whole being likewise. The multiple branches and traditions

---

178. Wuthnow, *After Heaven*.
179. Webber, *Ancient-Future Faith*, 24.
180. Demarest, *Four Views on Christian Spirituality*, 13 and 15.

of Christian faith, each with their own histories, perspectives, emphases, and consequent theologies, each perceive and promote their own understandings of spirituality. And "understandings" must remain plural, because of the further variance within the branches and traditions of Christian faith themselves. To overview the broadest possible comparisons, Bruce Demarest, an unapologetic evangelical, edited a contribution to the genre of multiple view books targeted to evangelicals, though all four contributors were white American males. *Four Views on Christian Spirituality*[181] summarized the perspectives of each of the Eastern Orthodox, Roman Catholic, Progressive Protestant, and Evangelical traditions, each by an adherent.[182] The intent of the book included advocating for the restoration of authentic spirituality as an equal focus alongside theology and ethics in Christian life.

First, spirituality in Eastern Orthodoxy was characterized by Bradley Nassif as simply "our life in Christ,"[183] with the final destiny of the Christian being deification—the ultimate communion with God. Spirituality thus produces an ever closer relationship with God and with each other, and is something "less taught than caught."[184] It is also a sacramental way of life that extends sacramentality to nature and all human existence. Second, spirituality in Roman Catholicism was characterized by Scott Hahn as a sense of belonging to something greater than oneself. The central motif is family—a close relational intimacy that encompasses all believers into the universal family of God. Though Catholic spirituality is conventionally understood as more about liturgy, tradition, and sacrament, the continual emphasis of Catholic spirituality is the importance of "sonship," and the continual cry is "Come to the Father."[185]

Third, within Protestantism, spirituality in Progressive Mainline Protestantism was characterized by Joseph Driskill as concerned with "the lived experience of faith, the communities that shape experience, the practices that sustain it, and the moral life that embodies it."[186] The life, death, and

---

181. Demarest, *Four Views on Christian Spirituality*.

182. Two earlier, turn-of-the-century anthologies also provide multiple views from multiple eras of church history. *Invitation to Christian Spirituality: An Ecumenical Anthology*, edited by John Tyson, includes representation of Roman Catholic, Protestant, feminist, and liberation theology perspectives. *Exploring Christian Spirituality: An Ecumenical Reader*, edited by Kenneth Collins, includes representation of Roman Catholic, Eastern Orthodox, Lutheran, Reformed, Anglican, Methodist, and Evangelical perspectives.

183. Demarest, *Four Views on Christian Spirituality*, 32.

184. Demarest, *Four Views on Christian Spirituality*, 49.

185. Demarest, *Four Views on Christian Spirituality*, 93.

186. Demarest, *Four Views on Christian Spirituality*, 115.

symbolic resurrection of Jesus serve as the ultimate model of compassion and justice, including care for the earth. Notably, Driskill's presentation was assessed by one evangelical critic as "framed in a tone of humility."[187] Fourth, spirituality in Evangelicalism was characterized by Evan Howard as holding conversion to be the most important element—"a mystical *union* with God, a joining of God *with* us."[188] Based on David Bebbington's seminal evangelical quadrilateral—biblicism, crucicentrism, conversionism, and activism—evangelical spirituality is then the reading, studying, meditating on, and listening to sermons about the Scriptures.[189]

In sum, Eastern Orthodox Christians adhere to a normative tradition, Roman Catholics to a normative community, progressive Protestants to freedom from normativity, and evangelical Protestants to a more private and personal spirituality.[190] In the end, all four views of spirituality are derived from the commonality that all Christians share, that of living all of life before God, but also from the discrepant theology and methodology of the respective traditions or branches of Christianity. Different individual Christians therefore experience a rather differentiated spirituality, "one that is personally authentic and empowering, but also positively located within a larger web."[191] Hence we are again back to talking about comparative theology instead of the actual consciousness of lived experience of individual spirituality—the values, dispositions, longings, and virtues toward which individual Christians aspire most—and are to that extent still failing to apprehend generic, defining characteristics of Christian spirituality itself.

Howard's concise, fundamental definition of Christian spirituality as relationship with God was common to three of the four views. But "relationship with God" begs further nuance and explication. Is it the modern notion of intimacy as continuous, mutual self-disclosure, or is it simply to love, honor, and obey God, and "follow Jesus" by modelling one's life after him? Is it really the two-way communication that constitutes communion, or the one-way commitment that constitutes covenant? Is it charismatic

---

187. Scorgie, Review, 292.

188. Demarest, *Four Views on Christian Spirituality*, 167.

189. Elsewhere, Glen Scorgie offered a fuller definition of evangelical spirituality as "a liberating consciousness of unconditional grace and divine embrace, and an expectation that this God of grace will continue to be encountered, and his voice heard, chiefly through Scripture. Also central to evangelical spirituality is a perception of God's pleasure when the gospel, the biblical narrative of grace, is shared with others, or when believers otherwise contribute to its credible dissemination." *Dictionary of Christian Spirituality*, 28.

190. Scorgie, Review, 293.

191. Scorgie, Review, 293.

experience of God or pietistic devotion to God? The progressive Protestant tradition has long questioned how meaningful claims of a "living, personal relationship with Jesus Christ" really are, suspecting it to be overreach and overstatement, or simple Christianese.[192] "Skeptical of such claims to intimacy with the divine, the liberal Protestant tradition has instead focused its energies on Kingdom-building social concern, and settled for nurturing hearts that beat in sync with the unselfish, compassionate, and justice-loving heart of God."[193] For example, as discovered posthumously in her personal, private writings, Mother Teresa, for one, never "felt" anything spiritually. Similar understandings of spirituality are increasingly permeating at least the more progressive wing of evangelicals as well. "Most evangelicals will agree that the dynamics of authentic Christian spirituality must culminate in doing—in vocation, in following the heart of God into the world . . . [Thus] there is a turn of uneasy evangelical consciences toward more 'embodiment' of the gospel in Christ-like ministries of compassion and justice."[194] Wyndy Corbin Reuschling's *Desire for God and the Things of God: The Relationships between Christian Spirituality and Morality* is one such expression.[195]

When a survey of various Christian spiritualities narrows from the three historic branches of Christianity to a typology which to some extent is present within each branch, the two Protestant views above reappear. Richard Foster, the Quaker author of the classic *Celebration of Discipline: The Path to Spiritual Growth*,[196] has also elucidated the essential practices of six great spiritual traditions of Christian faith.[197] Based on the words of Jesus in John 7:38, "Out of the believer's heart shall flow rivers of living waters," he described a "mighty river of the Spirit" that is "a deep river of divine intimacy, a powerful river of holy living, a dancing river of jubilation in the Spirit, and a broad river of unconditional love for all peoples."[198] The six spiritual traditions or "streams of living waters" feeding that river are

---

192. Christianese is a pejorative reference to Christian terminology. It is the argot, jargon, and clichés, such as "washed in the blood of the Lamb," that communicates comprehensibly in the context of a particular Christian sub-culture, but baffles non-Christians, at times deliberately. Full dictionaries are available online.

193. Scorgie, Review, 292.

194. Scorgie, Review, 293.

195. Reuschling, *Desire for God*.

196. Foster devotes one chapter each to the inward disciplines of meditation, prayer, fasting, and study, the outward disciplines of simplicity, solitude, submission, and service, and the corporate disciplines of confession, worship, guidance, and celebration. See Foster, *Celebration of Discipline*.

197. Foster, *Streams of Living Water*.

198. Foster, *Streams of Living Water*, xv.

a) the prayer-filled life of the Contemplative Tradition focused on "a life of loving attention to God,"[199] b) the virtuous life of the Holiness Tradition focused on living "whole, functional lives in a dysfunctional world,"[200] c) the Spirit-empowered life of the Charismatic Tradition focused on "a life immersed in and under the direction of the Spirit,"[201] d) the compassionate life of the Social Justice Tradition focused on "compassion and justice for all peoples,"[202] e) the Word-centered life of the Evangelical Tradition focused on "the living Word of God, the written Word of God, and the proclaimed Word of God,"[203] and f) the sacramental life of the Incarnational Tradition focused on "a life that makes present and visible the realm of the invisible spirit."[204] Notably, most of these traditions are better understood as spiritual practices than as spiritual experience, as something individuals do, not something done to them.

Self, Desire, and the Other

If, as Howard maintained, Christian spirituality is essentially "relationship with God," perhaps a deeper way of understanding it lies beneath its practices and experiences, beneath what it thinks and what it does. Personal relationship always entails a subject and an object, the self and the other, plus some kind of connection between the two, though that connection may not necessarily be thought or enacted but simply felt instead. A fuller illumination of relationship therefore requires a more detailed understanding of all three components of self, connection, and other. Who, more fully, is the self? What, more exactly, is the connection? And who, more precisely, is the other? Beneath its competing theologies, its various practices, and its inexplicable experiences, Christian spirituality is the transformed self in a relationship of desire for the mystical Other.

As already described, Christian spirituality transcends the self both vertically in relation to the transcendent divine as well as horizontally in relation to the immanent neighbor. But before it transcends the self, Christian spirituality transforms the self. In *Spirituality and the Awakening Self: The Sacred Journey of Transformation*, David Benner unpacked the profound

---

199. Foster, *Streams of Living Water*, 58.
200. Foster, *Streams of Living Water*, 96.
201. Foster, *Streams of Living Water*, 132.
202. Foster, *Streams of Living Water*, 182.
203. Foster, *Streams of Living Water*, 233.
204. Foster, *Streams of Living Water*, 272.

changes wrought by a "deeper consciousness of being in God."[205] Yet the self cannot be spiritually awakened apart from an equal and concurrent awakening of awareness of God, or as Merton put it, "If I find [God] I will find myself, and if I find my true self I will find [God]."[206] Writing about becoming and being instead of belief and behavior, Benner defined transformation of the self as "1) increased awareness, 2) a broader, more inclusive identity, 3) a larger framework for meaning-making, and 4) a reorganization of personality that results in a changed way of being in the world."[207] Such transformation, or what psychology regards as human development, unfolds by the self first identifying with its body, then its mind, then its soul, and ultimately its spirit. It is "more a gift than an achievement"[208]—not something effectively sought—and "best recognized after the fact."[209] Benner, who grew up in an evangelical milieu before journeying from more conservative theology to the expansiveness of Christian mysticism, nevertheless stated explicitly that he was trying "to hold his theology with humility and not confuse his belief with Truth."[210]

However, "being in God" does not yet adequately elucidate the relationship of self with the Other. Like the affect that precedes and mostly predetermines rationality, as described in Essay One, and the emotional intuition that precedes and mostly predetermines morality, as described in Essay Two, spirituality is not a tranquil, affectless state of being. It is rather, as Simmel described, a "powerful longing of the soul,"[211] a deep, driving desire for the Other that is only, barely comparable in the interpersonal human realm to erotic yearning. Covington was not wrong in detecting similarities between sexual ecstasy and the spiritual ecstasy of the snake-handlers. Nevertheless, the profound difference is that both sexuality and spirituality are ultimately not about the loss of self in momentary ecstatic experience, but rather about constant, consummate common-union with, and completion in, the other.

In *The Holy Longing: The Search for a Christian Spirituality*, Ronald Rolheiser observed that humans are "over-charged with desire . . . driven, forever obsessed, congenitally dis-eased, living lives, as Thoreau once

---

205. Benner, *Spirituality and the Awakening Self*, ix.
206. Benner, *Spirituality and the Awakening Self*, 113.
207. Benner, *Spirituality and the Awakening Self*, 59.
208. Benner, *Spirituality and the Awakening Self*, 59.
209. Benner, *Spirituality and the Awakening Self*, 71.
210. Benner, *Spirituality and the Awakening Self*, 110.
211. Simmel, "Conflict in Modern Culture," 23.

suggested, of quiet desperation."[212] He then defined spirituality as what we do with our desires, how we channel our eros, that "fire" within us, the restlessness that we cannot shake, and "the congenital all-embracing ache that lies at the center of human experience."[213] Sexual energy is "the most powerful of all fires, the best of all fires, the most dangerous of all fires, and the fire which, ultimately, lies at the base of everything, including the spiritual life."[214] Spirituality is an energy of desire that constantly functions both to motivate and empower us, as well as to join and adhere us. Rather than a discrete perception or a passing experience, spirituality is an integral part of everyday life.[215] By thus revealing the mystic in everyone, Rolheiser concurred with German theologian Karl Rahner that the time is fast approaching when each person will either be a mystic or an unbeliever.

Many other scholars have also expounded the significant commonality of yearning, of aching desire in both embodied sexuality and disembodied spirituality.[216] Both represent the human longing for completion in the other,[217] sexually in the complementary human other, spiritually in the ultimate divine Other. Sexual longing for consummation is therefore an earthy, corporeal manifestation of a higher, holier longing.[218] As William Butler Yeats lamented, "the tragedy of sexual intercourse is the perpetual virginity of the soul,"[219] leaving even the most sexually satisfied to continually mourn their ultimate incompleteness.[220] According to Rolheiser, "Rahner once said

212. Rolheiser, *Holy Longing*, 3.

213. Rolheiser, *Holy Longing*, 4.

214. Rolheiser, *Holy Longing*, 193.

215. James K. A. Smith developed this theme in *You Are What You Love: The Spiritual Power of Habit*, which was a condensation of his earlier works. Tish Harrison Warren popularized it in *Liturgy of the Ordinary: Sacred Practices in Everyday Life*. Whereas Warren's entire book is given to the spirituality of the various activities of a single ordinary day, many others have reflected on the spirituality of a single activity, such as the spirituality of running. For example, see Roger Joslin, *Running the Spiritual Path: A Runner's Guide to Breathing, Meditating, and Exploring the Prayerful Dimension of the Sport*.

216. Popular writers have observed the same. Rob Bell provided a characteristically postmodern rumination on the similarities in *Sex God: Exploring the Endless Connections between Sexuality and Spirituality*. Debra Hirsch, in *Redeeming Sex: Naked Conversations about Sexuality and Spirituality*, asserted that "our sexuality is so interlaced with longing for and experience of spirituality that we cannot access one without somehow tapping into the other" (23).

217. Nelson and Longfellow, *Sexuality and the Sacred*.

218. McMinn, *Sexuality and Holy Longing*.

219. Yeats, *Vision*, 398.

220. Ron Rolheiser provided a moving exposition of Judges 11, where Jephthah's daughter requests time, before he sacrifices her, to go into the desert to bewail the

that in the torment of the insufficiency of everything attainable we eventually realize that, here in this life, all symphonies remain unfinished . . . We are always in some way frustrated, in some way sleeping alone."[221]

As Taylor observed above, the three distinct historical epochs of pre-modernity, modernity, and postmodernity nonetheless shared in common a desire for connection with the transcendent.[222] However, the transformed self in a relationship of desire for the mystical Other is left with the wonder of who that transcendent Other might all be. Despite the assertion of theological anthropology that all humans and their concepts of God are finite and fallen, Christians throughout history have for the most part not been shy about specifying the theologically correct attributes of God. According to the Westminster Shorter Catechism (1646–1647), "God is a Spirit, infinite, eternal, and unchangeable in his being, wisdom, power, holiness, justice, goodness, and truth." But a fuller, alphabetical list of attributes ascribed to God in various times, places, and contexts includes the following: aseity (God is so independent that God does not need humans), eternity, goodness, graciousness, holiness, immanence, immutability, impassibility, impeccability, incomprehensibility, incorporeality, infinity, jealousy, love, mission, mystery, omnipotence, omnipresence, omniscience, oneness, providence, righteousness, simplicity, sovereignty, transcendence, Trinity, veracity, and wrath. Is this list definitive of the Other whom the spiritual self desires? Presumably the attributes of incomprehensibility, infinity, mystery, and transcendence qualify the other attributes, and leave the list open and incomplete.

Mysticism

As already documented above, few in the general population identify as religious but not spiritual, ever more identify as spiritual but not religious, and close to half of Americans (48 percent) and one quarter of Canadians (24 percent) identify as both religious and spiritual. When spirituality is understood to consist of personal mental beliefs, behavioral practices, or even emotional desires, many who identify as spiritual would likely be content to identify as such, and not identify as mystical. Yet in terms of experience, the number of Americans who claimed a mystical experience with the divine more than doubled from 22 percent in 1962 to 49 percent in 2009, a rise

---

fact that she is to die a virgin, incomplete and unconsummated. See "Mourning Our Virginity."

221. Rolheiser, *Holy Longing*, 204.
222. Taylor, *Secular Age*.

from less than a quarter to almost half in half a century.[223] Indeed, "mystical experiences are more common today among those who are unaffiliated with any particular religion (30%) than they were in the 1960s among the public as whole (22%)."[224] Like spirituality in general, mysticism in particular is also clearly resurgent, and more so outside traditional religion than within it. Indeed, while most Christians committed to theological correctness take the spirituality of "relationship with God" to be an inherent part of their lived faith, many Christians consider mysticism to be outside traditional Christianity. Wary of its ambiguities, they suspect mysticism to be heretical, and not so subtly attach derogatory connotations to it. And "sometimes 'mysticism' or 'mystic' has been used as a weapon to stigmatize"[225] those suspected or accused of vacuous faith.

Also like spirituality, mysticism must be understood as an entire way of life, a lived faith that cannot be reduced to particular beliefs, practices, or even particular types of experiences. As already cited, Howard defined Christian spirituality as "the entirety of lived relationship with God," and then proceeded to define Christian mysticism as a subset within spirituality. In his formulation, mysticism is

> conscious experience of the divine presence ... Both emphasize the experiential aspect of faith. Both mysticism and spirituality give special attention to the life of the spirit. But whereas mysticism finds its center in the consciousness of God's presence, spirituality refers to a broader reality ... Mysticism, unlike spirituality, is focally concerned with the human consciousness of the direct presence of God. Spirituality, on the other hand, is concerned with the entirety of the lived experience of an individual or group in relationship with God.[226]

The most cited and influential definition of Christian mysticism is from the distinguished scholar Bernard McGinn, who defined it as "a special consciousness of the presence of God that by definition exceeds description and results in a transformation of the subject who receives it."[227] As Julia Lamm noted, according to this definition, mysticism is consciousness, not only experience, it is related to divine presence, not divine absence, and it is "a transformative process and sustained way of living that is at once moral,

---

223. "Mystical Experiences."
224. "Mystical Experiences."
225. Lamm, "Guide to Christian Mysticism," 2.
226. Howard, *Brazos Introduction to Christian Spirituality*, 16.
227. McGinn, *Presence of God*, 26.

intellectual, and spiritual."[228] In similar tones, Benner defined Christian mysticism as "participation in the mystery of the transformation journey toward union with God in love,"[229] a journey that involves deep longing in contemplative stillness, aligns head and heart, and leads to a unified consciousness. Union with God remains a mystical union, just as God remains a mystical Other, as specifics about both that union and that Other remain beyond description. Nonetheless, "[w]ith shockingly bold language, Peter describes the mystical possibility of union with God as participating in the divine nature (2 Pet 1:4)."[230]

At the same time—here is further paradox—the self in union with God also remains embodied and embedded, as emphasized by feminist theology. Carol Christ questioned the emphasis on transcendence in conventional definitions of mysticism, because "women's mystical experiences [are] often found within the world . . . women's quest is for a wholeness in which the oppositions between body and soul, nature and spirit, rationality and emotion are overcome."[231] The mystical self is not surrendered, sacrificed, dissolved, or annihilated in a dualistic flight from immanence toward transcendence, but rather, the mystical self is affirmed in its physical materiality and social context.[232] Christ drew out two types of earthly mysticism: embodied nature mysticism and embedded social/communal mysticism. "Embodied mysticism is felt in the body, for example in eating and drinking or in dancing or making love or in climbing the peach tree . . . Embedded mysticism seeks to feel the feelings of other individuals in the world ever more deeply. [It] is the sense of being part of a larger whole that is infused with the presence of the divine."[233] As such, mystical consciousness of divine presence that transforms does not require escape from the here and now, because it can flourish within it.[234]

228. Lamm, "Guide to Christian Mysticism," 4.

229. Benner, *Spirituality and the Awakening Self*, 75.

230. Benner, *Spirituality and the Awakening Self*, 74.

231. Christ, "Embodied Embedded Mysticism," 161.

232. The "common core thesis" of mysticism is that "both within and outside of the great faith traditions is an experience of ego dissolution and union that is essentially identical, regardless of interpretation." See Hood and Chen, "Social Scientific Study," 584. Christ here refutes the thesis that ego dissolution is also true of Christian mysticism.

233. Christ, "Embodied Embedded Mysticism," 165. Diana Butler Bass developed a similar argument more fully in *Grounded: Finding God in the World—A Spiritual Revolution*.

234. Other perspectives not expressly feminist concur. For example, Rodney Clapp also articulated an embodied spirituality, and argued that "Classical Christian spirituality never rejects and never gives up on the body because of three key features of its

However, whatever the complexities and uncertainties of the Christian mystical self may be, or those of the character of its union with the Other, the most indeterminate aspect of Christian mysticism, by far, is who or what that holy, Wholly Other may be. As Lamm summarized, "[m]ystical discourse challenges any static, rote, or merely 'exterior' understanding of God. Mysticism is iconoclastic, rejecting the impulse to make God into one object (or subject) among many . . . [it] resists formalism."[235] Therefore, when seeking some understanding of the holy, Wholly Other, rationality must be a servant, not the master, and intellectual humility is a prerequisite.

Negative Theology

Understandably, most theologies are given to stating who or what God is. After all, definitions best detail positively exactly what entities are, not negatively what they are not. But that assumes the entity in question is definable, and therein lies the obvious problem with defining God. Most Christian theologies begin with the disclaimer that God is ultimately incomprehensible and undefinable, and then proceed unapologetically to attempt to do so. In contrast, mystical Christian theologies proceed by stating what God is not, or not only, and not only not just the attribute being described compared to other attributes, but not only that attribute itself. This distinction between affirmative theology (*kataphatic*—"according to images" or "saying") and negative theology (*apophatic*—"apart from images" or "unsaying") was first articulated by Pseudo-Dionysius the Areopagite in the sixth century in his enormously influential *The Mystical Theology*. He begins from the assumption that "the more we take flight upward, the more our words are confined to the ideas we are capable of forming; so that now as we plunge into that darkness which is beyond intellect, we shall find ourselves not simply running short of words but actually speechless and unknowing."[236] After a series of denials of who or what God is (only), and avowing that God falls within the predicate of neither being nor non-being, Pseudo-Dionysius concludes his treatise by asserting, "We make assertions and denials of what is next to it, but never of it, for it is both beyond every assertion, being the perfect and unique cause of all things, and, by virtue of its pre-eminently simple and

---

basic story and logic: creation, incarnation, and resurrection." *Tortured Wonders*, 34. Moreover, much of his book is as much about socially embedded spirituality as it is about physically embodied spirituality.

235. Lamm, "Guide to Christian Mysticism," 10.
236. Pseudo-Dionysius, *Mystical Theology*, 3.1033B.

absolute nature, free of every limitation, beyond every limitation; it is also beyond every denial."[237]

Kataphatic theology, the *via positiva*,[238] "refers to the path of knowing God by affirmation, namely, through his self-revelation mediated by the intellect and senses. This path affirms that truths about the Almighty are disclosed via biblical teaching, the sacraments, and other symbols of the faith."[239] Apophatic theology, the *via negativa*, "represents the path of knowing God by sheer negation.[240] Advocates aver that the divine Reality, dwelling in a realm beyond human comprehension, cannot be known by ideas, images, and language. Rather, God is known in the darkness by detachment, prayerful silence, and contemplation."[241] Said differently, apophatic theology is "the knowledge of God gained by means of the systematic, logical negation of attributes, properties, and qualities positively graspable by the human mind."[242] It "confesses God to be so utterly transcendent, so beyond our concepts and names for God, that we must in fact 'negate' them in order to free God from such cramped categories . . . we clear space within ourselves so that God can appear, so to speak, *as God*, that is, as the mystery God is and must be in order to be properly God."[243] One effect of living out apophatic theology that is notable here is its humble silence of unsaying.[244]

Together, kataphatic and apophatic theology are complementary, not contradictory. They are not separate, conflicting ways of talking about God in which one cancels out the other, because the negative presupposes the positive, and both are necessary for meaningful discourse about God. Both are needed simultaneously, because God, it is said, is both transcendent and immanent, both hidden and manifest. "It is the dialectical interplay between these two approaches that provides the impetus (upward) toward 'higher' knowledge of God and ultimately toward union with God . . . The mystic makes the unqualified affirmation of the goodness, love, and presence of God. The mystic often also utters the prophetic 'no' to reified, institutionalized, professionalized forms of speech and text about God."[245] Even God's

---

237. Pseudo-Dionysius, *Mystical Theology*, 5.1048B.

238. Leading proponents include Augustine, Luther, Calvin, and Ignatius.

239. Demarest, *Four Views on Christian Spirituality*, 19.

240. Leading proponents include Gregory of Nyssa (c. 335–c. 395), Meister Eckhart (c. 1260–c. 1328), John of the Cross (1542–1591), Jacob Boehme (1574–1624), and Thomas Merton (1915–1968).

241. Demarest, *Four Views on Christian Spirituality*, 18.

242. Fortin, "Christian Rationality," 340.

243. Stang, "Negative Theology," 161.

244. Burrows, "Words that Reach into the Silence."

245. Lamm, "Guide to Christian Mysticism," 16.

self-disclosure or revelation is "a trace or trail that we can follow back to the mysterious source of all revelation."[246] If and when that is achieved, negation does not only negate the affirmations of positive theology, but negation paradoxically negates itself. This more radical negation

> embodies the capacity to reject any word, any concept, be it positive or negative, as being fundamentally inappropriate to describe the divine . . . [and] culminates and ends with the immediate and therefore silent encounter of the human with God . . . It is at this point, where human reason must let go of all its conceptual and logical, argumentative apparatus in order to experience the absolute and transcendent God, that its deeper nature is revealed . . . In the end, then, human reason turns into love as it gives way to the affective, passive experience of the transcendent."[247]

In his introductory textbook on Christian spirituality, McGrath addressed the spiritual importance of being able to visualize the divine, to see the face of God, and to touch God.[248] Doing so understandably requires some affirmative, kataphatic theology. Yet McGrath began his discussion by first confronting the problematic challenge of idolatry. He first noted the absolute prohibition in the Second Commandment of producing any images of God: "You shall not make for yourself an idol, whether in the form of anything that is in heaven above, or that is on the earth beneath, or that is in the water under the earth. You shall not bow down to them or worship them" (Exod 20:4–5). Fearing the idolatrous worship of social constructions, the Reformed tradition (along with Islam), unlike the Orthodox and Catholic traditions, has discouraged any form of religious art, including the depiction of God or Jesus.[249] But of course, ideas and concepts of God are equally social constructions. Finally, after reviewing visualizations of God in the creation, the incarnation, the cross, and the sacraments, McGrath concluded his discussion with the "corrective" of the apophatic tradition,

---

246. Stang, "Negative Theology," 161.
247. Fortin, "Christian Rationality," 341–42.
248. McGrath, *Christian Spirituality*.

249. Apophatic theology is common to all three Abrahamic faiths, and not surprisingly, is being revitalized by postmodern theology, as noted by Karen Armstrong in *The Case for God*. Replying to the New Atheists, she tracked how historical *mythos* was usurped by *logos* in modernity, resulting in the phenomena of religious fundamentalism and atheism. She then contended that ultimate reality—God, Allah, Brahman, nirvana, or Tao—transcends human rationalism, and can only be known through devoted practice. In truth, Pi, from *Life of Pi* in the opening vignette of Essay One, was not far wrong.

and cited John Chrysostom's (347–407) treatise *On the Incomprehensibility of God*:

> Let us invoke him as the inexpressible God, incomprehensible, invisible and unknowable. Let us affirm that he surpasses all power of human speech; that he eludes the grasp of every mortal intelligence; that the angels cannot penetrate him; that the seraphim cannot see him clearly; that the cherubim cannot fully understand him. For he is invisible to the principalities and powers, the virtues and all creatures, without exception.[250]

Nevertheless, negative theology does not actually distance God from the personal life of the mystic. As Rowan Williams clarified, the "energy of conceptual negation is bound up with a sense of intimate involvement in the life of God, rather than absolute disjunction."[251] Union with God persists and is perfected as, metaphorically, "negative theology regards the transcendent God as intimately involved in our lives as the breath in our lungs—or perhaps better, regards the breath in our lungs as transcendently divine as any distant god we presume to imagine."[252] For the mystic, God is not (only) far removed from us, but is with us, indeed in us. Consciousness of that presence is the union with God that transforms us.

In "Christian Rationality: Embracing the Divine Mystery," Jean-Pierre Fortin anticipated in broad strokes the cumulative argument developed in the three essays comprising this book. He noted how "the postmodern criticism and overcoming of the modern canons and concepts of rationality and science have paved the way to a systematic reconsideration of the nature and status of faith and religion in relation to human reason."[253] He asserted that "[t]he mysterious character or incomprehensibility of God . . . is not to be counted as one attribute of the divine among many, but as something positively affecting and determining all divine attributes."[254] Or as Karl Rahner put it so succinctly, "This incomprehensibility is not one attribute of God alongside others, but the attribute of his attributes."[255] In the end, the only truly rational choice for the Christian is to humbly embrace the divine mystery, "because mystery has been shown to be the very definition, experience, and manifestation of ultimate rationality, that is, of God."[256]

250. McGrath, *Christian Spirituality*, 118.
251. Williams, *Arius*, 243.
252. Stang, "Negative Theology," 174.
253. Fortin, "Christian Rationality," 337.
254. Fortin, "Christian Rationality," 344.
255. Rahner, "Human Question of Meaning," 94.
256. Fortin, "Christian Rationality," 347.

From a Christian mystical perspective, but employing the terms of the meta-theoretical position of critical realism framing this whole analysis, God can be understood, roughly, as the "real," the Spirit as its subset of the "actual," and Jesus as its further subset of the "empirical." To review, the real is comprised of all the "mechanisms" that exist, whether humans are aware of them or not. The actual is comprised of all the mechanisms that have been activated, producing events in time and space, whether observed by humans or not. The empirical is comprised of all the mechanisms that have been both activated and observed, the domain of direct or indirect human experience of the real and the actual. In this sense, Jesus is the empirical that humans have observed, though he is not identical with all that happens by the actual Spirit, and neither Jesus nor the Spirit is identical to all that is real—God. Though not perfectly aligned with the doctrine of the Trinity, such a conception still deems each to be equally God, but also recognizes what Christian mystics deem unfathomable God to be.

The Cloud

Perhaps the archetypal, definitive expression of the apophatic tradition in Christian life, the polar opposite of the apologetic tradition, is an instructional text for cloistered monks written in the latter half of the fourteenth century. *The Cloud of Unknowing*, written in Middle English by an English monk who humbly chose to remain anonymous, is a spiritual guide to contemplative prayer.[257] Though the work is written in the fourteenth-century vernacular and "fraught with alliteration and metaphor,"[258] the author is "perhaps the most subtle and incisive, as well as the most original spiritual writer in the English language."[259] The way to know God, he suggests, is to abandon attempting to understand God's particular attributes and activities, humbly surrender one's mind and ego, and live a life of prayer.

The primary theme of *The Cloud of Unknowing* is "an experience of mystical union with God . . . in which one's awareness moves beyond anything that can be thought, imagined, or reflected upon,"[260] that is, beyond rational cognition and particular images. Two secondary themes that are most pertinent to what has been argued here are also prominent. One is the cultivation of the virtue of humility, and not merely the "imperfect humility which arises from reflection upon the nature of the [sinful] self," but the

---

257. The contemporary practice of Centering Prayer is one derivative.
258. Englert, "Desire and Symbol," 52.
259. Knowles, *English Mystical Tradition*, 67.
260. Young, "Forget Yourself," 9.

"perfect humility" which arises through attention to the divine.[261] "Humility is brought to perfection only when knowledge of self is superseded by awareness of God."[262] The other secondary theme is the author's theology of desire, which is the erotic yearning of the soul, the longing of love, the *desiderium*—love in the absence of the beloved.[263] In the end, readers are "drawn to rest in silence, but [are] also exposed to one of the most ornate descriptions of silence ever to be fashioned."[264] In the unknown author's own words,

> Lift up your heart to God with a gentle stirring of love. Focus on [God] alone . . . Don't let anything else run through your mind and will. Here's how. Forget what you know. Forget everything God made and everybody who exists and everything that's going on in the world, until your thoughts and emotions aren't focused on or reaching toward anything, not in a general way and not in any particular way. Let them be . . .
>
> The first time you practice contemplation, you'll only experience a darkness, like a cloud of unknowing. You won't know what this is. You'll only know that in your will you feel a simple reaching out to God. You must also know that this darkness and this cloud will always be between you and your God, whatever you do. They will always keep you from seeing [God] clearly by the light of understanding in your intellect and will block you from feeling [God] fully in the sweetness of love in your emotions. So, be sure you make your home in this darkness. Stay there as long as you can, crying out to [God] over and over again, because you love [God]. It's the closest you can get to God here on earth, by waiting in this darkness and in this cloud. Work at this diligently, as I've asked you to, and I know God's mercy will lead you there . . .
>
> [God] measures us and makes . . . divinity fit our souls, and our souls are able to take the measure of [God] because [God] created us in [God's] image and made us worthy. [God] alone is complete and can fulfill our every longing. God's grace restores our souls and teaches us how to comprehend [God] through love. [God] is incomprehensible to the intellect . . . Nobody's mind is powerful enough to grasp who God is. We can only know [God] by experiencing [God's] love.
>
> Look. Every rational creature, every person, and every angel has two main strengths: the power to know and the power

261. Young, "Forget Yourself" 10.
262. Young, "Forget Yourself," 11.
263. Englert, "Desire and Symbol."
264. Englert, "Desire and Symbol," 59.

to love. God made both of these, but [God is] not knowable through the first one. To the power of love, however, [God] is entirely known, because a loving soul is open to receive God's abundance . . . [God's] very nature makes love endless and miraculous. God will never stop loving us. Consider this truth, and, if by grace you can make love your own, do. For the experience is eternal joy; its absence is unending suffering.

I know you'll ask me, "How can I think on God as God, and who is God?" and I can only answer, "I don't know." Your question takes me into the very darkness and cloud of unknowing that I want you to enter. We can know so many things. Through God's grace, our minds can explore, understand, and reflect on creation and even on God's own works, but we can't think our way to God. That's why I'm willing to abandon everything I know, to love the one thing I cannot think. [God] can be loved, but not thought.

By love, God can be embraced and held, but not by thinking. It is good sometimes to meditate on God's amazing love as part of illumination and contemplation, but true contemplative work is something entirely different. Even meditating on God's love must be put down and covered with a cloud of forgetting. Show your determination next. Let that joyful stirring of love make you resolute, and in its enthusiasm bravely step over meditation and reach up to penetrate the darkness above you. Then beat on that thick cloud of unknowing with the sharp arrow of longing and never stop loving, no matter what comes your way . . .

No matter how sacred, no thought can ever promise to help you in the work of contemplative prayer, because only love—not knowledge—can help us reach God . . .

Become blind during contemplative prayer and cut yourself off from needing to know things. Knowledge hinders, not helps you in contemplation. Be content feeling moved in a delightful, loving way by something mysterious and unknown, leaving you focused entirely on God, with no other thought than of [God] alone. Let your naked desire rest there . . .

It doesn't matter how much profound wisdom we possess about created spiritual beings; our understanding cannot help us gain knowledge about any uncreated spiritual being, who is God alone. But the failure of our understanding can help us. When we reach the end of what we know, that's where we find

God. That's why St. Dionysius said that the best, most divine knowledge of God is that which is known by not-knowing.[265]

---

265. Butcher, *Cloud of Unknowing*, 11, 12, 14, 21–22, 28–29, 79, 156.

EPILOGUE

WHILE MOSES WAS SHEPHERDING his father-in-law Jethro's flock, his attention was captured by the burning bush. After removing his sandals because he was standing on holy ground, hiding his face because he was afraid to look at God, and hearing God send him to bring the Israelites out of Egypt, "Moses said to God, 'If I come to the Israelites and say to them, "The God of your ancestors has sent me to you," and they ask me, "What is his name?" what shall I say to them?' God said to Moses, "*ehyeh 'asher-'ehyeh*'" (Exod 3:13–14). God refused to be named, or even characterized, insisting simply that "I will be who I will be." Yet we humans likewise insist, contrarily, on having at least a word and preferably a name for God, because our minds require the symbol system that is language in order to function. Without language, we cannot think.[1] And without language, we are incapable of even an idea of God, despite how feebly insufficient our language for, and ideas about, the totality of God may be.

All we humans have are analogies and metaphors for God, figures of speech that are used to make comparisons between God and things we know more adequately with our reason and/or senses.[2] As noted in Essay Two, C. S. Lewis humbly acknowledged this truth in "A Footnote to All Prayers," when he implored God to translate all our "limping metaphors" for God.[3] Among the early metaphors for God in Genesis are spirit and

---

1. Like animals, humans possess multiple senses and a brain capable of functions such as perception and memory. Unlike animals, humans also possess a mind dependent on language for its realization, as dramatically exemplified by the famous historical case of Helen Keller, and as first expounded by George Herbert Mead in *Mind, Self and Society*. See also Sandstrom et al., *Symbols, Selves, and Social Reality*. Therefore, Ludwig Wittgenstein's famous aphorism that "The limits of my language mean the limits of my world" (White, *Wittgenstein's 'Tractatus Logico-Philosophicus,'* 98) would be more accurately rendered as "The limits of my language mean the limits of my mind."

2. I am indebted to my colleague Val Hiebert (no relation) for the following research and insights about metaphors.

3. Lewis, "Footnote to All Prayers," 129.

wind (*ruah* in Hebrew). Like God, wind is constantly moving around us, filling every space, animating the air we breathe, and thereby giving us life. But unlike the empirical nature of wind, God is more like the non-empirical character of spirit. Wanting to make God more comprehensible, relatable, and accessible, we therefore prefer the metaphor of personhood. God, we say, is a person, and not just any person, but a specifically male person, and not just any male person, but a father. Historically, the metaphor of God as father communicated most effectively to its original audience in the context of their ancient Near-Eastern social norm of *pater familias*, which was their social construction of family. They deemed a father to be all-knowing and all-powerful, having the power of life and death over wives and children. Needless to say, the metaphor of father does not convey those same characteristics and powers to us today.

Not unintentionally, the Christian institutionalization of the metaphor of God as father has come at the expense of God as mother, despite numerous mother metaphors in the biblical text. Patriarchal bias in translation has systematically obscured those mother metaphors. For example, the Hebrew word *rehem* means either womb or uterus, sometimes compassion or mercy, but when it appears in the biblical text, it has historically been translated as mercy, thereby ignoring the exclusively female organ it also signifies. Hence Jer 31:20, "my heart yearns for him, I will surely have mercy on him," can just as accurately and validly be translated as "my womb trembles for him, I will surely have mother-compassion upon him." Metaphorically, God has a womb.[4] In Isa 42:14; Rom 8:22; and Gal 4:19, God is like a woman groaning in labor pains. In Job 38:28–30 and Job 8, God is like a woman giving birth. In Isa 49:15 and Num 11:11–12, God is like a nursing mother. In Ps 131:1–2, God is like a mother with a weaned child. In Isa 66:12–13 and Luke 13, God is like a comforting mother. But of course, in overall essence, surely God is neither the binary of exclusively male nor exclusively female. God is both, and more.

The concept of God conveyed by Christian metaphors for God are narrowed and entrenched further by the patriarchy also implicit in the concept of the Trinity. Two of the three persons—Father and Son—are identified as male, even though Parent and Child would be more inclusive yet still limiting personifications of God. True, Jesus was a male, but it would have been even less comprehensible, and that much less effective, to incarnate God as a female in that patriarchal culture. Nevertheless, why was Jesus identified more as the son (male child) of God than simply as the child of God, if not

---

4. Other examples of "yearning heart" more appropriately translated as "trembling womb" include Isa 63:15–16 and Isa 46:3–4.

in deference to the patriarchal culture into which he was born? Was his maleness significant or even relevant in a way that would have disqualified a female incarnation? Is there something about being male that more fully reflects the image of God the parent? And if not, is not incarnation itself simply a means by which the spirit of God temporarily humanizes and personalizes itself in order to perform the functions of revealing itself and redeeming humanity? In overall essence, surely God is neither exclusively father, mother, person, wind, nor even spirit—metaphors all. God is I AM.

Furthermore, in the Kabbalah of Jewish mysticism, God is not even a noun; God is a verb.[5] Just as functional definitions demarcate religion by what it does, in contrast to substantive definitions which demarcate religion by what it is, and just as Fowler maintained that faith is a verb ("faithing"), and just as "love is something you do,"[6] so too God in this sense is an action, not an object. "I AM" is the first person form of the English verb "to be," just as Yahweh is a third person form of the Hebrew verb "to be."[7] In this sense it is more accurate to say that "God happens" than to say that "God is a thing." God is what God does.

When we humans strive to comprehend the supreme divine, the Great I AM, we understandably exercise all our capacities to their fullest extent. We earnestly employ every means of mind, body, and spirit possible to not only comprehend but experience all that we believe and/or hope possible. Ultimately, we not only long to comprehend and experience the divine, but also to connect to and become one with the divine. Yet who would dare claim that they can positively affirm all that God is, much less fully know God personally? As Essay Three made manifest, only a negative theology adequately addresses the incomprehensible mystery of God. As Essay One concluded, citing Cohen, our names for God are our conception of and construction of the divine, and are in need of healing.[8] When we exhaust our rationality and are confronted with its limitations, we are humbled by our finitude, and animated by our spirituality.

Psalm 46 describes multiple terrifying circumstances threatening humans—mountains trembling and kingdoms tottering—to which God calmly replies, "Be still." God's gentle but firm reproof of human anxiety and fretting is, "Stop it. That's enough. Quiet your mind, heart, and body." Jesus would later echo that command when he rebuked the wind and waves

---

5. Cooper, *God is a Verb*.

6. Bisagno, *Love is Something You Do*.

7. Yahweh, like "*ehyeh*," is an imperfect form of the Hebrew hyh "to be," which, though a name in Hebrew, can be conjecturally translated as "he will be." See Alter, *Hebrew Bible*, 222–23.

8. Cohen, "Come Healing."

pounding his boat, and his disciples in it, with "Peace! Be still!" (Mark 4:39). Likewise, only when we cease striving to master all truth and to maintain correct beliefs about God can we rest content that the Infinite "will be who I will be." As Psalm 46 begins and ends, God is our refuge—another metaphor. But of course the full phrase is not just "Be still," but "Be still and know that I am God." Some knowing remains involved, though what form that knowing takes is not specified, other than that it requires stillness, not frenetic mental, emotional, or physical activity. This is not a spirituality of dwelling, or seeking, or practice. This is a spirituality of being, the polar opposite of the madness and ecstasy of snake handling. This is God talking to us, telling us what (not) to do in order to know the only thing ultimately worth knowing.

Gravity: A Center for Contemplative Activism is an organization that promotes a reflective exercise adopted from Richard Rohr and based on Psalm 46:10.[9] The contemplative participant is first instructed to find a quiet place, gently close their eyes, and take a few deep breaths. They are then led to pray, either aloud or quietly to themselves, the following diminishing sentences, with an appropriate length of silence between them:[10]

> Be still and know that I am God.
>
> Be still and know that I am.
>
> Be still and know.
>
> Be still.
>
> Be.

A potential problem with this reflective prayer exercise is that it reduces to the individual existentialism of the atheist. As potential corrective, it can be used as a palindrome poem, or mirrored poem, which is first read forward, and then read backward.[11] The second reading then begins with "Be," the mindfulness of existence. "Be still" is the mindfulness that there is nothing we can actively do to achieve the ultimate. "Be still and know" is the mindfulness that there is something more to be known, through stillness. "Be still and know that I am" is the mindfulness that there is an Other to be

---

9. https://gravitycenter.com/practice/be-still/.

10. My friend Jake Friesen, to whom this book is dedicated, together with his wife Val Hiebert, would often use this reflection during the weeks when he was dying from cancer.

11. A well-known example of a palindrome poem is Jonathan Reed's "The Lost Generation."

known. "Be still and know that I am God" is the mindfulness of the divine transcendent, the holy, Wholly Other, the Great I AM. Thus,

> Be.
>
> Be still.
>
> Be still and know.
>
> Be still and know that I am.
>
> Be still and know that I am God.

This is thinking ourselves toward God, a mindfulness of self that begins with the existential human "be," and ends in relationship with the divine transcendent "I AM." And so, longingly,

> "My soul waits in silence for God alone."
>
> PSALM 62:1

BIBLIOGRAPHY

Adorno, Theodor W., et al. *The Authoritarian Personality*. New York: Harper, 1950.
Allender, Dan B. *Sabbath*. Nashville: Thomas Nelson, 2010.
Allport, Gordon W. *The Person in Psychology: Selected Essays*. Boston: Beacon, 1968.
———. "The Religious Context of Prejudice." *Journal for the Scientific Study of Religion* 5 (1966) 447–57.
Alston, William P. *Perceiving God: The Epistemology of Religious Experience*. Ithaca: Cornell University Press, 1993.
Alter, Robert. *Genesis: Translation and Commentary*. New York: W. W. Norton, 1996.
———. The Hebrew Bible: A Translation with Commentary. 3rd ed. New York: W. W. Norton, 2019.
"America's Changing Religious Landscape," Pew Research Center, May 12, 2015. http://www.pewforum.org/2015/05/12/americas-changing-religious-landscape/.
Ammerman, Nancey Tatom. *Sacred Stories, Spiritual Tribes: Finding Religion in Everyday Life*. New York: Oxford University Press, 2014.
Appelrouth, Scott A., and Laura Desfor Edles. *Classical and Contemporary Sociological Theory: Text and Readings*. 3rd ed. Thousand Oaks, CA: Sage, 2015.
Applegate, Kathryn. *How I Changed My Mind about Evolution: Evangelicals Reflect on Faith and Science*. Downers Grove, IL: InterVarsity, 2016.
Archer, Margaret, et al. "What is Critical Realism?" *Perspectives: A Newsletter of the ASA Theory Section*, December 23, 2016. http://www.asatheory.org/current-newsletter-online/what-is-critical-realism.
Armstrong, Karen. *The Case for God*. New York: Alfred A. Knopf, 2009.
Ashton, Michael C., et al. "A Six-Factor Structure of Personality-Descriptive Adjectives: Solutions from Psycholexical Studies in Seven Languages." *Journal of Personality and Social Psychology* 86 (2004) 353–66.
Baer, Jonathan R. "The Making of the New Spirituality: The Eclipse of the Western Religious Tradition." *Fides Et Historia* 37 (2005) 284–87.
Barber, Benjamin. *Jihad vs. McWorld*. New York: Times, 1995.
Barrett, Justin L. "Intellectual Humility." *The Journal of Positive Psychology* 12 (2017) 1–2.
Barton, Mukti. "I am Black and Beautiful." *Black Theology: An International Journal* 2 (2004) 167–87.
Bass, Diana Butler. *Christianity After Religion: The End of Church and the Birth of a New Spiritual Awakening*. San Francisco: HarperOne, 2012.

———. *Grounded: Finding God in the World—A Spiritual Revolution*. San Francisco: HarperOne, 2015.

Baudrillard, Jean. *Simulacra and Simulation*. Translated by Sheila Faria Glaser. Ann Arbor: University of Michigan Press, 1994.

Baue, Frederic W. *The Spiritual Society: What Lurks beyond Postmodernism?* Wheaton, IL: Crossway, 2001.

Baugus, Bruce P. "Paradox and Mystery in Theology." *Heythrop Journal* 54 (2013) 238–51.

Bauman, Zygmunt. *Modernity and the Holocaust*. Ithaca: Cornell University Press, 1989.

Becker, Dana, and Jeanne Marecek. "Positive Psychology: History in the Remaking?" *Theory and Psychology* 18 (2008) 591–604.

"Being Christian in Western Europe," Pew Research Center, May 29, 2018. http://www.pewforum.org/2018/05/29/being-christian-in-western-europe/.

Bell, Rob. *Sex God: Exploring the Endless Connections between Sexuality and Spirituality*. Grand Rapids: Zondervan, 2007.

Bellah, Robert, et al. *Habits of the Heart: Individualism and Commitment in American Life*. New York: Harper & Row, 1985.

———. "Religious Evolution." *American Sociological Review* 23 (1964) 358–74.

Benner, David. *Spirituality and the Awakening Self: The Sacred Journey of Transformation*. Grand Rapids: Brazos, 2012.

Benson, Robert. *In Constant Prayer*. Nashville: Thomas Nelson, 2010.

Berger, Peter L., ed. *The Desecularization of the World: Resurgent Religion and World Politics*. Grand Rapids: Eerdmans, 1999.

———. *The Sacred Canopy: Elements of a Sociological Theory of Religion*. Garden City, NY: Doubleday, 1967.

Berger, Peter L., and Thomas Luckmann. *The Social Construction of Reality: A Treatise in the Sociology of Knowledge*. Garden City, NY: Doubleday, 1967.

Bertrand, J. Mark. *(Re)Thinking Worldview: Learning to Think, Live, and Speak in this World*. Wheaton, IL: Crossway, 2007.

Bhaskar, Roy. *The Possibility of Naturalism: A Philosophical Critique of the Contemporary Human Science*. Atlantic Highlands, NJ: Humanities, 1979.

———. *A Realist Theory of Science*. London: Verso, 1975.

———. *Scientific Realism and Human Emancipation*. London: Verso, 1986.

Bibby, Reginald. *Resilient Gods: Being Pro-Religious, Low Religious, or No Religious in Canada*. Vancouver: UBC Press, 2017.

Bielo, James S. *Emerging Evangelicals: Faith, Modernity, and the Desire for Authenticity*. New York: New York University Press, 2011.

Bisagno, John R. *Love is Something You Do*. Houston: Lucid, 2010.

Blackburn, Simon, and Keith Simmons, eds. *Truth*. Oxford: Oxford University Press, 1999.

Bollinger, Richard A., and Peter C. Hill. "Humility." In *Religion, Spirituality, and Positive Psychology: Understanding the Psychological Fruits of Faith*, edited by Thomas G. Plante, 31–48. Santa Barbara: Praeger/ABC-CLIO, 2012.

Bomford, Rodney. "God and the Unconscious." Paper presented at "God and the Unconscious," St Marylebone, London, October 2000.

———. *The Symmetry of God*. New York: Free Association, 1999.

Bonhoeffer, Dietrich. *Papers and Letters from Prison.* Translated and edited by E. Bethge et al. New York: Macmillan, 1953.

Borchert, Donald Marvin. *Embracing Epistemic Humility: Confronting Triumphalism in Three Abrahamic Religions.* Lanham: Lexington, 2013.

Bothwell, Dave. "The McDonaldization of Christian Philosophy." *Maranatha*, 2013. https://dbot hwell.wordpress.com/2013/03/18/the-mcdonaldization-of-christian-philosophy/.

Boyd, Craig A. "Humility, Virtue Epistemology, and the New Atheism." *Theology and Science* 15 (2017) 162–76.

Branum, Josh. "Journal of Psychology and Theology 43." *Journal of Youth Ministry* 14 (2016) 97–100.

Breems, Brad. "Relational Being as Icon or Communal Freedom: Southern Africa's Ubuntu." *Journal of Sociology and Christianity* 6 (2016) 56–79.

"British Social Attitudes: Record Number of Brits with No Religion," NatCen Social Research, September 4, 2017. http://www.natcen.ac.uk/news-media/press-releases/2017/september/british-social-attitudes-record-number-of-brits-with-no-religion/.

Bruce, Steve. *God is Dead: Secularization in the West.* Oxford: Blackwell, 2002.

Bruni, Frank. "The Commander in Chief Who Buried Humility." *The New York Times*, January 22, 2017, SR1.

Bullard, Gabe. "The World's Newest Major Religion: No Religion." *National Geographic*, April 22, 2016. https://news.nationalgeographic.com/2016/04/160422-atheism-agnostic-secular-nones-rising-religion/.

Burge, Ryan, and Paul A. Djupe. "Emergent Church Practices in America: Inclusion and Deliberation in American Congregations." *Review of Religious Research* 57 (2015) 1–23.

Burns, David J. "Self-Construction through Consumption Activities: An Analysis and Review of Alternatives." In *The Self: Beyond the Postmodern Crisis*, edited by Paul C. Vitz and Susan M. Felch, 149–68. Wilmington, DE: ISI, 2006.

Burrows, Mark S. "Words that Reach into the Silence: Mystical Languages of Unsaying." In *Minding the Spirit: The Study of Christian Spirituality*, edited by Elizabeth A. Dryer and Mark S. Burrows, 201–14. Baltimore: Johns Hopkins University Press, 2005.

Butcher, Carmen Acevedo, trans. *The Cloud of Unknowing with the Book of Privy Counsel.* Boulder: Shambhala, 2009.

Byrne, James M. *Religion and the Enlightenment: From Descartes to Kant.* Louisville: Westminster John Knox, 1996.

Callen, Barry L. *Discerning the Divine: God in Christian Theology.* Louisville: Westminster John Knox, 2004.

Campbell, Antony F. *The Whisper of Spirit: A Believable God Today.* Grand Rapids: Eerdmans, 2008.

Carter, Erik C. "The New Monasticism: A Literary Introduction. *Journal of Spiritual Formation and Soul Care* 5 (2012) 268–84.

Casanova, Jose. "Religious Conviction and Intellectual Humility in Public Life: Socio-Theological Reflections." Intellectual Humility and Religious Conviction Workshop, University of Connecticut, 2017.

Cavey, Bruxy. *The End of Religion: Encountering the Subversive Spirituality of Jesus.* Colorado Springs: NavPress, 2007.

Chamberlain, Paul. *Why People Stop Believing*. Eugene, OR: Cascade, 2018.
Chancellor, Joseph, and Sonja Lyubomirsky. "Humble Beginnings: Current Trends, State Perspectives, and Hallmarks of Humility." *Social and Personality Psychology Compass* 7 (2015) 819–33.
Chittister, Joan. *The Liturgical Year*. Nashville: Thomas Nelson, 2010.
Chrisomalis, Stephen. "Philosophical Isms." *The Phrontistery*. http://phrontistery.info/isms.html#top.
Christ, Carol P. "Embodied Embedded Mysticism: Affirming the Self and Others in a Radically Interdependent World." *Journal of Feminist Studies in Religion* 24 (2008) 159–67.
Christen, Markus, et al. "The Semantic Space of Intellectual Humility." *European Conference on Social Intelligence* (2014) 40–49.
Church, Ian M. "The Doxastic Account of Intellectual Humility." In *Logos and Episteme* 7 (2016) 413–33.
Church, Ian M., and Justin L. Barrett. "Intellectual Humility." In *Handbook of Humility: Theory, Research, and Applications*, edited by Everett L. Worthington Jr. et al., 62–75. New York: Routledge, 2017.
Church, Ian M., and Peter L. Samuelson. *Intellectual Humility: An Introduction to the Philosophy and Science*. New York: Bloomsbury Academic, 2017.
Clapp, Rodney. *Tortured Wonders: Christian Spirituality for People, Not Angels*. Grand Rapids: Brazos, 2004.
Clark, Robert, and S. A. Gaede. "Knowing Together: Reflections on a Holistic Sociology of Knowledge." In *The Reality of Christian Learning: Strategies for Faith-Discipline Integration*, edited by Harold Heie and David L. Wolfe, 55–86. Grand Rapids: Eerdmans, 1987.
Clayton, Philip, and Steven Knapp. *The Predicament of Belief: Science, Philosophy, and Faith*. New York: Oxford University Press, 2011.
Clifford, William K. *Lectures and Essays*. London: Macmillan, 1879.
Clough, Patricia Ticineto, and Jean Halley, eds. *The Affective Turn: Theorizing the Social*. Durham: Duke University Press, 2007.
Cockburn, Bruce. "Forty Years in the Wilderness." *Bone on Bone*. Waterdown, ON: True North Records, 2017.
Cohen, Leonard. "Come Healing." *Old Ideas*. New York: Columbia Records, 2012.
Collins, Kenneth J., ed. *Exploring Christian Spirituality: An Ecumenical Reader*. Grand Rapids: Baker, 2000.
Cooper, David A. *God is a Verb: Kabbalah and the Practice of Jewish Mysticism*. New York: Riverhead, 1998.
Covington, Dennis. *Salvation on Sand Mountain: Snake Handling and Redemption in Southern Appalachia*. New York: Penguin, 1995.
Cowan, Steven B., ed. *Five Views on Apologetics*. Grand Rapids: Zondervan, 2000.
Cox, Harvey. *The Future of Faith: The Rise and Fall of Beliefs and the Coming Age of the Spirit*. San Francisco: HarperOne, 2009.
———. *The Market as God*. Cambridge: Harvard University Press, 2016.
Craig, William Lane. "Classical Apologetics." In *Five Views on Apologetics*, edited by Steven B. Cowan, 25–90. Grand Rapids: Zondervan, 2000.
Crick, Francis. *The Astonishing Hypothesis: The Scientific Search for the Soul*. New York: Simon & Schuster, 1994.

Crouch, Andy. *Playing God: Redeeming the Gift of Power.* Downers Grove, IL: InterVarsity, 2013.

Damasio, Antonio. *Descartes' Error: Emotion, Reason, and the Human Brain.* New York: Penguin, 2005.

———. *Looking for Spinoza: Joy, Sorrow, and the Feeling Brain.* New York: Harcourt, 2003.

Davis, Charles. *Temptations of Religion.* New York: Harper & Row, 1973.

Davis, Don E., et al. "Distinguishing Intellectual Humility and General Humility." *The Journal of Positive Psychology* 11 (2016) 215–24.

———. "Humility and the Development and Repair of Social Bonds: Two Longitudinal Studies." *Self and Identity* 12 (2013) 58–77.

———. "Relational Spirituality and Forgiveness: Development of the Spiritual Humility Scale (SHS)." *Journal of Psychology and Theology* 38 (2010) 91–100.

Davis, Don E., and Joshua N. Hook. "Humility, Religion, and Spirituality: An End Piece." *Journal of Psychology and Theology* 42 (2014) 111–17.

Demarest, Bruce, ed. *Four Views on Christian Spirituality.* Grand Rapids: Zondervan, 2012.

DeWall, C. Nathan. "Fostering Intellectual Humility in Public Discourse and University Education." In *Handbook of Humility: Theory, Research, and Applications,* edited by Everett L. Worthington Jr. et al., 233–45. New York: Routledge, 2017.

DeYoung, Kevin. "Christian Smith Makes the Bible Impossible." *The Gospel Coalition,* August 2, 2011. https://www.thegospelcoalition.org/blogs/kevin-deyoung/christian-smith-makes-the-bible-impossible/.

Dillon, Michelle. "Humility Regained: Public Catholicism with Francis." Intellectual Humility and Religious Conviction Workshop, University of Connecticut, 2017.

Dobbelaere, Karel. *Secularization: An Analysis at Three Levels.* Oxford: Oxford University Press, 2002.

Doherty, Carroll, and Jocelyn Kiley. "Key Facts about Partisanship and Political Animosity in America." Pew Research Center, June 22, 2016. https://www.pewresearch.org/fact-tank/2016/06/22/key-facts-partisanship/.

Doukhan, Abigail. "Christianity for Postmoderns: From Metanarrative to Storytelling." In *Revisiting Postmodernism: An Old Debate on a New Era,* edited by Bruce L. Bauer and Kleber O. Gonçalves, 43–52. Berrien Springs, MI: Andrews University Department of World Mission, 2013.

Drane, John. *After McDonaldization: Mission, Ministry, and Christian Discipleship in an Age of Uncertainty.* Grand Rapids: Baker Academic, 2008.

———. *The McDonaldization of the Church: Spirituality, Creativity, and the Future of the Church.* Macon, GA: Smyth & Helwys, 2008.

Dreher, Rod. *The Benedict Option: A Strategy for Christians in a Post-Christian Nation.* New York: Sentinel, 2017.

Drescher, Elizabeth. *Choosing Our Religion: The Spiritual Lives of America's Nones.* New York: Oxford University Press, 2016.

Dunnington, Kent. "Intellectual Humility and the Ends of Virtues: Conflicting Aretaic Desiderata." *Political Theology* 18 (2017) 95–114.

Durkheim, Emile. *The Elementary Forms of the Religious Life.* Translated by Joseph Ward Swain. New York: Free Press, 1912/1965.

Eliot, T. S. *The Waste Land.* New York: Horace Liveright, 1922.

Elkins, D. N., et al. "Towards a Humanistic-Phenomenological Spirituality: Definition, Description and Measurement." *Journal of Humanistic Psychology* 28 (1988) 5–18.

Englert, Robert W. "Desire and Symbol: Two Aspects of *The Cloud of Unknowing*." *The Way* 41 (2001) 52–60.

Enns, Peter. *The Sin of Certainty: Why God Desires Our Trust More Than Our "Correct" Beliefs*. San Francisco: HarperOne, 2016.

Entwistle, David N. *Integrative Approaches to Psychology and Christianity: An Introduction to Worldview Issues, Philosophical Foundations, and Models of Integration*. 3rd ed. Eugene, OR: Cascade, 2015.

Erlandson, Sven. *Spiritual but Not Religious: A Call to Religious Revolution in America*. Bloomington, IN: iUniverse, 2000.

Exline, Julie J., et al. "Humility and Modesty." In *Character Strengths and Virtues: A Handbook and Classification*, edited by Christopher Peterson and Martin E. P. Seligman, 461–75. New York: Oxford University Press, 2004.

Fisch, Menachem. "A Modest Proposal: Towards a Religious Politics of Epistemic Humility." *Journal of Human Rights* 2 (2003) 49–64.

Flanagan, Kieran. "Introduction." In *A Sociology of Spirituality*, edited by Kieran Flanagan and Peter C. Jupp, 1–21. Burlington, VT: Ashgate, 2007.

Flanagan, Kieran, and Peter C. Jupp, eds. *A Sociology of Spirituality*. Burlington, VT: Ashgate, 2007.

Flint, William C. "A Critical Sociology of Knowledge Paradigms: Comparing Premodern, Modern, and Postmodern Thought." *Free Inquiry in Creative Sociology* 21 (1993) 37–44.

Fortin, Jean-Pierre. "Christian Rationality: Embracing the Divine Mystery." *Toronto Journal of Theology* 29 (2013) 337–50.

Foster, Charles. *The Sacred Journey*. Nashville: Thomas Nelson, 2010.

Foster, Richard J. *Celebration of Discipline: The Path to Spiritual Growth*. HarperSanFrancisco, 1978.

———. *Streams of Living Water: Essential Practices from the Six Great Traditions of Christian Faith*. San Francisco: HarperOne, 2001.

Fowler, James W. *Stages of Faith: The Psychology of Human Development and the Quest for Meaning*. San Francisco: HarperOne, 1995.

Frankl, Victor. *Man's Search for Meaning*. Boston: Beacon, 1959.

Fricker, Miranda. *Epistemic Injustice: Power and the Ethics of Knowing*. New York: Oxford University Press, 2009.

Frye, Northrop. *The Double Vision: Language and Meaning in Religion*. Toronto: University of Toronto Press, 1991.

Fuller, Robert. *Spiritual but Not Religious: Understanding Unchurched America*. New York: Oxford University Press, 2001.

Gallagher, Nora. *The Sacred Meal*. Nashville: Thomas Nelson, 2010.

Gilligan, Carol. *In a Different Voice: Psychological Theory and Women's Development*. Cambridge: Harvard University Press, 1982.

Gingerich, Owen. *God's Planet*. Cambridge: Harvard University Press, 2014.

Ginsberg, Allen. *Howl and Other Poems*. San Francisco: City Lights, 1956.

Glicksberg, Charles Irving. *Literature and Religion: A Study in Conflict*. Dallas: Southern Methodist University Press, 1960.

Goffman, Erving. *Presentation of Self in Everyday Life*. Garden City, NY: Anchor, 1959.

Gorski, Philip S. "What is Critical Realism? And Why Should You Care?" *Contemporary Sociology* 42 (2013) 658-70.
Graham, Jesse, et al. "Liberals and Conservatives Rely on Different Sets of Moral Foundations." *Journal of Personality and Social Psychology* 96 (2009) 1029-46.
———. "Moral Foundations Theory: The Pragmatic Validity of Moral Pluralism." *Advances in Experimental Social Psychology* 47 (2013) 55-130.
———. "The Moral Stereotypes of Liberals and Conservatives: Exaggeration of Differences across the Political Spectrum." *PLoS ONE* 7 (2012) e50092.
Greeley, Andrew M. *The Catholic Imagination*. Berkeley: University of California Press, 2000.
———. *Religion as Poetry*. New Brunswick, NJ: Transaction, 1995.
Gregg, Aiden P., and Nikhila Mahadevan. "Intellectual Arrogance and Intellectual Humility: An Evolutionary-Epistemological Account." *Journal of Psychology and Theology* 42 (2014) 7-18.
Gregg, Melissa, and Gregory J. Seigworth, eds. *The Affect Theory Reader*. Durham: Duke University Press, 2010.
Grof, Stanislav. "Brief History of Transpersonal Psychology." *The International Journal of Transpersonal Studies* 27 (2008) 46-54.
Gschwandtner, Christina M. *Postmodern Apologetics? Arguments for God in Contemporary Philosophy*. New York: Fordham University Press, 2012.
Guhin, Jeffrey. "The Problem with 'Just a Theory': Creationism, Climate Change, and the Relation between Certainty and Action." Intellectual Humility and Religious Conviction Workshop, University of Connecticut, 2017.
Gushee, David P. *Changing Our Mind: Definitive 3rd Edition of the Landmark Call for Inclusion of LGBTQ Christians with Response to Critics*. Canton: Read the Spirit, 2017.
Gushee, David P., ed. *A New Evangelical Manifesto: A Kingdom Vision for the Common Good*. Atlanta: Chalice, 2012.
Habermas, Jurgen. *Knowledge and Human Interests*. Boston: Beacon, 1971.
Haidt, Jonathan. *The Righteous Mind: Why Good People are Divided by Politics and Religion*. New York: Pantheon, 2012.
Hall, Douglas J. *The End of Christendom and the Future of Christianity*. Eugene, OR: Wipf & Stock, 2002.
Hamilton, Victor P. *The Book of Genesis: Chapters 1-17*. Grand Rapids: Eerdmans, 1990.
Happold, F. C. *Mysticism: A Study and an Anthology*. 3rd ed. New York: Penguin, 1991.
Harner, Michael J. *The Way of the Shaman*. New York: Harper & Row, 1990.
Harris, Marvin. "History and Significance of the Emic/Etic Distinction." *Annual Review of Anthropology* 5 (1976) 329-50.
Harris, Sam. *Waking Up: A Guide to Spirituality Without Religion*. New York: Simon & Schuster, 2015.
Hartelius, Glenn, et al. "Transpersonal Psychology: Defining the Past, Divining the Future." *Humanistic Psychologist* 35 (2007) 135-60.
Hartley, John. "Bounded Intellectual Humility in Evangelical Struggles over Relations with Muslims and Islam." Intellectual Humility and Religious Conviction Workshop, University of Connecticut, 2017.
Hartman, Andrew. *A War for the Soul of America: A History of the Culture Wars*. Chicago: University of Chicago Press, 2015.

Hastings, Arthur. "Transpersonal Psychology: The Fourth Force." In *Humanistic and Transpersonal Psychology: A Historical and Biographical Sourcebook*, edited by Donald Moss, 192–208. Westport, CT: Greenwood, 1999.

Heelas, Paul, and Linda Woodhead. *The Spiritual Revolution: Why Religion is Giving Way to Spirituality*. Malden, MA: Blackwell, 2005.

Heft, James L., et al., eds. *Learned Ignorance: Intellectual Humility among Jews, Christians, and Muslims*. New York: Oxford University Press, 2011.

Heidegger, Martin. *The Question Concerning Technology and Other Essays*. Translated by William Lovitt. New York: Garland, 1977.

Henry, Gary. "Story and Silence: Transcendence in the Work of Elie Wiesel." *Public Broadcasting Service*. http://www.pbs.org/eliewiesel/life/henry.html.

Herrick, James A. *The Making of the New Spirituality: The Eclipse of the Western Religious Tradition*. Downers Grove, IL: InterVarsity, 2003.

Hewitt, John P., and Randall Stokes. "Disclaimers." In *Social Psychology Through Symbolic Interaction*, edited by Gregory P. Stone and Harvey A. Farberman, 363–74. New York: Macmillan, 1986.

Hick, John. *God and the Universe of Faiths* 2nd ed. London: Oneworld, 1993.

Hiebert, Dennis. "A Call for Civility in Public Dialogue." *Journal of Sociology and Christianity* 8 (2018) 1–5.

———. "The McDonaldization of Protestant Organizations." *Christian Scholar's Review* 29 (1999) 261–79.

———. "The Mechanisms and Morality of Capitalism: A Brief Christian Critique." *Journal of Sociology and Christianity* 9 (2019) 65–81.

———. "Truth and Love in Christian Life." *Journal for the Sociological Integration of Religion and Society* 6 (2016) 30–35.

Hill, Peter C., and Steven J. Sandage. "The Promising but Challenging Case of Humility as a Positive Psychology Virtue." *Journal of Moral Education* 45 (2016) 132–46.

Hirsch, Debra. *Redeeming Sex: Naked Conversations about Sexuality and Spirituality*. Downers Grove, IL: InterVarsity, 2015.

Hodges, Bert H. "Persons as Obligated: A Values-Realizing Psychology in Light of Bakhtin, Macmurray, and Levinas." In *The Self: Beyond the Postmodern Crisis*, edited by Paul C. Vitz and Susan M. Felch, 63–82. Wilmington, DE: ISI, 2006.

Holley, David M. "Confident Religious Faith and Intellectual Virtue." *International Philosophical Quarterly* 57 (2017) 211–26.

Hood, Ralph W., Jr., and W. Paul Williamson. *Them That Believe: The Power and Meaning of the Christian Serpent-Handling Tradition*. Berkeley: University of California Press, 2008.

Hood, Ralph W., Jr., and Zhuo Chen. "Mystical, Spiritual, and Religious Experiences." In *Handbook of the Psychology of Religion and Spirituality*, edited by Raymond F. Paloutzian and Crystal L. Park, 422–40. New York: Guilford, 2014.

———. "The Social Scientific Study of Christian Mysticism." In *The Wiley-Blackwell Companion to Christian Mysticism*, edited by Julia. A. Lamm, 577–91. Hoboken: Wiley-Blackwell, 2013.

Hook, Joshua N., and Don E. Davis. "Humility, Religion, and Spirituality: Introduction to the Special Issue." *Journal of Psychology and Theology* 42 (2014) 3–6.

———. "Intellectual Humility and Religious Tolerance." *Journal of Positive Psychology* 12 (2017) 29–35.

Hopkin, Cameron R., et al. "Intellectual Humility and Reactions to Opinions about Religious Beliefs." *Journal of Psychology and Theology* 42 (2014) 50–61.

Horton, Michael S. *The Christian Faith: A Systematic Theology for Pilgrims on the Way.* Grand Rapids: Zondervan, 2011.

Howard, Evan B. *The Brazos Introduction to Christian Spirituality.* Grand Rapids: Brazos, 2008.

Hoyle, R. H., et al. "Holding Specific Views with Humility: Conceptualization and Measurement of Specific Intellectual Humility." *Personality and Individual Differences* 97 (2016) 165–72.

Hunter, James Davison. *Culture Wars: The Struggle to Control the Family, Art, Education, Law, and Politics in America.* New York: Basic, 1991.

———. *To Change the World: The Irony, Tragedy, and Possibility of Christianity in the Late Modern World.* New York: Oxford University Press, 2010.

Hunter, James Davison, and Carl Desportes Bowman. *The Vanishing Center of American Democracy: The 2016 Survey of American Political Culture.* Charlottesville: Advanced Studies in Culture Foundation, 2016.

Hunter, James Davison, and Paul Nedelisky. *Science and the Good: The Tragic Quest for the Foundations of Morality.* New Haven, CT: Yale University Press, 2018.

Huntington, Samuel P. "The Challenger Civilizations: On the West's Declining Ability to Promote a Universal Culture." *Harvard Magazine* (1997). https://harvardmagazine.com/1997/01/forum.html.

———. *The Clash of Civilizations and the Remaking of World Order.* New York: Simon & Schuster, 1996.

Huss, Boaz. "Spirituality: The Emergence of a New Cultural Category and its Challenge to the Religious and the Secular." *Journal of Contemporary Religion* 29 (2014) 47–60.

Idris-Soven, Ahamed, et al. *The World as a Company Town: Multinational Corporations and Social Change.* Berlin: Mouton de Gruyter, 1978.

Imperatori-Lee, Natalia. "Father Knows Best: Theological 'Mansplaining' and the Ecclesial War on Women." *Journal of Feminist Studies in Religion* 31 (2015) 89–107.

Irlenborn, Bernd. "Religious Diversity: A Philosophical Defense of Religious Inclusivism." *European Journal for Philosophy of Religion* 1 (2010) 127–40.

Izzard, Susannah. "Holding Contradictions Together: An Object-Relational View of Healthy Spirituality." *Contact* 140 (2003) 2–8.

Jacobsen, Douglas, and Rhonda Hustedt Jacobsen. *Scholarship and Christian Faith: Enlarging the Conversation.* New York: Oxford University Press, 2004.

James, William. *Pragmatism: A New Name for Some Old Ways of Thinking.* New York: Longmans, Green, and Co., 1908.

———. *The Varieties of Religious Experience: A Study in Human Nature.* New York: Longmans, Green and Co., 1902.

Jarvinen, Matthew J., and Thomas B. Paulus. "Attachment and Cognitive Openness: Emotional Underpinnings of Intellectual Humility." *Journal of Positive Psychology* 12 (2017) 74–86.

Jaschik, Scott. "Calling Out Academic 'Mansplaining.'" *Inside Higher Ed*, October 16, 2012. https://www.insidehighered.com/news/2012/10/16/new-website-provides-outlet-victims-academic-mansplaining.

Johnson, Casey, et al. "Intellectual Humility." *Oxford Bibliographies* (2017). https://www.oxfordbibliographies.com/view/document/obo-9780195396577/OBO-9780195396577-0347.xml.

Johnson, Kathryn Ann, et al. "Intellectual Humility and Forgiveness of Religious Conflict." *Journal of Psychology and Theology* 43 (2015) 255–62.

Johnstone, Ronald. *Religion in Society: A Sociology of Religion*. 8th ed. New York: Routledge, 2006.

Jones, Tony. *The Church is Flat: The Relational Ecclesiology of the Emerging Church Movement*. Minneapolis: JoPa Group, 2011.

Joslin, Roger. *Running the Spiritual Path: A Runner's Guide to Breathing, Meditating, and Exploring the Prayerful Dimension of the Sport*. New York: St. Martin's Griffin, 2004.

Jung, Carl. "The Spiritual Problem of Modern Man." In *The Jung Reader*, edited by David Tracey, 217–31. New York: Routledge, 2012.

Kapuscinski, Afton, and Kevin S. Masters. "The Current Status of Measures of Spirituality: A Critical Review of Scale Development." *Psychology of Religion and Spirituality* 2 (2010) 191–205.

Keenan, William J. F. "A Phoney Holy War: Reflections on the Myth of Spiritual Revolution." *Implicit Religion* 19 (2016) 131–98.

Kelly, Kevin. *The Inevitable: Understanding the 12 Technological Forces That Will Shape Our Future*. New York: Penguin, 2017.

Kennedy, Rick. "Educating Bees: Humility as a Craft in Classical and Christian Liberal Arts." *Christian Scholar's Review* 42 (2012) 29–42.

Kierkegaard, Søren. *Concluding Unscientific Postscript to Philosophical Fragments*, edited and translated by Howard V. Hong and Edna H. Hong. Princeton: Princeton University Press, 1992.

———. *Philosophical Fragments / Johannes Climacus*, edited and translated by Howard V. Hong and Edna H. Hong. Princeton: Princeton University Press, 1985.

Kim-Prieto, Chu, ed. *Religion and Spirituality across Cultures*. New York: Springer, 2014.

Kinnaman, David, and Gabe Lyons. *Good Faith: Being a Christian When Society Thinks You're Irrelevant and Extreme*. Grand Rapids: Baker, 2016.

Klostermaier, Klaus. *Hindu and Christian in Vrindaban*. London: SCM-Canterbury, 1971.

Knowles, David. *The English Mystical Tradition*. New York: Harper, 1961.

Koenig, Harold G. "Religion, Spirituality, and Health: The Research and Clinical Implications." *ISRN Psychiatry* (2012) 1–33.

Kohlberg, Lawrence. "Stage and Sequence: The Cognitive-Developmental Approach to Socialization." In *Handbook of Socialization Theory and Research*, edited by D. A. Goslin, 347–480. Chicago: Rand McNally, 1969.

Krumrei-Mancuso, Elizabeth J. "Intellectual Humility and Prosocial Values: Direct and Mediated Effects." *Journal of Positive Psychology* 12 (2017) 13–28.

———. "We Know in Part: Debunking Myths About Intellectual Humility." *The Table*, September 15, 2014. https://cct.biola.edu/we-know-part-debunking-myths-about-intellect ual-humility/.

Krumrei-Mancuso, Elizabeth J., and Steven V. Rouse. "The Development and Validation of the Comprehensive Intellectual Humility Scale." *Journal of Personality Assessment* 98 (2016) 209–21.

Kubsch, Ron. "Why Christianity is an Emancipation Narrative for Francois Lyotard." *Philosophical Initiatives: MBS Texte* 93, 2008. https://www.researchgate.net/publication/327221684_Why_Christianity_is_an_Emancipation_Narrative_for_Francois_Lyotard.

Kugler, Matthew, et al. "Another Look at Moral Foundations Theory: Do Authoritarianism and Social Dominance Orientation Explain Liberal-Conservative Differences in 'Moral' Intuitions?" *Social Justice Research* 27 (2014) 413–31.

Kuhn, Thomas S. *The Structure of Scientific Revolutions*. 4th ed. Chicago: University of Chicago Press, 2012.

Kundera, Milan. *Immortality*. New York: Grove Weidenfeld, 1991.

Kuyper, Abraham. *Common Grace: God's Gifts for a Fallen World*. Bellingham, WA: Lexham, 2015.

Lamm, Julia A. "A Guide to Christian Mysticism." In *The Wiley-Blackwell Companion to Christian Mysticism*, edited by Julia A. Lamm, 1–23. Hoboken: Wiley-Blackwell, 2013.

Lamott, Anne. *Help, Thanks, Wow: The Three Essential Prayers*. New York: Riverhead, 2012.

———. *Plan B: Further Thoughts on Faith*. New York: Riverhead Trade, 2006.

Leary, Mark R., et al. "Cognitive and Interpersonal Features of Intellectual Humility." *Personality and Social Psychology Bulletin* 43 (2017) 793–813.

Leblanc, Douglas. *Tithing: Test Me in This*. Nashville: Thomas Nelson, 2010.

Lee, Kibeom, and Michael C. Ashton. "Psychometric Properties of the HEXACO Personality Inventory." *Multivariate Behavioral Research* 39 (2004) 329–58.

Lewis, Bernard. "'I'm Right, You're Wrong, Go to Hell: Religions and the Meeting of Civilizations." *The Atlantic Monthly* 291 (2003) 36–42.

Lewis, C. S. *The Abolition of Man*. San Francisco: HarperOne, 2015.

———. "The Apologist's Evening Prayer." In *Poems*, edited by Walter Hooper, 129. New York: Harcourt Brace Jovanovich, 1964.

———. "Footnote to All Prayers." In *Poems*, edited by Walter Hooper, 129. New York: Harcourt Brace Jovanovich, 1964.

———. *Mere Christianity*. San Francisco: HarperSanFrancisco, 2015.

———. *The Problem of Pain*. San Francisco: HarperOne, 1996.

Linafelt, Tod. "The Undecidability of *barak* in the Prologue to Job and Beyond." *Biblical Interpretation* 4 (1996) 154–72.

Lipka, Michael, and Claire Gecewicz. "More Americans Now Say They're Spiritual but Not Religious." Pew Research Center, September 6, 2017. http://www.pewresearch.org/fact-tank/2017/09/06/more-americans-now-say-theyre-spiritual-but-not-religious/.

Livingstone, D. N. "Farewell to Arms: Reflections on the Encounter between Science and Faith." In *Christian Faith and Practice in the Modern World: Theology from an Evangelical Point of View*, edited by Mark A. Noll and David F. Wells, 239–62. Grand Rapids: Eerdmans, 1988.

Luckmann, Thomas. *The Invisible Religion: The Problem of Religion in Modern Society*. New York: Macmillan, 1967.

Lyotard, Jean-Francois. *The Postmodern Condition: A Report on Knowledge*. Minneapolis: University of Minnesota Press, 1984.

———. *The Postmodern Explained*. Minneapolis: University of Minnesota Press, 2003.

Macaskill, Grant. "Humility for Creatures and Sinners: A New Testament Vision of Intellectual Humility." *The Table*, Biola University, 2016. https://cct.biola.edu/new-testament-vision-intellectual-humility/.

MacIntyre, Alasdair. *After Virtue: A Study in Moral Theory*. Notre Dame: University of Notre Dame Press, 1981.

———. *Whose Justice? Which Rationality?* Notre Dame: University of Notre Dame Press, 1989.

MacKenna, C. "Self Images and God Images." Paper presented at "God and the Unconscious," St Marylebone, London, October 2000.

Markofski, Wes. "American Evangelicalism, Social Reflexivity, and Intellectual Humility in Public Life." Intellectual Humility and Religious Conviction Workshop, University of Connecticut, 2017.

———. *New Monasticism and the Transformation of American Evangelicalism*. New York: Oxford University Press, 2015.

Marske, Charles E. "Durkheim's 'Cult of the Individual' and the Moral Reconstitution of Society." *Sociological Theory* 5 (1987) 1–14.

Martel, Yann. *Life of Pi: A Novel*. New York: Vintage, 2001.

Marti, Gerardo, and Gladys Ganiel. *The Deconstructed Church: Understanding Emerging Christianity*. New York: Oxford University Press, 2014.

Martin, Craig. *Capitalizing Religion: Ideology and the Opiate of the Bourgeoisie*. London: Bloomsbury, 2014.

Martin, Philip. *How to Write Your Best Story: Advice for Writers on Spinning an Enchanting Tale*. Milwaukee: Crickhollow, 2011.

Maslow, Abraham. *Motivation and Personality*. New York: Harper & Row, 1954.

Massumi, Brian. *Parables for the Virtual: Movement, Affect, Sensation*. Durham: Duke University Press, 2002.

Matthias, Laurie R. "Professors Who Walk Humbly with Their God: Exemplars in the Integration of Faith and Learning at Wheaton College." *Journal of Education and Christian Belief* 12 (2008) 145–57.

McCullough, Michael E., et al, eds. *Forgiveness: Theory, Research, and Practice*. New York: Guilford, 2001.

McDowell, Josh. *The New Evidence that Demands a Verdict*. Milton Keynes: Authentic, 2004.

McElroy, Stacey E., et al. "Intellectual Humility: Scale Development and Theoretical Elaborations in the Context of Religious Leadership." *Journal of Psychology and Theology* 42 (2014) 19–30.

McGinn, Bernard. *The Presence of God: A History of Western Christian Mysticism*, Vol. 3: *The Flowering of Mysticism: Men and Women in the New Mysticism, 1200–1350*. New York: Crossroad, 1998.

McGrath, Alister E. *Christian Spirituality: An Introduction*. Malden: Blackwell, 1999.

———. *Mere Apologetics: How to Help Seekers and Skeptics Find Faith*. Grand Rapids: Baker, 2012.

McGuire, Meredith B. *Lived Religion: Faith and Practice in Everyday Life*. New York: Oxford University Press, 2008.

———. *Religion: The Social Context*. 5th ed. Long Grove, IL: Waveland, 2002.

McKnight, Scot. *Fasting*. Nashville: Thomas Nelson, 2010.

McLaren, Brian D. *Everything Must Change: When the World's Biggest Problems and Jesus' Good News Collide*. Toronto: Nelson, 2009.

———. *Finding Our Way Again: The Return of the Ancient Practices*. Nashville: Thomas Nelson, 2010.

———. *A Generous Orthodoxy*. Grand Rapids: Zondervan, 2004.

———. *The Great Spiritual Migration: How the World's Largest Religion is Seeking a Better Way to Be Christian*. New York: Convergent, 2017.

———. *We Make the Road by Walking*. New York: Jericho, 2014.

McMinn, Lisa Graham. *Sexuality and Holy Longing: Embracing Intimacy in a Broken World*. San Francisco: Jossey-Bass, 2004.

McMinn, Mark R. *The Science of Virtue: Why Positive Psychology Matters to the Church*. Grand Rapids: Brazos, 2017.

Mead, George Herbert. *Mind, Self and Society: From the Standpoint of a Social Behaviorist*. Chicago: University of Chicago Press, 1934/1962.

Meagher, Benjamin R., et al. "Contrasting Self-Report and Consensus Ratings of Intellectual Humility and Arrogance." *Journal of Research in Personality* 58 (2015) 35–45.

"Meet Those Who 'Love Jesus but Not the Church,'" Barna Group, March 30, 2017. https://www.barna.com/research/meet-love-jesus-not-church/.

Mercandante, Linda A. *Belief Without Borders: Inside the Minds of the Spiritual but Not Religious*. New York: Oxford University Press, 2014.

Merritt, Jonathan. "Is AI a Threat to Christianity?" *The Atlantic*, February 3, 2017. https://www.theatlantic.com/technology/archive/2017/02/artificial-intelligence-christianity/515463/.

Miller, Kevin D. "Reframing the Faith-Learning Relationship: Bonhoeffer and an Incarnational Alternative to the Integration Model." *Christian Scholar's Review* 43 (2014) 131–38.

Miller, William R., and Carl E. Thoresen. "Spirituality, Religion, and Health: An Emerging Research Field." *American Psychologist* 58 (2003) 24–35.

Moore, Brooke N., and Richard Parker. *Critical Thinking*. 12th ed. New York: McGraw-Hill, 2017.

Moore, Stephen D. *God's Beauty Parlor: And Other Queer Spaces in and Around the Bible*. Stanford: Stanford University Press, 2002.

Moroney, Stephen. "Where Faith and Learning Intersect: Re-Mapping the Contemporary Terrain." *Christian Scholar's Review* 43 (2014) 139–55.

"Mystical Experiences." Pew Research Center, December 29, 2009. https://www.pewresearch.org/fact-tank/2009/12/29/mystical-experiences/.

Nelson, J. B., and S. P. Longfellow. *Sexuality and the Sacred: Sources for Theological Reflection*. Louisville: Westminster/John Knox, 1994.

Nelson, Robert H. *The New Holy Wars: Economic Religion vs. Environmental Religion in Contemporary America*. University Park: Pennsylvania State University Press, 2010.

Neufeld, Edmund K. "The Gospel in the Gospels: Answering the Question 'What Must I Do to be Saved?' from the Synoptics." *Journal of the Evangelical Theological Society* 51 (2008) 267–96.

Newbigin, Lesslie. *Foolishness to the Greeks: The Gospel and Western Culture*. Grand Rapids: Eerdmans, 1988.

———. *Proper Confidence: Faith, Doubt, and Certainty in Christian Discipleship*. Grand Rapids: Eerdmans, 1995.

Nietzsche, Friedrich. "Thus Spoke Zarathustra." In *The Portable Nietzsche*, translated and edited by Walter Kauffman, 103–440. New York: Viking, 1954.

Nisbett, Richard. *The Geography of Thought: How Asians and Westerners Think Differently . . . And Why*. New York: Free Press, 2004.

Norwine, Jim, et al. "Personal Identity: Postmodern or Transmodern? A Study of College and University Undergraduates at the Turn of the Millennium." In *The Self: Beyond the Postmodern Crisis*, edited by Paul C. Vitz and Susan M. Felch, 203–24. Wilmington, DE: ISI, 2006.

O'Dea, Thomas. *The Sociology of Religion*. Upper Saddle River, NJ: Prentice-Hall, 1966.

Oman, Doug. "Defining Religion and Spirituality." In *Handbook of the Psychology of Religion and Spirituality*, edited by Raymond F. Paloutzian and Crystal L. Park, 23–47. New York: Guilford, 2014.

Otto, Rudolph. *The Idea of the Holy*. Translated by J. W. Harvey. New York: Oxford University Press, 1923.

Packard, Josh, and Ashleigh Hope. *Church Refugees: Sociologists Reveal Why People are Done with Church But Not Their Faith*. Loveland, CO: Group, 2015.

———. *The Emerging Church: Religion at the Margins*. Boulder: First Forum, 2012.

Palmer, Parker J. *The Promise of Paradox: A Celebration of Contradictions in the Christian Life*. New York: Jossey-Bass, 2008.

Paloutzian, Raymond F., and Crystal L. Park. "Recent Progress and Core Issues in the Science of the Psychology of Religion and Spirituality." In *Handbook of the Psychology of Religion and Spirituality*, edited by Raymond F. Paloutzian and Crystal L. Park, 3–22. New York: Guilford, 2014.

Panikkar, Raimon. *The Intrareligious Dialogue*. New York: Paulist, 1978.

Pargament, K. I. "Of Means and Ends: Religion and the Search of Significance." *The International Journal for the Psychology of Religion* 2 (1992) 201–29.

Pascal, Blaise. *Pensées*. Translated by W. F. Trotter. Scotts Valley, CA: CreateSpace Independent, 2011.

Penner, Myron Bradley. *The End of Apologetics: Christian Witness in a Postmodern Context*. Grand Rapids: Baker Academic, 2013.

Peterson, Christopher, and Martin E. P. Seligman. *Character Strengths and Virtues: A Handbook and Classification*. New York: Oxford University Press, 2004.

Peterson, Michael, et al. *Reason and Religious Belief: An Introduction to the Philosophy of Religion*. 5th ed. New York: Oxford University Press, 2013.

Piedmont, Ralph L. "Looking Back and Finding Our Way Forward: An Editorial Call to Action." *Psychology of Religion and Spirituality* 6 (2014) 265–67.

Pieper, Josef. *The Silence of St. Thomas*. Chicago: Gateway, 1957.

Pinker, Steven. *Enlightenment Now: The Case for Reason, Science, Humanism, and Progress*. New York: Viking, 2018.

Plantinga, Alvin. "Pluralism: A Defense of Religious Exclusivism." In *The Philosophical Challenge of Religious Diversity*, edited by Kevin Meeker and Philip Quinn, 172–92. New York: Oxford University Press, 1999.

———. "Reason and Belief in God." In *Faith and Rationality: Reason and Belief in God*, edited by Alvin Plantinga and Nicholas Wolterstorff, 16–93. Notre Dame: University of Notre Dame Press, 1983.

———. *Where the Conflict Really Lies: Science, Religion, and Naturalism*. New York: Oxford University Press, 2011.

Pond, Lauren. *Test of Faith: Signs, Serpents, Salvation*. Durham: Duke University Press, 2017.
Porter, Steven L. "Religious Perspectives on Humility." In *Handbook of Humility: Theory, Research, and Applications*, edited by Everett L. Worthington Jr. et al., 47–61. New York: Routledge, 2017.
Pseudo-Dionysius. *The Mystical Theology*. In *Pseudo-Dionysius: The Complete Works*, translated by Colm Luibheid. New York: Paulist, 1987.
Putnam, Ruth Anna. "Perceiving Facts and Values." *Philosophy* 73 (1998) 5–19.
Race, Alan. *Christians and Religious Pluralism: Patterns in the Christian Theology of Religions*. Maryknoll, NY: Orbis, 1982.
Rahner, Karl. "The Human Question of Meaning in the Face of the Absolute Mystery of God." In *Theological Investigations*, translated by E. Quinn, 89–104. London: Darton, Longman, & Todd, 1983.
Rawls, John. *Justice as Fairness: A Restatement*. 2nd ed. Cambridge: Belknap, 2001.
———. *Political Liberalism*. New York: Columbia University Press, 2005.
Reed, Jonathan. "The Lost Generation." https://genius.com/Jonathan-reed-the-lost-generation-annotated.
Reitan, Eric. *The Triumph of Love: Same-Sex Marriage and the Christian Love Ethic*. Eugene, OR: Cascade, 2017.
"Religion and Faith in Canada Today," Angus Reid Institute, 2015. http://angusreid.org/faith-in-canada/.
Renton, Jennie. "Yann Martel Interview." *Textualities*, 2005. http://textualities.net/jennie-renton/yann-martel-interview.
Reuschling, Wyndy Corbin. *Desire for God and the Things of God: The Relationships between Christian Spirituality and Morality*. Eugene, OR: Cascade, 2012.
Riis, Ole, and Linda Whitehead. *A Sociology of Religious Emotion*. New York: Oxford University Press, 2010.
Ritzer, George. *Enchanting a Disenchanted World: Continuity and Change in the Cathedrals of Consumption*. 3rd ed. Thousand Oaks, CA: Pine Forge, 2010.
———. *The McDonaldization of Society: Into the Digital Age*. 9th ed. Thousand Oaks, CA: Pine Forge, 2018.
Ritzer, George, and Jeffrey Stepnisky. *Sociological Theory*. 10th ed. Thousand Oaks, CA: Sage, 2018.
Rizzuto, Ana-Maria. "Exploring Sacred Landscapes." In *Exploring Sacred Landscapes: Religious and Spiritual Experiences in Psychotherapy*, edited by Mary Lou Randour, 16–33. New York: Columbia University Press, 1993.
Roberts, Alexander, and James Donaldson, eds. *The Ante-Nicene Fathers: Volume III*. Translated by Peter Holmes. Grand Rapids: Eerdmans, 1951.
Roberts, Robert C., and W. Jay Wood. "Humility and Epistemic Goods." In *Intellectual Virtue: Perspectives from Ethics and Epistemology*, edited by Michael DePaul and Linda Zagzebski, 257–80. New York: Oxford University Press, 2003.
———. *Intellectual Virtues: An Essay in Regulative Epistemology*. 4th ed. New York: Oxford University Press, 2009.
Robinson, Brian, and Mark Alfano. "I Know You Are, But What Am I? Anti-individualism in the Development of Intellectual Humility and Wu-Wei." *Logos and Episteme* 7 (2016) 435–59.
Robinson, Marilynne. "Credo." *Harvard Divinity Bulletin* 36, Spring 2008. https://bulletin.hds.harvard.edu/articles/spring2008/credo.

Rolheiser, Ronald. *The Holy Longing: The Search for a Christian Spirituality*. New York: Image, 1998.

———. "Mourning Our Virginity." *Ron Rolheiser*, August 22, 2004. https://ronrolheiser.com/ mourning-our-virginity/#.XO4WPY97ntQ.

Rollins, Peter. *The Divine Magician: The Disappearance of Religion and the Discovery of Faith*. New York: Howard, 2015.

Ross, Andrew. "New Age Technoculture." In *Cultural Studies*, edited by Lawrence Grossberg, Cary Nelson, and Paula Treichler, 531–55. New York: Routledge, 1992.

Rothman, Lily. "A Cultural History of Mansplaining." *The Atlantic*, November 1, 2012. https:// www.theatlantic.com/sexes/archive/2012/11/a-cultural-history-of-mansplaining/264380/.

Rozental, Stefan, ed. *Niels Bohr: His Life and Work as Seen by His Friends and Colleagues*. Hoboken, NJ: Wiley, 1967.

Russell, Bertrand. *The Problems of Philosophy*. London: Oxford University Press, 1967.

Saint-Andre, Peter. *The Ism Book: A Field Guide to Philosophy*. N.p.: Monadnock Valley, 2013.

Samuelson, Peter L., et al. "Implicit Theories of Intellectual Virtues and Vices: A Focus on Intellectual Humility." *Journal of Positive Psychology* 10 (2015) 389–406.

Sandstrom, Kent L., et al. *Symbols, Selves, and Social Reality: A Symbolic Interactionist Approach to Social Psychology and Sociology*. 4th ed. New York: Oxford University Press, 2014.

Sayer, Andrew. *Realism and Social Science*. Thousand Oaks, CA: Sage, 2000.

Schaeffer, Francis. *How Should We Then Live? The Rise and Decline of Western Thought and Culture*. Wheaton, IL: Crossway, 2005.

Schellenberg, John L. *The Will to Imagine: A Justification of Skeptical Religion*. Ithaca: Cornell University Press, 2012.

———. *The Wisdom to Doubt: A Justification of Religious Skepticism*. Ithaca: Cornell University Press, 2012.

Schillinger, Jamie. "Intellectual Humility and Inter-Religious Dialogue Between Christians and Muslims." *Islam and Christian-Muslim Relations* 23 (2012) 363–80.

Schrödinger, Erwin. "Nature and the Greeks and Science and Humanism." Cambridge: Cambridge University Press, 2014.

Scorgie, Glen G., ed. *Dictionary of Christian Spirituality*. Grand Rapids: Zondervan, 2011.

———. Review of *Four Views on Christian Spirituality*, Edited by Bruce A. Demarest. *Journal of Spiritual Formation and Soul Care* 6 (2013) 288–95.

Seligman, Martin E. P., and Mihaly Csikszentmihalyi. "Positive Psychology: An Introduction." *American Psychologist* 55 (2000) 5–14.

Shaw, Bernard. *Too True to be Good: A Political Extravaganza*. New York: Samuel French, 1933.

Sheldrake, Philip, ed. *The New Westminster Dictionary of Christian Spirituality*. Louisville: Westminster John Knox, 2013.

Simmel, Georg. "The Conflict in Modern Culture." In *The Conflict in Modern Culture and Other Essays*, translated and edited by P. Etzkorn, 11–26. New York: Teachers College, 1918/1968.

———. *The Philosophy of Money*. Translated and edited by Tom Bottomore and David Frisby. London: Routledge and Kegan Paul, 1907/1978.

Slife, Brent D. "Religious Implications of Western Personality Theory." *Pastoral Psychology* 61 (2012) 797–808.

Smith, Christian. *American Evangelicalism: Embattled and Thriving*. Chicago: University of Chicago Press, 1998.

———. *The Bible Made Impossible: Why Biblicism is Not a Truly Evangelical Reading of Scripture*. Grand Rapids: Brazos, 2011.

———. *Moral, Believing Animals: Human Personhood and Culture*. New York: Oxford University Press, 2003.

———. *Religion: What It Is, How It Works, and Why It Matters*. Princeton: Princeton University Press, 2017.

———. *The Sacred Project of American Sociology*. New York: Oxford University Press, 2014.

———. *What is a Person? Rethinking Humanity, Social Life, and the Moral Good from the Person Up*. Chicago: University of Chicago Press, 2010.

———. "Why Christianity Works: An Emotions-Focused Phenomenological Account." *Sociology of Religion* 68 (2007) 165–78.

Smith, Christian, and Melinda Lundquist Denton. *Soul Searching: The Religious and Spiritual Lives of American Teenagers*. New York: Oxford University Press, 2005.

Smith, James K. A. *Desiring the Kingdom: Worship, Worldview, and Cultural Formation*. Grand Rapids: Baker Academic, 2009.

———. "The Future is Catholic: The Next Scandal for the Evangelical Mind." In *The State of the Evangelical Mind: Reflections on the Past, Prospects for the Future*, edited by Todd C. Ream et al., 141–60. Downers Grove, IL: InterVarsity, 2018.

———. *Imagining the Kingdom: How Worship Works*. Grand Rapids: Baker Academic, 2013.

———. *Thinking in Tongues: Pentecostal Contributions to Christian Philosophy*. Grand Rapids: Eerdmans, 2010.

———. *Who's Afraid of Postmodernism? Taking Derrida, Lyotard, and Foucault to Church*. Grand Rapids: Baker Academic, 2006.

———. *You Are What You Love: The Spiritual Power of Habit*. Grand Rapids: Brazos, 2016.

Smith, Wilfred Cantwell. *The Meaning and End of Religion*. New York: Macmillan, 1962.

Solnit, Rebecca. *Men Explain Things to Me*. Chicago: Haymarket, 2014.

Sorokin, Pitirim A. *Social and Cultural Dynamics: A Study of Change in Major Systems of Art, Truth, Ethics, Law, and Social Relationships*. New Brunswick, NJ: Transaction, 1985.

Spiegel, James S. "Open-mindedness and Christian Flourishing." *Christian Psychology* 8 (2014) 38–48.

———. "Open-mindedness and Intellectual Humility." *Theory and Research in Education* 10 (2012) 27–38.

Spufford, Francis. *Unapologetic: Why, Despite Everything, Christianity Can Still Make Surprising Emotional Sense*. London: Farber & Farber, 2012.

Stackhouse, John G. *Humble Apologetics: Defending the Faith Today*. New York: Oxford University Press, 2006.

Stang, Charles M. "Negative Theology from Gregory of Nyssa to Dionysius the Areopagite." In *The Wiley-Blackwell Companion to Christian Mysticism*, edited by Julia A. Lamm, 161–75. Hoboken: Wiley-Blackwell, 2013.

Stark, Rodney. "Secularization, R.I.P." In *The Secularization Debate*, edited by William Swatos Jr. and Daniel V. A. Olson, 41–66. Lanham: Rowman & Littlefield, 2000.

Stark, Rodney, and Roger Finke. *Acts of Faith: Explaining the Human Side of Religion*. Berkeley: University of California Press, 2000.

———. *How the West Won: The Neglected Story of the Triumph of Modernity*. Wilmington, DE: ISI, 2014.

———. *The Victory of Reason: How Christianity Led to Freedom, Capitalism, and Western Success*. New York: Random House, 2006.

Suhler, Christopher L., and Patricia Churchland. "Can Innate, Modular 'Foundations' Explain Morality? Challenges for Haidt's Moral Foundations Theory." *Journal of Cognitive Neuroscience* 23 (2011) 2103–16.

Sullivan, Andrew. "My Problem with Christianism." *Time*, May 15, 2006. http://www.time.com/time/magazine/article/0,9171,1191826,00.html.

Swatos, W. H., Jr. "Religiosity." In *Encyclopedia of Religion and Society*, edited by W. H. Swatos Jr., 406. Walnut Creek, CA: Altamira, 1998.

Swenson, Donald S. *Society, Spirituality, and the Sacred: A Social Scientific Introduction*. 2nd ed. Toronto: University of Toronto Press, 2009.

Tanesini, Alessandra. "'Calm Down Dear': Intellectual Arrogance, Silencing, and Ignorance." *Aristotelian Society: Supplementary Volume* 90 (2016) 71–92.

Tangney, June Price. "Humility: Theoretical Perspectives, Empirical Findings, and Directions for Future Research." *Journal of Social and Clinical Psychology* 19 (2000) 70–82.

Taylor, Charles. "A Catholic Modernity?" In *A Catholic Modernity?* edited by James Heft, 13–37. New York: Oxford University Press, 1999.

———. *The Ethics of Authenticity*. Cambridge: Harvard University Press, 1991.

———. *The Malaise of Modernity*. Toronto: House of Anansi, 1991.

———. *A Secular Age*. Cambridge: Belknap, 2007.

———. *Sources of the Self: The Making of the Modern Identity*. New York: Cambridge University Press, 1989.

Taylor, Daniel. *The Myth of Certainty: The Reflective Christian and the Risk of Commitment*. Downers Grove, IL: InterVarsity, 1999.

———. *The Skeptical Believer: Telling Stories to Your Inner Atheist*. St. Paul: Bog Walk, 2013.

Taylor, Justin. "Why the Christian Narrative is not a 'Metanarrative.'" *The Gospel Coalition*, March 12, 2015. https://www.thegospelcoalition.org/blogs/justin-taylor/why-the-christian-narrative-is-not-a-metanarrative/.

Taylor, Steve. "Moving Beyond Materialism: Can Transpersonal Psychology Contribute to Cultural Transformation?" *The International Journal of Transpersonal Studies* 36 (2017) 147–59.

Taylor, Steve, and Krisztina Egeto-Szabo. "Exploring Awakening Experiences: A Study of Awakening Experiences in Terms of their Triggers, Characteristics, Duration, and After Effects." *Journal of Transpersonal Psychology* 49 (2017) 45–65.

Teasdale, Wayne. *The Mystic Heart: Discovering a Universal Spirituality in the World's Religions*. Novato: New World Library, 2001.

Thiessen, Joel, and Sarah Wilkins-Laflamme. "Becoming a Religious None: Irreligious Socialization and Disaffiliation." *Journal for the Scientific Study of Religion* 56 (2017) 64–82. https://onlinelibrary.wiley.com/doi/pdf/10.1111/jssr.12319.

Thornton, Bruce S. *Greek Ways: How the Greeks Created Western Civilization*. New York: Encounter, 2002.
Tickle, Phyllis. *The Great Emergence: How Christianity is Changing and Why*. Grand Rapids: Baker, 2008.
Trumbull, Henry Clay. *Practical Paradoxes*. Philadelphia: John D. Wattles, 1889.
Tyson, John R., ed. *Invitation to Christian Spirituality: An Ecumenical Anthology*. New York: Oxford University Press, 1999.
Vacek, Edward Collins. "Orthodoxy Requires Orthopathy: Emotions in Theology." *Horizons* 40 (2013) 218–41.
Vago, Steven. *Social Change*. 5th ed. Toronto: Pearson, 2003.
Van Elk, Michiel, and Andre Aleman. "Brain Mechanisms in Religion and Spirituality: An Integrative Predictive Processing Model." *Neuroscience and Biobehavioral Reviews* 73 (2017) 359–78.
Van Tongeren, Daryl R., et al. "Humility Attenuates Negative Attitudes and Behaviors toward Religious Out-group Members." *Journal of Positive Psychology* 11 (2016) 199–208.
Vance, J. D. *Hillbilly Elegy: A Memoir of a Family and Culture in Crisis*. New York: Harper, 2016.
Varga, Ivan. "Georg Simmel: Religion and Spirituality." In *A Sociology of Spirituality*, edited by Kieran Flanagan and Peter C. Jupp, 145–60. Burlington, VT: Ashgate, 2007.
Vaughan, Frances. "Spiritual Issues in Psychotherapy." *The Journal of Transpersonal Psychology* 23 (1991) 105–19.
Verter, Bradford. "Spiritual Capital: Theorizing Religion with Bourdieu Against Bourdieu." *Sociological Theory* 21 (2003) 150–74.
Vitz, Paul C. "The Future of the University: From Postmodern to Transmodern." In *Rethinking the Future of the University*, edited by David Lyle Jeffrey and Dominic Manganiello, 105–16. Ottawa: University of Ottawa Press, 1998.
———. *Psychology as Religion: The Cult of Self-Worship*. 2nd ed. Grand Rapids: Eerdmans, 1994.
Voas, David, and Steve Bruce. "The Spiritual Revolution: Another False Dawn for the Sacred." In *A Sociology of Spirituality*, edited by Kieran Flanagan and Peter C. Jupp, 43–62. Burlington, VT: Ashgate, 2007.
Wallace, Ruth A., and Alison Wolf. *Contemporary Sociological Theory: Expanding the Classical Tradition*. 5th ed. Upper Saddle River, NJ: Prentice Hall, 1999.
Waltz, Alan K. "Wesleyan Quadrilateral." *A Dictionary for United Methodists*. Nashville: Abingdon, 1991. http://www.umc.org/what-we-believe/wesleyan-quadrilateral.
Warren, Tish Harrison. *Liturgy of the Ordinary: Sacred Practices of Everyday Life*. Downers Grove, IL: InterVarsity, 2016.
Webber, Robert E. *Ancient-Future Faith: Rethinking Evangelicalism for a Postmodern World*. Grand Rapids: Baker, 1999.
Weber, Max. *Economy and Society: Vol. I and II*, edited by Guenther Roth and Claus Wittich. Berkeley: University of California Press, 1978.
———. *The Methodology of the Social Sciences*, edited by Edward Shils and Henry Finch. New York: Free Press, 1949.
———. "Science as a Vocation." In *From Max Weber: Essays in Sociology*, translated and edited by Hans H. Gerth and C. Wright Mills, 129–56. New York: Free Press, 1946.

———. *The Sociology of Religion*. Translated by Ephraim Fischoff. Boston: Beacon, 1964.

Wender, Andrew M. "Learning Through Upheaval: Strategies for Analyzing and Construing Emerging Sociopolitical Transformations in the Middle East." *Digest of Middle East Studies* 21 (2012) 300–312.

Wenham, Gordon J. *Genesis 1–15*. Nashville: Thomas Nelson, 1987.

Westphal, Merold, "Post-Kantian Reflections on the Importance of Hermeneutics." In *Disciplining Hermeneutics: Interpretation in Christian Perspective*, edited by Roger Lundin, 57–66. Grand Rapids: Eerdmans, 1997.

Whitcomb, Dennis, et al. "Intellectual Humility: Owning Our Limitations." In *Philosophy and Phenomenological Research* 94 (2017) 509–39.

White, Roger M. *Wittgenstein's 'Tractatus Logico-Philosophicus': A Reader's Guide*. New York: Bloomsbury Academic, 2006.

Wiesel, Elie. *Night*. New York: Bantam, 1982.

———. *One Generation After*. New York: Schocken, 2011.

———. "A Prayer for the Days of Awe." *The New York Times*, October 2, 1997. https://www.nytimes.com/1997/10/02/opinion/a-prayer-for-the-days-of-awe.html.

Wilber, Ken. *Sex, Ecology, Spirituality: The Spirit of Evolution*. 2nd ed. Boston: Shambhala, 2001.

Williams, Rowan. *Arius: Heresy and Tradition*. Grand Rapids: Eerdmans, 2002.

———. "The Benedict Option: A New Monasticism for the 21st Century." *New Statesman*, May 1, 2017. https://www.newstatesman.com/politics/religion/2017/05/benedict-option-new-monasticism-21st-century.

Wilson, Jonathan R. *Living Faithfully in a Fragmented World: From After Virtue to a New Monasticism*. Eugene, OR: Cascade, 2010.

Wilson, Marvin R. *Our Father Abraham: Jewish Roots of the Christian Faith*. Grand Rapids: Eerdmans, 1989.

Witte, John, Jr., and Frank S. Alexander, eds. *Christianity and Human Rights: An Introduction*. Cambridge: Cambridge University Press, 2010.

Wolfteich, Claire E., et al. "Humility: Empirical Psychological Research in Dialogue with Practical Theology—Part II." *International Journal of Practical Theology* 20 (2016) 184–202.

Wolterstorff, Nicholas. *Reason Within the Bounds of Religion*. 2nd ed. Grand Rapids: Eerdmans, 1988.

Wood, Matthew. "The Sociology of Spirituality: Reflections on a Problematic Endeavor." In *The Sociology of Religion*, edited by Bryan S. Turner, 267–85. Malden: Blackwell, 2010.

Wood, Richard L. "Passion and Virtue in Public Life, or A Sociological View of the Political Holiness of World Needs." Intellectual Humility and Religious Conviction Workshop, University of Connecticut, 2017.

Woodruff, Elissa, et al. "Humility and Religion: Benefits, Difficulties, and a Model of Religious Tolerance." In *Religion and Spirituality Across Cultures*, edited by Chu Kim-Prieto, 271–85. New York: Springer, 2014.

Worthen, Molley. *Apostles of Reason: The Crisis of Authority in American Evangelicalism*. New York: Oxford University Press, 2013.

———. "The Evangelical Roots of our Post-Truth Society." *The New York Times*, April 16, 2017, SR8.

Worthington, Everett L., Jr., et al. "Introduction: Context, Overview, and Guiding Questions." In *Handbook of Humility: Theory, Research, and Applications*, edited by Everett L. Worthington Jr. et al., 1–15. New York: Routledge, 2017.

Worthington, Everett L., Jr., et al., eds. *Handbook of Humility: Theory, Research, and Applications*. New York: Routledge, 2017.

Wright, N. T. *The New Testament and the People of God: Christian Origins and the Question of God*. Minneapolis: Fortress, 2004.

———. *The Resurrection of the Son of God: Christian Origins and the Question of God*. Vol. 3. Minneapolis: Fortress, 2002.

———. *Simply Christian: Why Christianity Makes Sense*. San Francisco: HarperOne, 2006.

Wuthnow, Robert. *After Heaven: Spirituality in America Since the 1950s*. Berkeley: University of California Press, 1998.

———. *The God Problem: Expressing Faith and Being Reasonable*. Berkeley: University of California Press, 2010.

Yamane, David. "Spirituality." In *Encyclopedia of Religion and Society*, edited by W. H. Swatos Jr. 492. Walnut Creek, CA: Altamira, 1998.

Yanofsky, Noson S. *The Outer Limits of Reason: What Science, Mathematics, and Logic Cannot Tell Us*. Cambridge: MIT, 2013.

Yeats, William Butler. *A Vision: The Revised 1937 Edition: The Collected Works of W.B. Yeats*. New York: Simon & Schuster, 2015.

Young, Glenn. "Forget Yourself and Your Deeds for God: Awareness and Transcendence of Self in the Cloud of Unknowing." *Mystics Quarterly* 31 (2005) 9–22.

Young, R. V. "The Stark Truth about Western Civilization." *Modern Age* 56 (2014) 62–67.

Zagzebski, Linda Trinkaus. *Virtues of the Mind: An Inquiry into the Nature of Virtue and the Ethical Foundations of Knowledge*. New York: Cambridge University Press, 1996.

Zinnbauer, Brian J., et al. "The Emerging Meanings of Religiousness and Spirituality: Problems and Prospects." *Journal of Personality* 67 (1999) 889–919.

Zinnbauer, Brian J., and Kenneth I. Pargament. "Religiousness and Spirituality." In *Handbook of the Psychology of Religion and Spirituality*, edited by Raymond F. Paloutzian and Crystal L. Park, 21–42. New York: Guilford, 2005.

INDEX

ability-specific humility, 59, 65
The Abolition of Man (Lewis), 49
Abrahamic faiths, 5, 82, 86, 141
actions, 7–8, 10–11, 14, 24–28, 33–34, 49, 117–18
affective turn, 37
affect theory, 37
affectual action, 26
affirmative theology, 153–55
After McDonaldization (Drane), 33
After Virtue (MacIntyre), 142
age of authenticity, 129–30
Age of Belief, 21–22, 138
Age of Faith, 21–22, 138
age of mobilization, 129
Age of Spirit, 22, 48, 138
Aleman, Andre, 121
Alfano, Mark, 66
Allport, Gordon, 72, 109
alternative faith, 48–49
ambivalence, 124
Ammerman, Nancy, 113
Ancient-Future Faith: Rethinking Evangelicalism for a Postmodern World (Webber), 143
The Ancient Practices Series, 141
angels, 133
apologetics, 39–41, 95–96, 157
"The Apologist's Evening Prayer" (Lewis), 97–98
apophatic theology, 154–57, 155n249
Apostles of Reason: The Crisis of Authority in American Evangelicalism (Worthen), 34
Archaic religion, 5

arrogance. See intellectual arrogance
artificial intelligence, 79n130
attachment, 69
authority, 28–30, 64, 64n50, 75–76, 126, 136–37

Baer, Jonathan R., 135
Bandura, Albert, 118–19
barak (to bless), 90–91
Barna Group, 114
Barrett, Justin, 61–62
Bass, Diana Butler, 22–24, 116, 138
Baue, Frederic, 132–33
Baugus, Bruce, 47
Bauman, Zygmunt, 31–32
Bebbington, David, 145
behavior, 19, 22–23, 25–26, 67–68
behaviorism, 26, 118–19
belief(s)
 and action, 26
 church movement, 49
 conceptual, 17–18
 contradictions, 45–46
 control beliefs, 34–35
 cultural shifts, 21–24
 intellectual arrogance, 62–64
 intellectual humility, 57–61
 interpersonal effects, 84–85
 intrapersonal effects, 83–84
 isms, 12–14
 rational choice theory, 27–28
 rationalism in, 33–44
 rationality, 7–8, 33–35
 relational, 17–18
 social practices, 10–11

belief(s) *(continued)*
   truth, 8–10
   See also religion; spirituality
Bellah, Robert, 5, 130
belonging, 22–23
Benedict option, 142
Benner, David, 147–48, 152
bereshit (in the beginning), 90
Berger, Peter, 10, 15
Bergson, Henri, 36–37
Berlin Conference, 76
biblical narratives/passages, 3–4, , 87–89
biblicism, 43, 91
Bohr, Niels, 46n178
Bonhoeffer, Dietrich, 33
Borchert, Donald, 85
Bruce, Steve, 127, 137

Canada, 111
Catechism, Westminster Shorter, 150
Cavey, Bruxy, 138
certainty, 17–18, 48–49, 51, 83–84, 95
character strengths, 56, 64–65
Character Strengths and Virtues (Peterson and Seligman), 64–65
charismatic authority, 29–30
Chen, Zhuo, 122–23
Choosing our Religion: The Spiritual Lives of America's Nones (Drescher), 112–13
Christ, Carol, 152
Christen, Markus, 66
Christianism, 12, 12n43
Christianity
   alternative faith, 48–49
   apologetics, 39–41, 95–97
   authority, 29
   biblical passages, 87–89
   contradictions, 45–47
   cultural shifts, 21–24
   cultural theories, 134–39, 143
   evidentialism, 84
   hermeneutics, 91
   ideational culture, 133
   intellectual humility, 58, 99
   and Islam, 86
   metanarratives, 2–3n8, 3–4

   modernity, 78
   moralistic therapeutic deism, 131
   mysticism, 151–52
   negative theology, 153–57
   non-rationalistic, 44–52
   practices, 91–94
   and rationalism, 33–35, 40–41, 44
   rationalistic biblical hermeneutics, 43–44
   rationality, 6, 44–52
   rationalization of, 32–33, 44
   spirituality, 103–4, 139–60
   theologies of religion, 81–82
   truth, 9–10
   values, 99
   See also belief(s), God
Christianity After Religion: The End of Church and the Birth of a New Spiritual Awakening (Bass), 138
Christianity Today (magazine), 40
"Christian Rationality: Embracing the Divine Mystery" (Fortin), 156
Chrysostom, John, 156
Church, Ian, 61
church refugees, 113–14
Clayton, Philip, 18
The Cloud of Unknowing, 157–60
cognition, 7–8, 35–36, 37, 48, 69, 83, 110
cognitive behavioral therapy, 124
cognitive behaviorism, 118–19
Cohen, Leonard, 51–52
coherence theory, 8–9
collective action, 33, 117
colonialism, 76
"Come Healing" (Cohen), 51–52
communities, 113–14, 129, 133, 142
Comprehensive Intellectual Humility Scale (CIHS), 68
conceptual beliefs, 17–18
conformist faith, 41–42
Conjunctive Faith, 42
constructivist theory, 9–10
context-specific humility, 59, 65
contradictions, 45–47, 50, 129
control beliefs, 34–35
convictions, 57, 80–81, 83, 93–94, 95
correspondence theory, 8

Covington, Dennis, 100–102, 123, 138–39
Cox, Harvey, 21–22
Craig, William Lane, 51
Crick, Francis, 109–10
critical realism, 13–14, 24, 46–48, 51, 55–56, 87, 103, 157
Cromwell, Oliver, 87
culture, 21–24, 28, 73–80, 110, 127–33, 134–39, 143

Damasio, Antonio, 37
Davis, Don, 68
deconstructed church, 49
deductive reasoning, 7–8, 12–13
deep reflexivity, 71
Demarest, Bruce, 143–44
denominations, 9n31
Denton, Melinda Lundquist, 130
Descartes' Error (Damasio), 37
desire, 148–50, 158
Desire for God and the Things of God: The Relationships between Christian Spirituality and Morality (Reuschling), 146
determinism, 25
dialogue, 72
dikaiosune (righteousness), 91
divine, 22, 45–47, 86–87, 88, 139–40, 150–52, 155–56
dones, 113–14
Doukhan, Abigail, 2–4
Drane, John, 32–33
Dreher, Rod, 142
Drescher, Elizabeth, 112–13
Driskill, Joseph, 144–45
dualism, 36
Durkheim, Emile, 13, 14–15, 106

Early Modern religion, 5
Eastern Orthodoxy, 144–45
Eastern religions, 45
education, 59–60, 96–97
ego
  egoism, 68, 79
  egotism, 59
  involvement in belief, 62–64

embedded mysticism, 152
embodied cognition, 37, 69
embodied mysticism, 152
Embracing Epistemic Humility (Borchert), 85
emergent church movement, 49, 142
emic-etic distinction, 104, 134, 137
emotions/emotionalism, 14, 26, 37–38, 40, 48, 69
empiricism, 13–14, 103, 157
The End of Apologetics: Christian Witness in a Postmodern Context (Penner), 40–41
The End of Religion: Encountering the Subversive Spirituality of Jesus (Cavey), 138
Enlightenment modernity, 30, 34
Enlightenment Now: The Case for Reason, Science, Humanism, and Progress (Pinker), 77
Enlightenment rationalism, 12–14, 38–39, 41, 43, 95
Enlightenment rationality, 6, 7, 14, 18, 24, 34, 36, 77, 84
Enns, Peter, 17, 39
epistemologies, 14, 36, 50, 58, 96
ethos, 19–20
evangelicalism, 34–35, 49, 81, 91, 92–94, 114, 142, 144–47
evidentialism, 18, 51, 84, 92
evolution, 69, 90, 92
excluded middle, 45
exclusivism, 81–83, 115
experientialism, 18

faith
  alternative, 48–49
  cultural shifts, 21–24
  definitions, 16–18
  intellectual arrogance, 95
  intrapersonal effects, 83–84
  personal, 41–42
  rationalism, 40–41
  rationality, 41–42, 50–51
  spiritual experiences, 122
feminist theology, 152
fideism, 18, 84, 132

Finding Our Way Again: The Return of the Ancient Practices (McLaren), 141
Flanagan, Kieran, 105–7
"Footnote to All Prayers" (Lewis), 98
forgiveness, 68, 73, 85
Fortin, Jean-Pierre, 156
Foster, Richard, 146
foundationalism, 13, 34–35
Four Views on Christian Spirituality, 144
Fowler, James, 16–17, 22, 41–42, 51, 83
friendship, 11
frozen reflexivity, 71
fundamentalism, 34, 43, 48, 86, 92–93, 132, 133

gender, 63–64, 75
general humility
    definition of, 58–59
    evangelicalism, 93
    intellectual humility, 64
    modernity, 73
    positive psychology, 65
    research, 56–58, 69
    self-esteem, 71
    sociological perspectives, 70
A Generous Orthodoxy (McLaren), 49
Gilligan, Carol, 75
globalization, 31, 76
Gnosticism, 35
God
    apologetics, 39–40
    biblical passages, 87–89
    in Christianity, 44
    The Cloud of Unknowing, 157–60
    contradictions, 45–48
    cultural shifts, 22–23
    faith, 95
    intellectual humility, 81–83, 98–99
    intercultural effects, 85–86
    metaphors, 161–65
    moralistic therapeutic deism, 130–31
    mysticism, 151–53
    negative theology, 153–57

    spirituality, 124–25, 139–40, 144–50
    translations, 90
    truth, 10, 39
    See also religion, spirituality
Gravity: A Center for Contemplative Activism, 164–65
Great Reversal, 23
Gregg, Aiden, 62–63, 69

Habits of the Heart (Bellah), 130
Hahn, Scott, 144
Haidt, Jonathan, 74, 93
Handbook of Humility: Theory, Research, and Applications, 65
Harris, Sam, 116
Heelas, Paul, 125–27, 140
Heidegger, Martin, 33
hermeneutics, 43, 91
Herrick, James, 135, 137–38
HEXACO Personality Inventory, 66–67
higher education, 96–97
Hodge, Charles, 92
holistic milieu, 125–27
Holocaust, 31–32, 53–54
the holy, 20–21, 123
The Holy Longing: The Search for a Christian Spirituality (Rolheiser), 148–49
Holy Spirit, 50–51
Hood, Ralph, Jr., 122–23
Hope, Ashleigh, 113
Howard, Evan, 139, 145, 151
How I Changed My Mind about Evolution: Evangelicals Reflect on Faith and Science (Applegate), 92
How the West Won: The Neglected Story of the Triumph of Modernity (Stark), 78
Hoyle, R. H., 68
human capacities, 36
humanistic psychology, 119–20
Humble Apologetics (Stackhouse), 96
humility
    apologetics, 95–96
    biblical passages, 87–89
    in Cloud of Unknowing, 157–58

INDEX

cultural dynamics, 73–74
interpersonal effects, 84–85
introduction to, 53–58
measure of, 67–68
Muslim accounts of, 86
personality trait theory, 66–67
philosophical perspectives, 58–64
psychological perspectives, 64–70
religious studies, 80–87
research, 56–58
social science, 117–18
sociological perspectives, 70–80
theory, 55–56
virtue of, 80–81
See also general humility, intellectual humility
Huntington, Samuel, 76–77
hypostatic union, 46

idealistic culture, 132–33
The Idea of the Holy (Otto), 20–21, 123
idolatry, 155
Imperatori-Lee, Natalia, 63–64
imperialism, 31, 76
inclusivism, 81–83
inconsistencies, 46
individualism, 23, 73–74, 91, 129–30
Individuative-Reflective Faith, 41–42
inductive reasoning, 7–8
industrialization, 31, 79
institutionalization, 30, 49
instrumental rationality, 27, 31, 33
intellectual arrogance
  apologetics, 96
  convictions, 95
  fundamentalism, 92–93
  hermeneutics, 91
  higher education, 96–97
  intellectual humility, 60–61
  interpersonal effects, 85
  intrapersonal effects, 83–84
  Jesuits, 92
  measurement issues, 68
  modernity, 78–79
  moral foundations theory, 75
  overview, 62–64
  poetic prayers, 98–99

research, 69
science, 92
self and identity, 71–72
theologies of religion, 82
intellectual diffidence, 61
intellectual humility
  Christian virtue of, 87–99
  convictions, 57–58
  cultural dynamics, 73–74
  definition of, 59–62
  faith, 83
  higher education, 97
  intercultural effects, 85–87
  measurement issues, 67–68
  philosophical perspectives, 58–64
  poetic prayers, 98–99
  psychological definitions, 66–67
  relational dynamics, 73
  religious studies, 80–87
  research, 69–70
  science, 79–80
  self and identity, 71–72
  sociological perspectives, 70–80
  sound judgments, 56
  spirituality, 103–4, 124
  virtues, 65–66
Intellectual Humility Scale (IHS), 68
intellectual limitations, 61–62
intercultural effects, 85–87
interpretation, 91
interspirituality, 115
irrationality, 4–5, 8, 13–14, 31–32, 43
irreligious identification, 111–18
Islam, 86
isms, 12–14, 18
Izzard, Susannah, 124

James, William, 9, 106, 114, 123
Jarvinen, Matthew, 69
Jesuits, 91–92
Johnstone, Ronald, 15
judgmental rationality, 55–56

Kapuscinski, Afton, 123
kataphatic theology, 153–55
Kendal Project, 125–27
kenosis, 87–88
kenotic Christology, 46

kerygmatic mission, 81
Klostermaier, Klaus, 85–86
Knapp, Steven, 19
knowledge, 13–14, 35–36, 48, 55–56, 87, 88, 128–29
Kohlberg, Lawrence, 75
Krumrei-Mancuso, Elizabeth, 68, 70
Kugler, Matthew, 75–76
Kuhn, Thomas, 57
Kundera, Milan, 37–38

Lamm, Julia, 151–52, 153
Larson, Sheila, 130
laws of logic, 45–46, 45n174
learned ignorance, 86
legitimacy, 2–4, 28–29
Lewis, C. S., 46, 49, 59, 89, 97–99
"life-as," 21, 125–27, 140
Life of Pi (Martel), 1–4
literalism, 43, 90
literalist faith, 41–42
literature, 37–38
logical rationality, 7
logic of conviction, 17, 49, 51
logic of rational certainty, 17
Looking for Spinoza (Damasio), 37
Luckmann, Thomas, 10
Lyotard, Jean-François, 2–3

MacIntyre, Alasdair, 142
Mahadevan, Nikhila, 62–63, 69
The Making of the New Spirituality: The Eclipse of the Western Religious Tradition (Herrick), 137–38
malaise of modernity, 78
mansplaining, 63
Markofski, Wes, 70
marriage, 126
Martel, Yann, 1–4
Maslow, Abraham, 119–20
Masters, Kevin, 123
McDonaldization, 30–31, 32–33
McElroy, Stacey, 68
McGinn, Bernard, 151
McGrath, Alister, 40, 141, 155–56
McLaren, Brian, 17, 49, 98, 141
McMinn, Mark, 95

means-end rationality, 26–27
mental health, 124
mental materialism, 63, 95
Mercadante, Linda, 115
Mere Apologetics (McGrath), 40
Merton, Thomas, 47
metanarrative, 2–3n8, 2–5
mind-body interactivity, 36–37
modernity
  apologetics, 40
  cultural change, 132
  cultural dynamics, 78–79
  Enlightenment, 30, 34
  Holocaust, 31–32
  the Other, 150
  postmodern critique, 2–3
  rationality, 6, 14, 25, 31–32, 51
  theories of culture, 128–29
modern rationalism, 35–36
modern rationality, 24, 31–32
Modern religion, 5
modesty, 59
monasticism, 136, 142
monotheism, 82, 86
morality
  intellectual humility, 58, 62
  moral foundations theory, 74–76, 85, 93
  moralism, 132
  moralistic therapeutic deism, 130–31
  moral order, 11, 14–15, 22
mysteries, 47, 156
The Mystical Theology (Pseudo-Dionysius), 153
mysticism
  embedded, 152
  embodied, 152
  experiences, 86–87, 110, 122–24
  mystics, 154–57
  negative theology, 156–57
  the Other, 147–50
  SBNRs, 114–15
  spirituality, 150–53, 152n232
  theories of culture, 131–32
Mythic-Literal Faith, 41–42
myths, 19–21, 43

Nassif, Bradley, 144
National Study of Youth and Religion, 130
natural scientists, 96
negative theology, 153–57
neurocognitive basis of spirituality, 121
New Atheism, 41, 96, 116
Newbigin, Lesslie, 34, 84
A New Evangelical Manifesto, 43
new monasticism, 142
New Religious Synthesis, 135
Nietzsche, Friedrich, 36
Night (Wiesel), 53
nihilism, 84
Nisbett, Richard, 45
non-contradiction, 45–46
nones, 112–13, 122
non-rationality, 7–8, 13–14, 16–21, 26–27, 29–30, 44–52, 58, 102–4
numinous experience, 122–23, 138

obedience, 22–23
objective culture, 131
OCEAN personality trait analysis, 67
O'Dea, Thomas, 20
Oman, Doug, 108–9
omnipotence paradox, 46
On the Incomprehensibility of God (Chrysostom), 156
ontology, 10, 40
open-mindedness, 60, 82, 95
orthopathy, 49, 136
Otto, Rudolph, 20–21, 123

Packard, Josh, 113
Palmer, Parker, 47, 88
paradigm shifts, 57n13
paradoxes, 46–47, 50
Pargament, Kenneth, 108–9, 111
Paulus, Thomas, 69
Penner, Myron, 40–41
Pentecostalism, 48–49
personal faith, 41–42
personality trait theory, 66–67
Peterson, Christopher, 65
philosophy, 33–34, 36–37, 56, 58–64, 92

Pinker, Steven, 77–78
Plantinga, Alvin, 18, 121
pluralism, 27, 74, 81–83, 91
poetic prayers, 97–99
polytheistic religions, 82
Pope Francis, 94
positive psychology, 56–57, 64–65, 124
positivism, 13
postmodernism
   apologetics, 40
   church movement, 49
   cultural shifts, 21
   cultural theories, 128–29, 132–33, 136
   Enlightenment rationalism, 39
   faith, 42
   metanarratives, 2–3
   and modernism, 35–36
   self, 38
   spirituality, 143
   transcendence, 150
power and authority, 28–30, 29n107
practical rationality, 8
pragmatic theory, 9
The Predicament of Belief (Clayton and Knapp), 18
premodernity, 128–29, 132, 143, 150
pride, 87, 89, 97
priests, 30
Primitive religion, 5
profane, 19, 106, 109
prophets, 30
proselytizing faiths, 82, 85
Protestants/Protestantism, 20, 23, 33–34, 49, 144–46
Psalm 46, 163–64
Pseudo-Dionysius, 153–54
psychology
   behaviorism, 26
   faith, 50–51
   history of, 118–21
   humanistic, 119–20
   moral foundations theory, 75–76
   perspectives on humility, 64–70
   positive, 56–57, 64–65, 124
   research, 56–58, 69–70
   self, 38

psychology *(continued)*
  spirituality, 107–9, 110, 118–25
  transpersonal, 120–21, 129

quantum-relativistic physics, 120

Race, Alan, 81
Rahner, Karl, 149–50, 156
rational argumentation, 72
rational certainty, 17, 51
rational choice theory, 27–28
rationalism
  and alternative faith, 48–49
  in belief, 33–44
  in Christian faith, 33–35, 40–41, 44
  Enlightenment, 12–14, 38–39, 41, 43, 95
  and fideism, 18
  modern, 35–36
  and non-rationality, 51–52
  and social practices, 24
  and sound judgment, 55
  theological, 51
rationalistic biblical hermeneutics, 43
rationality
  action, 26–27
  of belief, 7–8, 33–35
  character of, 7–14
  and Christianity, 6, 44–52
  faith, 41–42, 50–51
  God, 156
  instrumental, 27, 31, 33
  intellectual humility, 58
  introduction, 4–6
  isms, 12–14
  judgmental, 55–56
  logical, 7
  means-end, 26–27
  modernity, 6, 14, 25, 31–32, 51
  and philosophy, 33
  postmodernism, 36, 43–44
  practical, 8
  rational choice theory, 27–28
  in religion, 5–6, 14–24, 28
  and science, 12–13
  social practices, 10–12
  spirituality, 103
  story, 1–4
  truth, 8–10
rationalization
  of action, 24–28, 49
  authority, 28
  of Christianity, 32–33, 44
  extremes of, 30–32
  Holocaust, 53
  and non-rationality, 51–52
  and rationalism in belief, 33–34
  sound judgment, 55–56
rational-legal authority, 29–30
realism. See critical realism
reason
  apologetics, 41
  biblical stories, 3–4
  contradictions, 47
  deductive, 7–8, 12–13
  Enlightenment rationalism, 12–13
  inductive, 7–8
  intrapersonal effects, 83–84
  isms, 18
  mind and body, 36–37
  modern and postmodern, 35–36
  modernity, 34–35
  rationality, 7–8
  religious evolution, 5–6
  sound judgment, 55–56
  theoretical, 8
reductionism, 13, 110
relationality, 17–18, 70, 73, 83, 84–85
relationships, 23, 70, 73, 147, 151
religion
  authority, 29–30
  convictions, 94
  cultural shifts, 21–24
  definitions, 14–18
  elements of, 19–21, 105–6
  evolution, 5–6
  humility, 80–87
  identification, 111–18
  Kendal Project, 125–27
  mysticism, 150–51
  psychological perspectives, 107–11
  rational choice theory, 27–28
  rationalism, 33–35
  rationality, 5–6, 14–24, 28
  rationalization, 30
  relational dynamics, 73

religionless Christianity, 33
research, 56–58
Smith on, 11–12
theologies of, 81–83
theories of culture, 128–39
See also spirituality
Religion: What It Is, How It Works, and Why It Matters (Smith), 11–12
research, 56–58, 69–70, 111–18, 121, 126–27
The Resurrection of the Son of God (Wright), 84
Reuschling, Wyndy Corbin, 146
revelation, 86, 132, 155
revitalization, 132
The Righteous Mind (Haidt), 74
rituals, 19–21
Ritzer, George, 30–31, 32–33
Roberts, Robert, 61
Robinson, Brian, 66
Rohr, Richard, 164–65
Rolheiser, Ronald, 148–50
Roman Catholic Church, 29–30, 34, 63–64, 94, 144–45
Romanticism, 14
Rouse, Steven, 68

sacralization, 125–26, 140
the sacred, 15–16, 19–21, 106, 108–9, 111, 112–13, 126–27
Salvation on Sand Mountain (Covington), 100–102
Samuelson, Peter L., 66
SBNRs, 114–15, 122
Schleiermacher, Friedrich, 114
Schrödinger, Erwin, 79–80
science, 12–13, 57–58, 79–80, 92, 109–11, 120–21. See also social science
Second Commandment, 155
A Secular Age (Taylor), 129
secularism, 35
secularization, 20, 33, 35, 125–27, 137
self
 authority, 107, 119
 Christian concept of, 23
 faith, 17

general humility, 58–59, 65
identification, 111–18
and identity, 71–72
intellectual arrogance, 64
intellectual humility, 66–67
mind and body, 38
mysticism, 152–53
poetic prayers, 98
reporting, 66–68
self-esteem, 71
spirituality, 147–50
transcendence, 122–23
Seligman, Martin, 65
semantic mapping technique, 66
semantic range, 89–90
sensate tendencies, 132–33
servility, 62
sexuality, 89, 148–50
shared stories, 48
Shaw, George Bernard, 16
Sheilaism, 130–31
Simmel, Georg, 131–32
skeptical religion, 57n16
Skinner, B. F., 118–19
Smith, Christian, 11–12, 15–16, 22, 36, 48, 91, 107, 130
Smith, James K. A., 93
snake handling, 100–101, 138–39
The Social Construction of Reality: A Treatise in the Sociology of Knowledge (Berger and Luckmann), 10
social constructions, 10, 48, 88, 155
social practices, 10–14, 18, 24, 51, 58, 141–42
social reflexivity, 70–71
social science, 19–20, 51, 104–5, 117–18, 121, 127–28
A Sociology of Spirituality, 104–5
"The Sociology of Spirituality" (Wood), 107
Sodom, 89
Sorokin, Pitirim, 132
sound judgment, 7, 55–56
Specific Intellectual Humility Scale (SIHS), 68
Spinoza, Baruch, 36–37
Spiritual Humility Scale (SHS), 68

spirituality
    alternative faith, 48–49
    Christian perspectives, 139–60
    the cloud, 157–60
    contrasting, 133–34
    cultural shifts, 21–24
    cultural theories, 127–33, 134–39
    definitions of, 104–11
    of dwelling, 133–34, 142
    elements of religion, 19
    evangelicalism, 144–47
    experience of, 122–25
    history, 140–43
    intellectual humility, 68
    introduction to, 100–104
    Kendal Project, 125–27
    levels of analysis, 109–11
    mysticism, 150–53
    negative theology, 153–57
    of practice, 133–34, 143
    psychological perspectives, 107–9, 118–25
    questions, 102–4
    and rationality in religion, 15–16
    of seeking, 133, 142
    self, desire, and the other, 147–50
    and sexuality, 148–50
    sociological perspectives, 104–7, 125–39
    spiritualist faith, 42
    types of, 111–18
    views and streams, 143–47
    See also religion
Spirituality and the Awakening Self (Benner), 147–48
The Spiritual Revolution: Why Religion is Giving Way to Spirituality (Heelas and Woodhead), 125–27
Spufford, Francis, 40
Stackhouse, John, 96
stages of faith, 41–42
Stark, Rodney, 78
state humility, 65
The State of the Evangelical Mind (Smith), 93
storytelling, 3–4, 50
streams of living waters, 146–47

The Structure of Scientific Revolutions (Kuhn), 57
studiositas, 59
subjective culture, 131
subjective-life, 21, 126–27, 140
subjectivization thesis, 125–26
Swenson, Donald, 15, 20, 30
syllogism, 7–8
syncretism, 115
Synoptic Gospels, 23
Synthetic-Conventional Faith, 41–42

Tangney, June Price, 59
Taylor, Charles, 21, 78, 125, 129–30, 138, 139, 150
Taylor, Daniel, 50
temperance, 65
territoriality, 63
Tertullian, 18
The Myth of Certainty: The Reflective Christian and the Risk of Commitment (Taylor), 95
theological rationalism, 51
theoretical reason, 8
therapeutic activities, 115, 127
The Sin of Certainty: Why God Desires Our Trust More than Our "Correct Beliefs" (Enns), 95
"Thus Spoke Zarathustra" (Nietzsche), 36
Tickle, Phyllis, 135–36, 138
Too True to be Good (Shaw), 16
traditional action, 26
traditional authority, 29–30
trait humility, 65
trait-relevant behavior, 67–68
transcendence/transcendentalism
    Christianity, 44, 139–40, 147
    isms, 14
    mysticism, 152
    negative theology, 154–55
    the Other, 150
    psychology, 120
    spiritual experience, 122
    theories of culture, 129–32
transitive, 47–48
translation, 89–91, 162
transmodernism, 38, 129

transpersonal psychology, 120–21, 129
Trumbull, Henry Clay, 46–47
Trump, Donald, 93–94
trust, 17, 73, 83–84, 95
truth
  biblical stories, 3–4
  cultural shifts, 23–24
  intellectual humility, 64
  isms, 12–13, 18
  judgmental rationality, 55
  knowledge, 88
  postmodernism, 38–39
  rationality, 8–10, 44
  spirituality, 124–25
  theologies of religion, 81, 83–84

Unapologetic: Why, Despite Everything, Christianity Can Still Make Surprising Emotional Sense (Spufford), 40
uncertainty, 44, 85
universality, 35, 76–77

value-rational action, 26–27
value-relevance in social science, 104
van Elk, Michiel, 121
Verter, Bradford, 108

virtues, 58–62, 65–66, 70, 74, 80, 85, 87–99
Voas, David, 127

Waking Up: A Guide to Spirituality Without Religion (Harris), 116
warfare metaphors, 63–64
Webber, Robert, 143
Weber, Max, 5–6, 25–26, 28–29, 30, 32–33, 104, 129
Wesleyan quadrilateral, 34
What is a Person? (Smith), 36
Whitcomb, Dennis, 61–62
Wiesel, Elie, 53–54
Wilson, Jonathan, 41
Wood, Jay, 61, 119
Wood, Matthew, 107
Woodhead, Linda, 125–27, 140
word association, spirituality and religion, 116–17
Worthen, Molley, 34
Worthington, Everett, 68
Wright, N. T., 84
Wuthnow, Robert, 133, 142–43

Zinnbauer, Brian, 108, 111

www.ingramcontent.com/pod-product-compliance
Lightning Source LLC
Chambersburg PA
CBHW031359230426
43670CB00006B/590